Addiction

In Context

A PHILOSOPHICAL PERSPECTIVE

MARIA ARTIZ, PH.D.

Order this book online at www.trafford.com
or email orders@trafford.com

Most Trafford titles are also available at major online book retailers.

Printed in the United States of America.

ISBN: 978-1-4120-6014-1 (sc)
ISBN: 978-1-4269-6232-5 (hc)
ISBN: 978-1-4269-6229-5 (sc)

Library of Congress Control Number: 2011904673

Trafford rev. 08/03/2011

 www.trafford.com

North America & international
toll-free: 1 888 232 4444 (USA & Canada)
phone: 250 383 6864 ✦ fax: 812 355 4082

ACKNOWLEDGMENTS

This book draws from a variety of source experiences. Credit is hereby given to those sources. The Evergreen State College, created by the Washington State legislature as an experimental college for advanced undergraduates, conducted innovative programs of college study, one of which, *Mind and Body*, provided a novel curriculum approach that combined the fields of Medicine and Psychology into a composite course of study. The holistic perspective of this book draws from that consciousness-raising experience.

During the course of the writing of this book, I learned that the concept of mind and body became a Catholic philosophical tradition in modernity; as such, there exists a body of work among the Catholic that explores the notions of mind and soul, and the relationship to the body, from which I draw reference. The concept derives from the philosophical republicanism of the ancient Greeks[1]; specifically, the Socratic belief in the unity of body and soul and the fundamentality of this unity to successful healing[2]. The perspective of body and soul, and its modern-

---

[1]   Rosen, Stanley. Introduction by Paul Rahe, *The Examined Life: Readings From Western Philosophers From Plato To Kant.* Random House, Inc.: New York, New York, 2000, p. 5.

[2]   *Encyclopedia of Catholicism.* Richard P. McBrien (Ed.). HarperCollins Publishers, Inc.: New York, 1995.

day attribute of mind and body, or, as I term it, mind/body, therefore originates with Socrates, the Greek philosopher. The concept of spirit/mind/body presented in this work represents a philosophical expansion of the original concept.

A course in *Consumer Education* at Lane Community College in Eugene, Oregon, provided the foundation for consideration of the role of consumerism.

Undergraduate experimental psychology courses conducted by Carol Szaslow at Oregon State University in Corvallis, provided the foundation for consideration of operant conditioning principles and the nature of human psychophysiology.

While a graduate student at the University of Oregon, I conducted a cross-cultural research study that included the development of a graduate practicum, entitled *Cross Ethnic Encounters*, under the auspices of Norman Sundberg and the clinical psychology wing of the Department of Psychology. The experience provided the foundation for consideration of cultural differences.

Suggested reading by Carolin Keutzer from the social and personality psychology wing of the Department of Psychology of the University of Oregon introduced me to the tao of physics. The book learning provided the foundation for consideration of the Buddhist perspective.

Graduate training in clinical psychology under the scientist-practitioner model established by the American Psychological Association in Boulder, Colorado, which was atdopted by the University of Oregon, provided the foundation for a dual perspective (research/practice) consideration of the psychological.

An internship in clinical psychology under the auspices of the Department of Psychiatry at Baylor College of Medicine in Houston, Texas, administered and directed by Paul Baer and Michael Cox, provided the foundation for consideration of the psychodynamic perspective.

Postdoctoral training at the Biodyne Institute in South San Francisco, California, under the auspices of former American Psychological Association president, Nicholas Cummings, provided the foundation for consideration of the addictive personality and treatment effectiveness. Clinical management positions with American Biodyne, Inc., of San Francisco, California, and Medco Behavioral Care Corporation of New York, New York, provided the foundation for consideration of clinical experience and case studies.

The suggestion to engage in addiction-related research by Carol Houston, Texas Area Director for American Biodyne, Inc. led to my development of addiction research and treatment programs in Corpus Christi and San Antonio, Texas. The experience provided the foundation for consideration of addiction treatment outcome and recidivism.

The Houston Public Library's Reference and Information service was sine qua non in their assistance researching bibliographic references.

I credit my father, Ernest Artiz, with coming to my rescue, when, upon learning of my frustration, he managed to locate online a reference that had eluded both the Houston Public Library and myself.

PROLOGUE

So many things happen in the course of one's life, that to attempt an explanation for why one has done a thing, is to touch upon one or another aspect of the totality of contributants. Such is the case with the writing of this book, which has various perspectives presented in composite, for an equally various number of reasons. Without explaining to the nth degree the whys and wherefores, let it suffice to say, that like the diamond of the analogy that the reader will encounter in Chapter 13, they are all a part and parcel of the whole and my intellectual perceptions regarding them.

The concept of the context of culture upon which *Addiction In Context* is based begins with my multicultural experience as a Spanish Basque descendant of Cuban-born parents growing up in the United States of America, surrounded primarily by Scottish-Americans. The experience provides the basis for the multicultural awareness herein presented.

The multidimensional concept I attribute to two tendencies; my tendency towards the analytical, which is inherent, and my tendency towards the holistic; with which I have been intrigued as a possible source of explanation for the unexplained from the moment I understood the word *Zeitgeist,* and realized the relevance of the ages; that is, the distinct time periods among civilizations that have been discerned by their prevailing social currencies of thought. As in the psychological perceptual gestalt exercise of perceiving figure versus ground, and the modern equivalent of discerning hidden and embedded three dimensionality, it was an intellectual hop, skip, and jump to apply multicultural and multidimensional lenses of perspective to the matter of addiction.

I drafted the first version of *Addiction In Context* in1,996 C.E. over the course of two months while conducting intensive research to confirm and/or disconfirm my contentions. It included Parts 1-6; 2 of which I have dropped as unnecessary. Securing publication proved fruitless, despite a positive review of the manuscript by the Harvard University Press. Editing, update, and reference revisions were made to the original manuscript in 2,003 and 2,005 C.E., respectively. Having finally secured a Canadian publishing contract, I discovered to my dismay that I was no longer satisfied with the text as it stood; my writing struck me as insufficiently explanatory; an holistic skeleton in need of philosophical flesh and blood. I added anecdotes from experience, and proceeded to hone the concepts into a more comprehensive understanding. It is my rendered opinion that, while the essential perspectives remain the same, the delay has resulted in a more complete presentation.

The references for *Addiction In Context* are largely available through the American public library system, where much of the research was conducted, in combination with numerous publications, primarily New York-based, as well as publicly unavailable professional research, treatment, and clinical training materials. Given that some of the modern references cited in this book have referred to concepts and statements deriving from more classical works, and such cross-referencing can become confusing, I have endeavored to cite both the modern authors and the original authors or works. At the risk of boring the reader with these multiple references, I contend that to be true to original authorship of conception, such holistic referencing is essential. In such case, the modern author is either cited as referring to the classical author or both sources are footnoted. Those seeking to explore the original sources, in addition to the modern commentaries, can seek the original authors' works by name, or refer to the modern sources for titles. My own commentaries are interspersed with the perspectives of the cited sources.

In consideration of the recently established maxim by the American Psychiatric Association to adopt a stance of political correctness in the addressing of various disorders,[3] I profess to the reader that while I support such sensitivity with respect to the labeling of individuals in psychiatric practice; for example, referring to an individual as having a substance use disorder versus referring to them as an addict; I nonetheless adopt a position of editorial license as an author which may or may not conform with considerations of political correctness.

This book is primarily concerned with wholeness of perspective; with the filling in of the gaps of belief, and the rounding out of the limitations of view, combining what may

---

[3]   Refer to the American Psychiatric Association's *Diagnostic and Statistical Manual IV-Text Revised, 4th ed.* Michael B. First et al. (Eds.). APA: Washington, D.C., 2000.

at first read appear to be an oddly related assortment of knowns and unknowns, in the generating of possibilities for consideration, and the elucidation of a paradigm for comprehension. While it is not exhaustive in its research, as say in a comprehensive search of the respective literatures, it is sufficiently clear in its establishment of what I consider to be a proper paradigmatic perspective for a comprehension of addiction that reflects wholeness of being. In this respect, it constitutes a book of philosophy, providing a fresh-perspective for applicable considerations.

I dedicate this book to my daughter, Veronica; the only child of a divorced parent, who was always there, while I was acquiring the experiential foundations for the thinking that went into the making of this book. In that respect, it is as much a part of her life as it is of mine. I have unceasing admiration for her tolerance; given the eccentricity of the life we shared.

It is a testament to frustration, after three discovered incidents of identity fraud, that I belabored the matter of name designation for this book longer than any other decision pertaining. My maiden name resides on the cover, in keeping with the international name standard.

Maria Artiz, Ph.D.
Houston, Texas, USA

TABLE OF CONTENTS

PART ONE

THE CONTEXT OF CULTURE

CHAPTER ONE

The Context of Illness

To comprehend addiction in a holistically meaningful way, we must understand its context within culture. Intellectually, this is comparable to understanding illness in the context of the totality of the person presenting with a problem. The holistic examination of a phenomenon requires that this be the essential perspective, as opposed to the traditional scientific perspective of isolation, that is, isolating respective parts for study. There are other methodological perspectives that deviate from the traditional scientific, including the single case study perspective; the study of a phenomenon based upon intensive scrutiny of an individual subject, and the phenomenological perspective; the study of a phenomenon based upon the self-interpretations (or self-reports) of the individual. Much of psychology is based upon the latter. The analysis of addiction presented in this book is based upon a nontraditional holistic perspective, intended to provide an umbrella of understanding in the form of a contextual paradigm for holistic comprehension that covers the gamut of what is meant by addiction; going beyond traditional assessments without undue elaboration; in order to achieve a greater understanding of the phenomenon as a whole. Towards this end, I view addiction as inseparable from context; be it the context of the person, the community, and et cetera. This is a unique perspective, which I find essential to the establishment of a genuinely holistic paradigm for study. As such, it deviates from the normative study approach in significant ways, incorporating variables of nontraditional responses, religious and social beliefs. It also deviates by considering the matter of perspective; how one views the world; from a variety of angles, deliberately presented to foster openness to new ways of thinking by loosening the hold of the rigid assumptions of other paradigms. In this respect, the holistic perspective of contextual analysis on the matter of addiction herein presented may be experienced initially as odd, confusing, and/or uncomfortable. With repeated consideration over time, it may become less so, as comprehension in the true sense of the word replaces the confusion that results from the paradigm shift. This book constitutes a different way of viewing a very old phenomenon.

To make this point clear, I cite Thomas S. Kuhn, whose book, *The Structure of Scientific Revolutions*, first published in 1,962 C.E. clarified, when I read it in 2,010 C.E., the nature of what I have set about accomplishing.

The invention of other new theories regularly, and appropriately, evokes the same response from some of the specialists on whose area of special competence they impinge. For these men the new theory implies a change in the rules governing the prior practice of normal science. Inevitably, therefore, it reflects upon much scientific work they have already successfully completed. That is why a new theory, however special its range of application, is seldom or never just an increment to what is already known. Its assimilation requires the reconstruction of prior theory and the re-evaluation of prior fact, an intrinsically revolutionary process that is seldom completed by a single man and never overnight.[4]

---

[4]   Kuhn, Thomas S. *The Structure of Scientific Revolutions*. 3rd ed. "Introduction: A Role for History," The University of Chicago Press: Chicago, 1996, p. 7.

Having duly established the philosophical and scientific contexts of this work, we proceed to consider the matter of addiction in context.

Addiction, as substance dependence, is officially classified by the medical community as an illness; specifically, a psychiatric disorder. Addiction, as phenomenon, has the multiple status of being regarded and treated by both the medical and nonmedical research and treatment communities, including government statisticians. As such, there are a variety of perspectives and approaches to the topic of addiction; as an illness, as a personality problem, as a personal problem, as a social problem, et cetera. This chapter considers the context of illness generally, as a foundation for holistically comprehending what is regarded as the specific *illness* of addiction. In all cases, one must necessarily exercise good judgment in determining and discerning the etiology of the phenomenon, particularly a complicated one such as addiction.

In my years as a practicing clinical psychologist, I was repeatedly struck by the impossibility of isolating *patient* from *milieu*, and *problem* from *context*. As Norman D. Sundberg declares in his book, *Assessment of Persons*, the matter of psychological assessment needs to regard the client as a person who brings to treatment, along with the presenting problem, his or her set of family experiences, values, and culture, that may or may not be addressed by standard psychological assessment measures.[5]

From a psychodynamic perspective, it is important, as a practicing clinician to know oneself; one's personal biases, inclinations, limitations, et cetera, and to maintain an ongoing awareness of one's own reactions to a patient, to minimize interference with the therapeutic process. As a practicing clinician, I was personally, as well as professionally, sensitive to the matter of cultural family context; and recognized my own propensity to attend to the differences, be what

---

[5] Sundberg, Norman. *Assessment of Persons*. Englewood Cliffs, New Jersey: Prentice Hall, 1977.

they may. I encountered a curious relationship between phenomenologically-experienced cultural differences and patient backgrounds. Patients who, on a statistical basis, would have been recognized as Caucasian, American, and cultural mainstream, experienced as much or more cultural dissonance as did patients from so-labeled ethnic minority cultural backgrounds. The universe of presenting patients is a self-selecting one, and these cultural dissonances in many, not all, cases were what necessitated treatment, albeit unrecognized as such, particularly among those experiencing problems of personal adjustment. This indicated a greater degree of cultural difference within culture than was indicated by the professional literature at the time, which tended to focus upon the more obvious ethnic minority cultural differences.

As a matter of personal and professional sensitivity, I brought to therapeutic understanding my own family's cultural differences. These include my family of origin's experiences pertaining to our Spanish and Basque origins, life in pre-revolutionary Cuba, life in pre-revolutionary Miami, Florida; experientially different from the Cuba and Miami of today. As a Spanish- American, I have experienced the mispronunciation, false hearing (replacement of the stated name with a similar name, e.g. Ortiz, Sanchez; that is more familiar to the listener), misspelling, e.g. Artz, Artez, Salenz, Sanez, Seanz, and gobbledegook misprinting (probably computer-generated) that resulted in something like Spfjk, of my surnames. This type of experience never occurred while I was married and using my husband's Scottish surname of McNally. These experiences comprise a part of the totality of what I have experienced in the way of culture. Relating how these cultural experiences of difference impacted my view of life to the matter of persons presenting with their own peculiarities of experience enabled appreciation of their differences and the importance of these to the life of the person.

In addition to what is traditionally considered to comprise cultural difference; cultures of varying ethnicity; there are other types of cultural experiences which influence the individual, and as such comprise additional contexts for consideration in an holistic approach to a phenomenon. In my family, for example, ghostly and psychic experiences are relevant aspects of reality. Phenomenologically, how one perceives and views the world is different for persons who have experienced such phenomena and those who accept these experiences as valid. In the writing of this book, I discovered that ghostly and psychic experiences are more prevalent than I previously realized, and the most publicized cases have been professionally documented.[6] Nonetheless, they are not commonplace occurrences; affecting primarily persons of European origin; randomly skipping across generations without any discernible pattern of manifestation.

As to the way in which American culture regards such phenomena, it has variously over the years been publicized, accepted and ignored, with resurgences of interest. Professionally, the experiences are relegated to an unincorporated branch of exploration entitled *parapsychology*; the semantic translation of which is *related to or similar to psychology*; they fall into a separate category with no officially recognized place of their own in the realm of academia. This does not render parapsychology a quasi-science. It does, however, render it apart from the mainstream of academic study. Kuhn makes an interesting and relevant point when he states, *How could history of science fail to be a source of phenomena to which theories about knowledge may legitimately be asked to apply?*[7]

---

[6] Holzer, Hans. Ghosts: *True Encounters With The World Beyond; Haunted Places, Haunted Houses, Haunted People.* Black Dog & Leventhal Publishers, Inc.: New York, 1997.

[7] Kuhn, Thomas S. *The Structure of Scientific Revolutions.* 3rd ed. The University of Chicago Press: Chicago, IL, 1996, p. 9.

Whereas, such experiences are genuine, albeit referred to as paranormal phenomena, persons who have them share a unique context of experience which inevitably affects the ways in which they view reality; comprising a subcultural heritage of their own. For the purpose of clarifying the importance of attending to contexts when studying a particular phenomenon holistically, the example demonstrates the need to attend to cultural experiences, including those considered paranormal.

Research regarding the behavior of people in organized groups has identified the capacity for groups to become ethnocentric; that is, to view their group, and at times, their view of the world as superior to that of others. This phenomenon is evident in political groupings; where the ethnocentric percept encourages members of the group to think in alliance. There are many groups that use this phenomenon to advantage, including cults, military companies and corps, and political parties, as a way of separating *us* from *them*. Most dramatically, ethnocentrism is visible during times of war. In this respect, the context of group affiliation, and group cultural identity is relevant to the matter of cultural assessment, which will be further addressed in the next chapter.

The ways in which we perceive the world are influenced by our experiences within it; given the existence of considerable differences in experiential reality, it stands to reason that there are considerable differences in attitudes among and between people, as well as a variety of attitudes of superiority among various groups of peoples. We can apply this knowledge about the phenomenon of ethnocentricity to the assessment of illness; in contextual terms as it may or may not pertain to individuals we identify as ill and as it may or may not pertain to branches or schools of thought directly or indirectly involved in conducting the assessment.

People don't become psychologically or physically ill, imbalanced, or develop difficulties in living and coping in a vacuum; they become so within the context of social reality. Similarly, what happens to the body may affect the mind, may affect the spirit, and vice versa. This book makes grammatically incorrect usage of the terms mind/body and spirit/mind/body to indicate the potential interactivity between them. What happens to the one may impinge upon the other, because what happens, happens to the whole person; the totality of the who and the what of the individual being.

People exist within the context of what we may scientifically define as a universe that comprises all human culture; which in turn contains subsets we may call subcultures. To define the extent of all possible subcultures would be a tedious exercise that requires constant revision, as old subcultures vanish and new ones emerge, and is unnecessary for the purposes of this book. For example, we could define all manner of cultural affiliations as subsets of the universe of all possible cultures; country of origin, family of origin, ethnic and racial background, group membership, religious identification, political identification, primary language, educational attainment, vocational category, residential categories (by country, by region, by municipal vs. rural, by zip code, etc.).This is the universe; the context; of social factors of influence.

There is also the universe; the context; of personal factors of influence; such factors as belief, capability, personality and temperament, and preference. Both the cultural and personal universes of influence comprise definable contexts for the purposes of comprehending a phenomenon in context; therefore, they are herein considered as aspects of experience which impinge upon human consciousness.

When a person within a particular cultural milieu is diagnosed ill, without examining the characteristic nature of the milieu, or the relationship between the manifested illness and its cultural and subcultural contexts, we are inferring and diagnosing illness on the basis of symptomatology devoid of cultural considerations. This constitutes standard practice, based upon accepted nosologies. Fundamentally, we treat the presenting patient, in accordance with acceptable practices. To do otherwise has the potential to put the patient and the treating professional at risk.

Nonetheless, there is ample opportunity, without violating the standards of professional practice, to go beyond the fundamentals, in order to respond more holistically. The notion of alternative approaches to standard medical practice is not a new one and is not without foundation; for example, osteopathic medicine is such a discipline which has gained the stature of legitimacy. It is *a system of medical practice based on a theory that diseases are due chiefly to loss of structural integrity which can be restored by manipulation of the parts supplemented by therapeutic measures (the use of medicine or surgery).*[8] Naturopathy, *a system of treatment of disease that avoids drugs and surgery and emphasizes the use of natural agents (as air, water, and sunshine) and physical means (in manipulation and electrical treatment)*[9] is another. The practice of the doctor of osteopathy and the doctor of naturopathy differs from the practice of the doctor of medicine, based upon differences in belief about what causes illness and what methods should be used to effect a cure. There are other alternative forms of medical practice; my mention of osteopathy and naturopathy as examples derives from their stature as acceptable medical practices in America. In similar regard, it is my contention that holistic consideration of the phenomenon called addiction has the potential for translation into acceptable practice. This is not to say that it will appeal to all practitioners.

From an holistic perspective, an holistic approach to assessment and treatment involves attending to the contextual factors as they pertain to symptomatology; methodologically distinct from traditional medical practice.

---

[8]   *Merriam-Webster's Collegiate Dictionary. 10th ed.* Merriam-Webster, Inc.: Springfield, Massachusetts, USA, 2001, p. 821.

[9]   *Merriam-Webster's Collegiate Dictionary. 10th ed.*, p. 773.

In holistic perspect, viewing symptomatology isolated from its context, reduces; to use the analogy of photography; the picture of the illness to a selected frame for viewing. This narrowing of the viewing field shuts out perception of the factors of context; with the traditional exception of medical history. Assuming an holistic perspective, when symptomatology is separated; medically dissected from the hypothetically perceivable totality of relevant contextual factors of influence; it provides us with a portion of the whole; a partial picture of the condition. Symptomatology viewed out of context provides a limited picture of conditions of illness and the social and personal factors which impinge upon their manifestation.

For example, consider the situation of a man who walks into an emergency room with a broken leg. Presume that the ER staff attends to the presenting symptomatology of his broken leg without obtaining an history regarding its occurring context. That is, they mend the broken leg without answering the questions of how and why the man came to break his leg, apart from the standard question of *What happened?*, and the standard answers that *I fell* or *I was in an accident.* The ER staff may not want to address presenting physical problems holistically, for philosophical or practical reasons, and that is their prerogative. The point of the example is that for purposes of holistic healing, such considerations count; the holistic assessment of problems of health necessitate assessment of cultural contexts.

Assuming an holistic health perspective, did the man break his leg because he was distracted by personal concerns and not paying attention to what he was doing; perhaps, because of marital or employment problems? If this were the case, his treatment could be expanded to include a referral to address these underlying sources of psychological disturbance in his life which are the primary contributants to the etiological onset of the broken leg. Did the man break his leg because of unacknowledged fear of succeeding, carelessness, or risk-taking in a skiing competition? If this were the case, treatment would be enhanced by referral to a professional well-versed in sports psychology with the capability to understand and treat the idiosyncratic aspects of his competitive sports experience.

The ER staff might view the circumstance of the man's broken leg differently if, in the course of obtaining a medical history, they responded to relevant information about prior injuries. For example, he reports that he broke his right arm the prior year, and his clavicle the year before that. Presuming the medical history-taking is thorough and the reporting is accurate, the man is assessed to have had a significant bodily injury each of the previous six years. In this case, an holistic response would generate concern regarding possible accident-proneness. If the man is treated for the currently presenting symptom; the broken leg; his leg will heal, but his accident proneness is likely to continue, given that treatment has not responded to the sources of his accident proneness.

An holistic approach would assess etiological sources pertaining to the symptomatology of the presenting physical problem, assuring that relevant aspects of the whole person are included in considerations regarding treatment. An holistic approach is less practical than the standard medical approach to treatment, and is not necessary to the mending of the broken leg. It is, in fact, more time- and cost-consuming for the provider and the patient. In this sense, selecting the path of an holistic approach to illness generally, is akin to selecting the path of long-term psychoanalysis for mental health specifically. It serves as a more comprehensive approach with a greater potential for lasting cure. The difference is one of healing versus mending; of curing versus treating.

Practically, how does one holistically approach the matter of illness in context? An holistic approach begins with a change in one's perspective. From this change in perspective, derives a change in one's overall goal; and from this change in one's overall goal, derives a change in one's applications, including assessment orientation and methodology. The first contact, then, is the contact with one's own consciousness, and a determination of the rightfulness of an holistic perspective for one's own view. From this determination, one is then able to proceed on the path towards holistic healing; be it for oneself or for others; beginning with educational preparation.

In the quest to seek cures for illness, there exists the potential to lose sight of the overriding goal. The current Zeitgeist in America of regulated health care, with its stringent strictures regarding diagnoses and compensable treatments, while providing a measure of protection from fraudulent practice for persons seeking care, simultaneously increases the risk potential of circumscribed treatment stymieing cure. The situation is analogous to the dilemma that primary and secondary school teachers face when presented with test achievement standards for their students to master. In Texas, public school principals and teachers have been provided with statistical printouts of their school and class achievement test standings relative to the school district and the state as a whole, with resultant pressures brought to bear to improve test scores. The risk potentials to education consist of teaching to the norm and teaching to the test; that is, circumscribing education with stringent curriculums designed to foster the passage of achievement tests. Whether such practice compromises the overriding goal of education is the crux.

The provision of health care has become more nationally standardized than at any prior time in American history. Individual practitioners face the potential risk, in treating to the standard, of ignoring important resources, including contextual factors, relevant to effecting cure. The risk inherent in standardization is that such uniformity can become exclusionary; a criticism historically rendered against standardized testing. With respect to practice, the risk lies in the potential to override clinical judgment. In the quest to treat, as in the quest to educate, where teaching to a test to assure student test passage and accreditation, and where treating to a standard to assure outcome checklist standards and accreditation, we risk shortchanging the original goals of teaching to teach and treating to treat; wherein learning and healing are the penultimate considerations. Prevailing attitudes of practicality in the practices of education and mental health threaten professionalism, and in so doing, threaten the natural avenues by which professions and sciences evolve. This split within the professions; between applied and research; generates from and resides with national government. From an holistic perspective, such split creates the potential for reduced effectiveness.

The illnesses of man, like man himself, are not islands unto themselves. They have a context, and that context resides in the idiosyncratic circumstances of the life of the individual. In and of themselves, presentations of illness may or may not mean anything beyond their actual symptomatologies of occurrence. That is, they may not be reflections of something beyond what is presented. At the same time, they may impact the individual's psychology. The fact that one aspect of organismic functioning can affect the other (mind and body), and the fact that aspects of culture can affect the person, are the relevant considerations.

In these various respects, if we address illness from the perspective of context, we are much more likely to understand and treat the whole person, not just as a body of parts, but as an experiencing and interpreting *idiosyncraticus* in need of our comprehending attention. As pertains to the interpretation of experience, a theoretical revolution occurred within the field of psychology that fits the description of scientific revolutions provided by Thomas Kuhn. Albert Bandura published *Social learning theory* in 1,977 C.E.; contending that the theoretical basis of the behavioral psychology which ensued from the pioneering animal behavior studies of the Russian physiologist, Ivan Petrovich Pavlov (1,849-1,936 C.E.); of cause and effect; in and of itself, was inadequate to explain human response.[10] Bandura presented a new conceptual model building upon the existing model, which added the intervening variable of human cognition, to account for the fact that, in human beings, a stimulus does not translate into behavioral response, the way it does in other animals. Human beings, being of higher consciousness, think and interpret, and in so doing, influence outcome; their responses to circumstances are not circumscribed by cause and effect. Bandura's work established the field of cognitive behavioral psychology. The role of human cognitions is now firmly established as an important factor. With regards to contexts of culture, we know that the phenomenology of the experience of the individual is supremely important.

Historically, the related notion of *the individual* having privileged ontological status; of having status on the basis of being and existing as an individual; an underlying philosophical perspect of Catholicism; dates back to the Greek philosopher, Aristotle (384- 322 B.C.E.).[11] Its origins in recorded thought date from this time period. The Greek notion is that a human being is born to exist as an individual; a privileged status in relation to what was known about other animals; and that this privileged status begins at birth. The perceived superiority of human beings within the animal kingdom, and the perceived importance of the beingness of the individual, is at the core of the historic development of Athenian principles of democracy, wherein developed a

---

[10] Bandura, Albert. *Social learning theory.* Englewood Cliffs, New Jersey: Prentice-Hall, 1977.

[11] Velkley, Richard. "Introduction" to "Metaphysics", Part 4, In Rosen, Stanley, (Ed.) *The Examined Life: Readings From Western Philosphers From Plato To Kant.* Random House: New York, 2000, p. 315.

high regard for individual opinion. With respect to illness, the opinion of the individual is a relevant consideration.

The search for holistic approaches to the phenomenon of illness has an historic basis. The works of Socrates and Freud exemplify the search for solutions to the problems of mind, body, and soul. The challenge in modernity is the same as it was in antiquity; how to reconcile philosophy and practice in the service of healing. In Socrates' time, medicine was based upon the founding work of Hippocrates, the Greek physician (460-377 B.C.E.) credited with being the father of medicine. Socrates philosophically contended that the practice of Hippocratic medicine aimed at healing illness via the body was insufficient; that the body cannot be healed without the soul. Freud, the Austrian neurologist who lived from 1,856 to 1,939 C.E., philosophically contended that the body; the soma; cannot be healed without the mind. Freud is credited with being the father of both psychiatry and psychosomatic medicine, based upon his pioneering treatment of hysteria and conversion reactions. The pioneering works of both Socrates and Freud derive from their respective confrontations with the inadequacies of extent practices; spurring them to seek alternative philosophies of approach.

As an aside, it is relevant to note that the legal notion of sound mind and body, that is/was expressed by the Latin phrase, mens sana in corpore sano; a sound mind in a sound body; has been codified into law for over 2,000 years. The extent to which such codification has impacted philosophies and practices of healing is not within the scope of this book; although it is here recognized as yet another of the factors in the universes of social and personal contexts. As practitioners are aware, legalities influence practice. With regard to phenomenons of illness; while practitioners may render diagnoses, the judicial system retains the supreme right to declare competence/incompetence.

The body/soul and mind/body approaches of Socrates and Freud serve as historic models in the search for holistic healing. In later chapters, the reader will consider discussion of these historic concepts of holistic health, as they are expounded; with the resolution to include the essence of spirituality; in a defined notion and model termed *spirit/ mind/body.*

In addition to the combined historic models, the notion and model of *illness in context* will be explored and developed; at times generally, at times with respect to the phenomenon of addiction; as part of a comprehensive umbrella, in the presentation of a more holistic philosophic perspect and approach to the matter of healing; with specific implications for the phenomenon of addiction.

CHAPTER TWO

The Holistic Perception of Reality

How we perceive reality affects our comprehensions of what we consider to be real. We can perceive reality as a composite of parts; which, like the functioning of the eye of the fly, with its multiple viewing angles, provides us with a variety of perspectives. We have already discussed the possibility of viewing reality from a zooming in, or closeup perspective of a selected part. This book, in progression, provides overviews of a variety of factors, or aspects of reality for viewing, to provide the reader with contextual understandings that enable composite thinking, from which s/he can progress to an holistic perception.

We can also perceive reality as a totality; a comprehensive panorama that is all-inclusive. While perceiving the whole is a more difficult enterprise, given the enormity of the universe of possible factors and influences, we commit an injustice against truth, when, in attempting to explain a phenomenon, we ascribe cause without at least attempting to obtain as complete a view as possible. Even then, our understanding of the truth is inherently limited by extent knowledge, extent belief, and our capabilities to perceive and comprehend.[12]

Truth is not an absolute. It has a variety of definitions; the applicable of which is, *the property of being in accord with fact or reality*[13] It is based upon our capability of obtaining knowledge and our interpretive comprehension of what we learn or know; affected by the manner in which we obtain knowledge and the scope of our view. In assessing causality, if we lack sufficient knowledge, then we may reach erroneous conclusions. Depending upon how we go about seeking truth; that is, the manner in which, and the scope from which we proceed, we may delimit our conclusions about causality.

Truth is a relative. Thus, what is true for one may not be true for all. And what is true at one point in time is very likely not to be true at another. This is because we differ and we change; between and within individuals and over time; we reinterpret the old, learn the new, and reinvent what we consider to be the truth as we proceed through time. We, and the world we inhabit, are living entities; with diverse opinions, constantly in motion, ever-changing. At any given point in time and space, we are confronted by a universe of possibilities from which we and our world select to view, to study, and to actualize. At another point in time and space, we and our world again select from a universe of possibilities. We are somewhat limited in our capacity to choose by both our previous choices, and by our capability to perceive the full range of possibilities. Despite these fundamental limitations of physics and physiology, there is still considerable leeway for us to exercise freedom of thought and consequently, freedom of choice.

---

12 Fritjof Capra, *The Tao of Physics: An Exploration of the Parallels Between Modern Physics and Eastern Mysticism, 2nd ed.* Shambhala Publications, Inc.: Boston, MA, 1983, p. 2.

13 *Merriam-Webster's Collegiate Dictionary, 10th ed.* Merriam-Webster, Inc.: Springfield, Massachusetts, 2001, p. 1265.

This is the semantic essence of the Canadian philosopher, Marshall McLuhan's, contention that, *There is absolutely no inevitability as long as there is a willingness to contemplate what is happening.*[14] This perception comes from the man who earlier insightfully stated that *The medium is the message.*[15] If one were to consider recorded history as the medium by which the message of man's comprehension of reality is conveyed; its importance to the process of truth is undeniable; in terms both reflective and contemplative.

Our perception of reality, and consequently, our understanding of truth is affected, not only by experience, but also by the development of our inherent capacities and by the limitation of our inherent physiology. Such phenomena as alien experience, metaphysics, parapsychology, spirituality, and theoretical physics challenge our awareness and extend the outer limits of our perceptions of reality; and in so doing, aid in the development of our inherent capacities. Quantum physicists have mathematically *proven* the theoretical existence of ten dimensions of reality, and posited the existence of yet another, despite the fact that human physiology limits man to perceiving three dimensions.[16]

The majority of the peoples of planet Earth believe in a god of one form or another, who dwells in a place or dimension different from our own. In this respect, people have come to *know* that additional dimensions of reality exist on a religious basis rather than on a sensory perception basis. Over the course of future millenia, humanity, or

---

[14] McLuhan, Marshall. The original reference for this quotation was not available through the public library system, as the book in question had been stolen; however it was found posted online at *www.thecanadianencyclopedia.com.*

[15] McLuhan, Marshall. *Understanding Media.* McGraw Hill: New York, 1969. Book based on June 30, 1959, speech at the University of British Columbia.

[16] Kaku, Michio. *Parallel Worlds: A Journey Through Creation, Higher Dimensions And The Future Of The Cosmos.* Doubleday: New York, 2005.

what succeeds humanity, may eventually evolve with the physiological capacity to perceive more dimensions; if, in fact, they do exist; and be able to perceptually experience these dimensions of reality in a more direct, and one would expect, meaningful, way.

It is anyone's guess what such beingness, were it to eventuate, would look like. Would it end up with very strange-looking eye apparatuses? Recall the kaleidoscopic vision of the fly. Flies have multiple capacities of vision; a composite of multiple eye viewing screens, so to speak, to accommodate their need for multiple perception. What would eye apparatuses require to be able to fully envision eleven dimensionality? Eleven eyes within an eye? It's an intriguing question.

One would expect to encounter an accompanying development in the brain that would facilitate the actuation. One day, we, or another form of beingness, might go beyond our current experiences of sixth senses and mind's eyes, and be able to actually see extra-dimensionality forthrightly. Should such an eventuation scenario come to pass, it will do so slowly, as an evolution over time; or suddenly, as an anomaly of emergence. In the meantime, we can and do experience limitations in our capacity and ability to perceive the possibilities of reality.

In temporal terms, as pertains to human heritage and history, we may or may not know what actually happened in the past; historical records are data summaries, incomplete with regard to details, and not always accurate; they reflect the perspective of the historian which may or may not be holistic in its rendering. With regard to the present, while we may record what we believe it is important to record for the future, we may miss recording some of what is important because of prejudice against its inclusion; as in the case of which side had the greater glory or the greater victory; and/ or because we fail to recognize its importance; due in part to the fact that understanding increases with hindsight. With regard to the future, prognostication is an inaccurate science; what we anticipate will happen, may not actually happen. Historical records as resource provide the most accurate reflections of humanity's perceptions of reality, yet they are not without flaw. Holistically speaking, our perceptions of reality are incomplete.

With regard to our perceptions in the present about what is true, we uphold our beliefs to be true with or without actual experience, based upon evidentiary support from other sources. Were this not the case, learning would be limited to hands-on experience and first-hand reporting, as it was in times of antiquity. As it stands, we are primarily vicarious learners; learning from others what they are willing to share, via books, computers, schools, television, et cetera. Thus, the existence of God is presumed to be true on the basis of historical account; primarily that of the disciples of Jesus Christ. The existence of alien life forms is also presumed to be true on the basis of historical account; primarily that of military documentation of alien craft sightings, crashing, and alien being encounters. The fact that, according to a poll taken in America, the majority of adults believe in the existence of alien beings is testament to our capacity to believe in the veracity of reported events without requiring the *proof* of direct experience. In the current era, as in prior eras, human beings are demonstrable believers; we believe each other to a far greater extent than we may realize or reflect upon. The positive side of this natural tendency to believe is that we are better able to help each other; which is advantageous to human survival. The negative side is that we are just as capable of believing untruths as we are of believing truths, and this puts us at risk of being deluded and manipulated. Our human propensity for believing enables us to both perceive and misperceive reality.

There is another aspect to the holistic perception of reality which pertains to those experiences which would generally be considered seemingly unreal. I refer to these as unreality experiences; genuine experiences that individuals regard as having an unreal or surreal quality. My characterization of examples is not absolute; there may be readers and others who regard such phenomena as normal; while they are normal in the sense that they genuinely occur, they do deviate from the norm or average, and in this regard, can be considered abnormal experiences. When the frequency of such occurrences increases, as has been the case with identity fraud, such experiences may cease to fit the abnormal characterization, and the argument could be made that the experience of identity fraud has already reached this point. Were it not for the fact that parapsychological experiences have been extensively studied and accepted, they too would fall into the abnormal category. In the interest of holistic inclusion, albeit of unusual aspects of reality, these kinds of experiences are mentioned; in this regard, recognition for inclusion is of first importance; how they may best be characterized is subsequent, and will be influenced by prevalence and perspective.

For example, the discovery by the individual that one has a double; a look-alike; is an uncanny experience. The effect is that it startles the individual; there is a sense of incredulity regarding the fact that it has happened. This and other types of seemingly unreal experiences which will be discussed have the capacity to be both unsettling and consciousness-expanding; in that they loosen the hold of firmly held perceptions about what is real. Suddenly, one is confronted with new possibilities; the universe of possible experiences expands to include more than what the individual expected. To literally or vicariously experience, and therefore, to know, such possibilities exist opens one's inner mind to expansion; a greater awareness, an increased perception, of reality. Such experiences arrest the attention with their strangeness; providing substantial cause for reflection.

At the age of 13, a junior high school teacher showed me a LIFE magazine article and asked me to look at the photograph. I glanced at the photo, then at him, and said, "You're in LIFE magazine?" He chuckled. The answer was a paradoxical no/yes. No, he wasn't the individual whose picture was taken and featured; yes, the photograph was an exact replica. I was undeniably startled. He let me read the accompanying text; I learned that the look alike was Russian and the photo was taken in Russia. My teacher lived and worked in the Cape Canaveral bedroom community of Satellite Beach, Florida, had no Russian relatives, and had never been to Russia. He was as flabbergasted by the discovery as I was. His remarks to me were these: *It has been said that everyone has a double*; and, *It must be true.* I accepted the experience as true, because it was. I never expected that I would one day experience the same phenomenon. In fact, I had forgotten about it, until it happened.

In 2,001 C.E., while viewing Headline News; a CNN channel affiliate; I watched news clips about the Queen of Oman; her visit to England to see Queen Elizabeth, her visit to the city of New York, clips of her in Oman, and listened to a recorded interview with her. I was stunned by the experience. It was the first time in my life that I had ever heard about her, much less seen her. There, on recorded television news, was my double.

I was speechless and shaken. I couldn't comprehend its meaning; why did this woman look, act, and to some extent, think like me? I didn't know her; I still don't. As far as I know, we are not related. I honest to God didn't know what to think or make of it. I turned off the television set and laid down to rest; resisting the urge to ruminate; there were so many thoughts impinging upon my consciousness about what was happening and what it could mean, that I decided to clear my mind from these intrusive distractions, and allow whatever awarenesses presented themselves. It was then that I recalled the experience of my junior high school teacher, and realized that I was not alone in the experience. This provided a modicum of reassurance, despite the fact that I was still quite shaken and continued to be for some time afterwards.

How does one reconcile such an unreal yet real event that parodies one's own life? Such an event fosters a new sensibility; a new awareness about life. My perspective on the world changed at the moment of recognition that I had a double. I felt vulnerable in a way I previously had not. Perhaps it is the same kind of vulnerability that a natural born twin experiences; I do not know. I do know that I feel protective towards my *other.* I still do not quite know what to make of it, other than that the almighty powers of creation must have a reason. Subsequent to the knowing, I find myself more attuned to noticing such occurrences. I expect that they occur more often than is realized, because we fail to notice. Certainly, the advent of worldwide media coverage has enabled a greater opportunity for people to discover these truths.

In my own case, it was as if life itself had decided that I should be shown certain truths for my own edification. God only knows why. Was it because I was writing this book and had decided to include a chapter on the holistic perception of reality? For whatever reason, I was led to the discovery of truths that I would not otherwise have known existed.

After the experiences, over time, of learning that people have doubles and that I myself have a double, I subsequently learned that a relative of mine also has a double. In November of 2,003 C.E., on the anniversary of the assassination of the American president, John F. Kennedy, the television menu was laden with JFK-related viewing options. I selected a documentary, entitled *The Oswald Story,* to watch. As the story unfolded, I was suddenly faced with the prerecorded interview of a woman who was the spitting image of a paternal aunt. Here, in historical interview, was her double. I was stunned. It was both startling and disconcerting to realize that the woman in this recorded interview reflected exactly how my aunt had looked and acted in the early 1960s; when the interview was conducted and the documentary was made.

Author Maria Artiz

Aunt Estella Artiz

Maria Artiz, Ph.D.

According to the documentary, Lee Harvey Oswald; the communist sympathizer arrested on suspicion of assassinating the president; had visited the Cuban Embassy in Mexico City prior to the time of the assassination. In response to questions regarding Oswald's visit to the embassy, the woman, a diplomatic employee of the Cuban government, reported that it was she with whom Oswald had spoken and to whom he had directed his inquiries. This information was presented as potentially relevant to the discussion of who Oswald was, the events and circumstances leading up to the assassination of JFK, and whether or not Oswald was, in fact, his assassin.

Apart from the fact that my paternal aunt was born in Cuba, the Cuban diplomat and my aunt had nothing else in common except this uncanny fact of looking and speaking alike. They were doubles of each other as clearly as if they had been identical twins.

How does one reconcile such startling realities of experience? As bizarre and unreal as they seem, they are nonetheless true instances of actual occurrences. From such experience, it is apparent that there are aspects to reality which are not typical; the experience of which is uncanny. In this respect, what I have termed unrealities of experience co-exist with what are considered to be typical realities in a kind of paradox. With respect to knowing and not knowing, we *know* typical realities in the sense that they are familiar to us. We are not as familiar with, and in this sense, do not really *know* the atypical realities.

I read a fictional passage in a *Reader's Digest Condensed Book* wherein a female Middle Eastern diplomat was described as a visual double of the Italian actress, Sophia Loren. While this fictionalized account does not constitute actual experience, it indicates a consciousness about the existence of such occurrences.

Natan Sharansky, who was born in the Ukraine, was imprisoned nine years in the Gulag for supporting dissident activities at a time (circa 1,978 C.E.) when the Soviet Union

26

was cracking down on anti-USSR human rights dissidents and Israel was advising Zionists to be true to their Jewish identities and refrain from participating in dissident activities. Sharansky, a self-described former Soviet Jew now living in Israel, refused the societal pull to make an either/or decision; that is, to categorize himself as either a dissident or a Zionist. Instead he made, and continues to make the decision to be both a human rights dissident and a Jewish activist[17] In his recent book, *Defending Identity*, Sharansky states that *One universal quality of identity is that it gives life meaning beyond life itself. It offers a connection to a world beyond the self.*[18] In effect, Sharansky makes a case for the necessity of identity in transcending the travails of living life in an imperfect world. In his own words, reflecting upon the Russian Jewish experience, Sharansky contends that, in the quest to aid mankind, Jews lost sight of the preeminent importance of identity.

Many Jews originally joined the communist revolution because they were determined to work for the benefit of all mankind. They could go beyond their ghetto or shtetl and be part of the dream of universal brotherhood, as befitting the descendants of the Hebrew prophets. So they cut off their own roots and joined the Communist Party. But in the end, those who did so helped to build one of the most bloodthirsty regimes in the world, and they found themselves among its first victims.[19]

Sharansky's contention is that identity is essential to freedom. As a democratist, he contends that freedom cannot exist without the existence of clear identity. While it is not so directed, Sharansky's portend is relevant to the matter of identity theft. Without the safety and security of an intact

---

[17] Sharansky, Natan. *Defending Identity: Its Indispensable Role In Protecting Democracy.* PublicAffairs; Perseus Books Group: New York, New York, 2008.

[18] Ibid, p.5.

[19] Ibid, p.15.

identity, one falls victim to a turbulent maelstrom of life-upheaving activity that undermines normalcy; entrapping its victims in a meaningless circularity of fighting an unseen assailant in the quest to escape its ravages. The experience is unsettling in a way that is qualitatively different from other experiences of entrapment; as in the case of political imprisonment, including the incarceration of persons due to war-defined enemy status, as was the case in America with Spanish residents during the Spanish-American War and Japanese residents during World War II. I say this with knowledge of the former from family experience. Members of my Spanish family, while not incarcerated, were nonetheless entrapped in New York City during the Spanish-American War, and denied communication with relatives in Cuba and Spain; the experience was mortifying. I myself have experienced an accumulation of over 30 years of interrupted communications with relatives in Cuba, despite the legal right to do so, and despite the allowance of others' communications. As a result of what I have come to term *the unseen hand*, I feel that I have, to an extent, experienced what it is like to be freedom-restricted by secretive warfare; why else the denial of communication, if not to disrupt family relationship in the service of beating an identified enemy target? I have concluded from the experience that the unseen hand identifies Spanish Cubans on all sides to be the enemy, given that relatives in Cuba are equally anguished by the illegal restriction of communication. While such experiences are mortifying in the real sense, the experience of identity theft is mortifying in the unreal sense.

There are yet other, documented unusual realities of experience, and I will not endeavor to include them all. For instance, Hans Holzer, the New York parapsychologist, documents the experience of *bilocation;* the unknowing astral travel projection of a living person to another location where they are observed, usually by persons known to them, and

28

from where they typically evaporate.[20] The anecdotes which precede and which follow serve to validate the existence of such experiences, in the hopes of raising the reader's consciousness pertaining to perception of what is real and what is not.

At the time of the discovery that I had a double, I was in a rather hypersensitive state; from maintaining due diligence in fending off instances of identity fraud. In other words, I was already experiencing a form of existential angst. Why were all these people defrauding my identity? Who were they and why were they doing it to me? At the time, identity fraud was rampant in Houston, Texas. The experiences were uncanny.

Such usage of one's name identity and other personal identifying information, as occurs in cases of identity fraud, is one kind of unreality experience. The effect upon the person who is so victimized is various; including the possible experiencing of a range of emotions, from stun, startle, and surprise, to annoyance, anger, and animosity, to anguish, angst, and alarm. No matter how stoic, one cannot help but be affected by the audacity of such conduct.

According to psychologist and sociologist, Robert Hammond, identity theft is an extensive phenomenon. He cites the finding of a 1,999 C.E. study commissioned by Image Data LLC that one out of every five Americans, or a member of their families, have been victimized by identity theft.[21] Another study commissioned by Identico Systems estimated that identity thieves had victimized 13 percent of Americans. The figure, according to Hammond, is greater than the 32 hundreds of a percent (.32%) of Americans victimized by robbery in 2,000 C.E..[22] Investigation by

[20] Holzer, Hans, pp. 729-731.

[21] Hammond, Robert. *Identity Theft: How To Protect Your Most Valuable Asset.* Career Press: Franklin Lakes, New Jersey, 2003, p.21.

[22] Ibid.

postal inspectors yielded the finding that a significant portion of identity fraud was undertaken by organized crime syndicates operating nationally to support drug trafficking.[23] The problem is so extensive that a 1,999 C.E. poll by the Wall Street Journal reported that loss of privacy was Americans' greatest fear. The relevance was supported by a 2,000 C.E. Harris poll finding that almost 90 percent of people were concerned about threats to their privacy; up from 34 percent in 1,970 C.E.[24]

Thievery has long plagued society; its history is an integral part of recorded human history. The thieving of identities is a modern phenomenon, with dangerous repercussions. For over two thousand years, man has been plagued by thieves who confiscate his property. Now, after almost two thousand years, man is also plagued by thieves who confiscate his identity. The experience of being preyed upon by thieves in this manner is surreal; in the nature of a bad dream that does not go away upon awakening. To the contrary, the process of reclaiming one's life when it has been thus stolen is arduous, lengthy, and ripe with the potential for additional injury, as has happened in cases where the victimized person has been accused of being the thief of their own identity. Can one imagine the experience of such insult added to injury in the defiling of one's own unique and individual life? One cannot help but wonder why; Why did such a thing happen? Why has God and the supernatural allowed such a terrible thing to happen?

The entertainment industry in America has made legal use of the parody of famous persons through comedic mimicry. Comedic acting-like and looking-like well-known persons has become an art form in and of itself; a form of visual cartooning. The past decades have borne witness to comedic representations of America's presidents, pundits, and stars. Thus and so, television has broadcasted a

---

[23] Ibid., p.20.

[24] Ibid.

variety of look-and-act-alike events. These entertainment events, dramatically deliberate and exaggerated in their presentations, are not harmful, do not constitute fraudulence, and do not result in experiences of unreality.

Reflecting upon perceptions of reality calls to mind Psychiatrist R. D. Laing's book, *The Politics of Experience*, which I read as an undergraduate psychology student during a course on abnormal behavior at Oregon State University.[25] Laing's perspective on schizophrenia, based upon phenomenological considerations, results in a re-characterization of the abnormality of schizophrenic behavior, wherein he explains its functionality for the individual. It requires a certain measure of courage to intellectually venture beyond the pillars of circumscribed professional thought in order to explore such views, as Laing clearly does. His perspective is all the more valuable for its uniqueness. In providing a new way of perceiving an old phenomenon, he provides additional stimulation for thinking about reality, different from the tried and true. According to Kuhn, *Acquisition of a paradigm and of the more esoteric type of research it permits is a sign of maturity in the development of any given scientific field.*[26]

In considering the holistic perception of reality, we must necessarily attend, not only to the obviously real, and the seemingly unreal, but to the supernatural as well. I have read that the majority of Earth's people believe in the existence of supraordinate powers in the world. Whether people believe in a pantheon of Gods, one God or supreme being, an omniscient intelligence, or an unspecified metaphysical; they believe in supernatural power, and they do so on the basis of accumulated cultural, world, and personal knowledge and teachings that pertain to the supraordinary experiences of

---

[25] Laing, R. D. *The Politics of Experience*. Pantheon Books: New York, 1967.

[26] Kuhn, Thomas S. *The Structure of Scientific Revolutions,* 3rd ed. The University of Chicago Press: 1996, p. 11.

human beings; past and present. These beliefs, as stated in the previous chapter, comprise a consensus of thought regarding what is truth. In this case, the truth is held to be that the supernatural exists, that the supernatural is powerful, and that experience of the supernatural is part of the reality of human experience. These beliefs regarding these perceived truths are found to be based primarily upon the knowledge, experience, and expertise of others. They comprise an important perspective which carries considerable influence upon human development.

While belief in the supernatural is primarily manifested as a belief in a God of some kind, there are other perceptions of supernatural reality, which may or may not be attributed to a God. For example, the belief in Satan or the Devil, the belief in witches and warlocks, and the belief in spirit beings that are neither angel, ghost, or demon. Human heritage records many an unusual experience which has occurred and has been attributed to be the result of visitations by Satan, witches and warlocks, or spirit beings.

Perhaps the least known of such occurrences, outside of tribal populations, are those involving spirit beings. In America, the world of spirit beings has been popularized by Carlos Castaneda and Dr. Alberto Villoldo.[27] In the 1,971 C.E. Castaneda account, spirit beings appear in response to the practicing of certain Yaqui Indian rites designed to facilitate altered consciousness. In the 2,005 C.E. Villoldo account, spirit beings are called upon and encountered in a process of shamanistic journeying within a state of altered consciousness in order to heal one's own or another's soul.

In 2,005 C.E., I happened to be waiting in the Charlotte, North Carolina, airport to board a return flight home to

---

[27] See Castaneda, Carlos. *A Separate Reality.* Washington Square Press: New York, 1971; and Villoldo, Ph.D., Alberto. *Mending the Past and Healing the Future with Soul Retrieval.* Hay House, Inc.: Carlsbad, CA, USA, 2005.

Houston. While I was seated in the front row of the designated boarding gate that faces passersby, I watched as, over the course of a span of fifteen or so minutes, three different *people* passed by, then passed by again as if they hadn't previously passed by; walking or riding a tram in the same direction a few minutes after the first passing. This occurred without their having retraced their routes; under normal circumstances, a physically impossible feat. I wasn't alone in my perception; an African-American couple who had seated themselves to my right witnessed the repeated passing of the last of the three. I heard the man ask the woman he was with, *Did you see that?* They subsequently engaged in incredulous laughing, head-shaking, and pondering the bizarreness of such a witnessed event.

Given what I have read in the Castenada and Villoldo accounts regarding such phenomena, spirits appeared to them when they were either deliberately called upon, as in the Castenada case, or as a result of deliberate journeying into their spirit world, as in the Villoldo case. From this, I presume that my reading of Villoldo's book aboard my flight to Charlotte served as a kind of psychic call to the spirit world, despite the fact that I was not of altered consciousness, with the result that these spiritual beings or apparitions presented themselves. In appearance, they were as bodily present as any other person in the airport. Yet, the fact that they each traversed the same route twice without having doubled back was a clear indication that they were not of the normal people variety. The fact that they deliberately gained my attention indicated that they wanted me to be aware of their presence. I was rather floored by the occurrence. I pondered it for some time, in an effort to comprehend its meaning. I sensed that they were there to watch over me.

The night before my departure from Houston, I noticed that the oil light indicator in my car had gone on, and added several quarts of oil. When I departed the next day to go to the airport, my car began billowing huge clouds of white smoke that attracted several police cars. I was informed that my car was in violation of air emission standards, and would not be permitted to be driven until inspected by a mechanic. I was told that the vehicle would have to be towed because of the potential for it to explode. The police made the arrangements and called for a cab to see me safely to the airport.

Was this the reason the spirits had appeared at the Charlotte airport? Had they sensed that I had been in danger? I never expected to experience a visitation by spirit beings that looked and acted just like normal people, yet that is what occurred, once again startling my perceptions of reality. I am convinced that we are truly not alone in this world.

The world and the cosmos within which we live; what we know as home; continues to be as mysterious as it is comprehensible. Each moment, each day, each year, there is the potential for us to learn more about the realities of the world within which we live. In the process, we adjust and clarify our perceptions of reality, adding in depth and dimensionality to our recognitions and comprehensions, towards an ever greater understanding which may never, in our mortal states of beingness, be complete.

The natural changes of our living planet and expanding universe add to this incompleteness in our knowingness. As we continue to experience the previously unexperienced, our knowledge and understanding expand to include more of the entire universe of genuine reality. Cosmically, for example, we experienced the unusual, with its scientifically notable effects, when, at the end of the last millenium, planet Earth was impacted by unusual sun bursts of energy, and the planetary magnetic polarities traded places. It has been forecasted that more such cosmic effects are likely in 2,012 C.E.; the year in which the ancient Mayan Calendar prophesies the end of their world; when the planet aligns with the center of our Milky Way galaxy. Such unusual, yet natural, cosmic happenings provide continual temporal opportunities to learn more about the phenomena of our world and home; enhancing our holistic perceptions of reality.

In the sense that we have come to know, yet do not fully know, the realities of our existence, the same can be said about the phenomenon of addiction in society. While accumulated studies and composite knowledge yield a general consensus of truth, the truth of addiction as we know it is incomplete; not yet whole, either in its currency or its composite. Over time, perspectives fluctuate with experiences, interests, knowledge, laws, and methodologies.

Given that the prevailing Zeitgeist in the world today is primarily a practical one; a probable consequence of globalization; in which there dominates a preference for cost-effective practical approaches and solutions over experimental or philosophical ones, the future direction of addiction research and treatment will reflect this attendant practicality; in approach and funding. On a practical basis then, will the three primary fields of attention that have branched likely grow stronger; the field of psychology (mind), the field of medicine (body), and the field of spirituality (spirit).

In viewing the phenomenon of addiction through the lens of technical and scientific inquiry, we narrow our focus of attention. When we zoom our inquisitive lens on *addicted* individuals and *addictive* families, we lose sight of the broader perspective of addiction within the context of culture; and relevant consensuses of thought therein. We find evidence of such narrow angle viewing tendency and an explanatory basis for its application in Latin. The phrase, *ex pede Herculem*, or, from the foot we may judge of the size of Hercules, indicates the existence of a perception that we may draw inferences about the whole from the part. In Greek mythology, from whence this Latin percept derives, the mythic figure of Hercules was ordered by the Goddess

Hera to perform twelve extraordinary labors, upon which success, the notion of herculean strength resides. Thus, we find the perspective of inferential analysis; from part to whole, from specific to general, integral to modern thought, medical practice, and opinion polling; already extent in classical times. Recalling that Hippocrates, the credited father of medicine, was Greek, it is not surprising that such perspective predominates; our perspective of reality has lineage in antiquity.

As true as this often is, it is also true that in so doing, we selectively ignore a vital part of the whole picture. The potential for mis-perception exists when we perceive addiction as *separate from* the cultural context within which it occurs. In the zealous pursuit of *handles* with which to open doors to cure addiction, we too narrowly focus our sights upon treating the symptoms. The historic narrowness of our field of focus has resulted in a loss of perception; of the vital role of the contextual influence of culture, including cultural knowledge, that contributes, interactively, with individual and family factors. It has limited the opening of our minds and hearts to other possibilities; something we must necessarily do if we are to get out of the rut we have, through habituation, created for ourselves, in order to holistically view addiction as a spirit/mind/body phenomenon.

CHAPTER THREE

The Cross-Cultural Perspective

Whether or not we consciously reflect upon the fact that we are all a part of culture, we are. Such culture, in terms of its influence, may be historic or modern; it may be distinct or indistinct; overt or subtle; traditional or chosen. In addition to predominant cultural differences based upon ethnicity, origins, race, and sex, there are familial cultural differences, such as the difference between educator families, military families, religious families, small business families, sports enthusiast families, et cetera, wherein there is a consistent pattern of vocational devotion. From the perspective of culture, there are many variations upon the theme.

Cross-cultural studies provide glimpses into the ways in which predominant cultural differences influence perceptions about the world in which we live. From these we may derive insight into the influence of culture on the manifestation of a spirit/mind/body phenomenon, such as addiction, and compare how such manifestations are regarded. The pioneering cross-cultural works of Albert Schweitzer in medicine, and Margaret Mead in anthropology, among still-living tribal peoples, while demonstrating a greater humanity, served to educate the world about fundamental fallacies in our perceptions and key differences in our cultural attitudes.

Their accomplishments represent a break with the tradition of studying the past; via the archaeologic. Their efforts are reminiscent of the detailed records of the early Spanish explorers regarding the peoples they encountered in the New World, with a new world intention of science versus the old world intention of exploration.

The cross-cultural research of Paul Pedersen,[28] Stanley Sue,[29] and Norman Sundberg[30], among others, supports the contention that awareness of and sensitivity to cross-cultural differences in beliefs, expectations, and values is important to psychology, and should comprise a particular understanding among helping professionals who treat individuals from different cultural backgrounds.

The cross-cultural psychology literature promotes the realization that, in order to accurately understand an individual's presenting problem or symptoms, the helping professional needs to recognize how the symptoms he or she sees are influenced by the cultural background from which the person comes, and with which the person identifies. In other words, the person's presenting problem cannot be viewed outside of the context of her/his phenomenological reality of experience, without a vital loss of understanding.

Individual consciousness is in large measure an interactive feature of cultural background. This can be clearly understood from the practice of educational immersion experiences, such as that provided by the American Field Service (AFS), wherein students engage in language study abroad in order to more fully comprehend language within

[28] Paul Pedersen, *The Five Stages of Culture Shock: Critical Incidents Around the World.* Contributions in Psychology Series, vol. 25. Greenwood Publishing Group, Inc.: Westport CT, 1994.

[29] Stanley Sue and James K. Morishima. *The Mental Health of Asian Americans: Contemporary Issues in Identifying and Treating Mental Problems.* Jossey-Bass, New York, 1982.

[30] Norman D. Sundberg. *Assessment of Persons.* Englewood Cliffs, New Jersey: Prentice Hall, 1977.

its context of origin. Such cultural immersion experience generates nuances of understanding that promote facility in the foreign language. Cultural experience is comprised of many nuances; of which the individual is only partially consciously aware. While persons from different cultures may learn the language of another culture, they are not automatically attuned to the nuances of the culture itself. And, in the case of the professional, they may need to be open to learning from the individual of another culture how it is for them personally in order for an appropriate level of sensitivity to occur. Cross-cultural sensitivity practices have been applied in diplomatic and international business circles out of concern for the maintenance of culturally appropriate decorum and the avoidance of insult.

With respect to the assessment of persons presenting for assistance from cultural backgrounds different from one's own, the following questions are relevant considerations. What does the problem represent within the context of the person's culture? How does the person interpret the problem and what is its meaning to them personally? How is the problem related to cultural expectations, beliefs, and values? In any given situation, such cross-cultural issues may or may not apply, but they often do, and when they do, they play a significant role in the course of resolution. Curiously, in this day and age of globalization, one also needs to be sensitive to the backlash; that is, the possibility that the posture of the presenting person is one of assuming a role of affinity-seeking, wherein the possibility exists that the helper may miss the true gist of the situation.

Popular culture is ripe with examples that illustrate the potential misunderstandings that can arise from the failure to comprehend the role of the individual's cultural experience in affecting her/his circumstance. Such cross-cultural idiosyncracies are relevant for consideration in helping situations, including treatment.

The 1,993 C.E. movie, *The Joy Luck Club*, based on Amy Tan's 1,989 C.E. book by the same name,[31] portrays a group of Chinese women and their daughters struggling to resolve the interpersonal conflicts between them. The Chinese daughters, reared in the United States, and the Chinese mothers, reared in strife-ridden pre-revolutionary China, are challenged by the differences between their respective attitudes, beliefs, choices, desires, experiences, and lifestyles. As their stories unfold, they confront the differences arising from their distinctly different cultural life experiences.

The inter-generational conflicts are eased, and in some cases transcended, as the pairs of mothers and daughters begin to reflect upon their experiences. The daughters learn what it is their mothers experienced and suffered; comprehending then the mothers' attitudes and choices. The mothers, in turn, learn how their daughters are struggling in their current experiences with biculturality. Despite their genuine differences, they gain depth in their perceptions; the one about the other; engendering a climate of mutual appreciation, the comprehension fostering forgiveness. The two generations of women come to terms with the different realities of their life circumstances on the shared ground of cultural struggle. The cultural contexts of their respective life circumstances is relevant (Chinese, American) as are the contexts of their struggles (revolution, acculturation).

In the book, *Mutant Message Down Under*, Marlo Morgan illustrates the role of cultural context in shaping the understanding of what it means to be symptomatic, as defined by a cultural system of belief. Morgan relates the beliefs of a remote Australian aboriginal tribe; that they are direct descendants of the first people on the planet, that their culture is 50,000 years old, that they are the only *real* people, that everything exists in a state of oneness, that

---

[31] Tan, Amy. *The Joy Luck Club*. Ballantine Books: New York, 1989.

everything happens for a purpose, that there are no freaks, misfits, or accidents, that there are only things that we, as humans, don't fully understand[32].

With regard to illness, these aborigines believe people are not random victims of ill health; that the physical body is the only means by which the higher level of eternal consciousness has to communicate with individual personality consciousness. They view the slowing down of the body by illness as a message that the individual needs to mend spiritual wounds; wounded relationships, gaping holes of disbelief, tumors of fear, eroded faith in the creator, and hardened emotions such as unforgiveness.[33]

From this cross-cultural difference we learn that what we commonly ascribe as physical illness, in the Australian aboriginal worldview, is a reflection of something else; something that affects the individual at the core level of her/ his well-being; and that the unwellness is considered to be spiritual, not physical, in nature. In Morgan's account, the aborigines ascribe our notion of "symptoms" as "imbalances" that derive from what is spiritually not right within the life circumstance of the individual. Whereas they perceive their tribal culture as balanced, deeply-rooted in nature, and interdependent with other living beings, they perceive non-aboriginal cultures as imbalanced, out of touch with essential oneness, and comprised of mutant beings. The cultural context of their life experience (Australian aboriginal) is relevant, as is the context of their shared belief (spiritual).

The religion of Christian Science, founded by Mary Baker Eddy in 1,866 C.E., continues to be practiced in North America. The Christian Scientists are naturalists who practice spiritual healing. Their belief is that spiritually unhealthy cognitions are the root cause of illness, and that illness can only be cured through the spiritual cleansing and

---

[32] Marlo Morgan. *Mutant Message Down Under.* HarperCollins Publishers, Inc.: New York, 1994, p. 68.

[33] Morgan, p. 96.

healing of the mind. Their insistence upon natural versus medical healing, including when a member is faced with a life-threatening condition, has resulted in publicized conflict with government authorities over the civil law that contends life-threatening conditions justify emergency response and enforced hospitalization by government authorities. The conflict between the religious tenet of the Christian Scientist and American civil law poses an interesting moral dilemma regarding jurisdiction. Who has the right to decide whether or not an individual receives emergency medical treatment under conditions that are life-threatening; the individual or the government?

The situation is far less typical than that of the individual who, lacking in financial resources, seeks emergency care as a solution for everything that ails them, knowing that the law protects them from being refused treatment. In the case of the Christian Scientist it is s/he who refuses medical treatment, on the grounds of religious belief. The cultural context of religion is relevant (Christian Science) as is the context of healing (naturalistic).

In each of the cultural contexts mentioned, the perception that when all is not well this constitutes an aberration from normalcy is consistent with Western notions of dysfunction and illness as aberrations from the normalcy of wellness; though this varies with respect to beliefs regarding the source, nature, and solutions for the aberrations. Thus, in the particular case, the Chinese women's view is that the solution depends upon a within-family resolution versus a resolution from without. In the aboriginal view, it depends upon one's connection to the world without, and being in balance with nature. In the view of the Christian Scientist, it depends upon understanding and practicing the divine principle of Jesus's teaching and healing. These examples from different cultural contexts demonstrate the relevance of different points of view that arise from cultural experience.

It is also relevant to note that decisions, even of individuals who appear to be out of cultural context, may nonetheless pertain to cultures of origin. Anecdotally, my own family of origin exemplifies this tendency. What is notable is the degree to which effort is extended on the basis of cultural proclivity. For instance, my maternal grandparents, living in New York City, made the decision that my aunt and mother would be born in Cuba, from where they had emigrated during the Depression. My grandmother returned to the family home in Cuba for the midwife-assisted births, in the traditional manner of home birth. The outbreak of World War II precluded her from doing so for the birth of my uncle. The effort and expense involved in enacting their decision underscores its importance to them. The cultural context of culture of origin (noble Spanish) is relevant, as is the context of traditional family (home birth-oriented Spanish). The influence of the cultures of origin upon decision-making are self-evident.

My paternal grandparents also made decisions based upon cultural proclivities. After the turn of the last century, it became popular among Spanish families to educate their children in America. My grandfather in Havana sent my father and his brother, who lived in New York, to Fork Union Military Academy in West Virginia, at considerable expense, in keeping with this cultural Zeitgeist, in hopes they would be well-disciplined as well as well-schooled. According to my father, my grandfather got his wish. Their adventures off-premises during high school at times resulted in what they considered to be harsh disciplinary measures; pacing for hours at a time with heavy rifles. As he tells it, they had a lot of company. The cultural context of family of origin (noble Spanish) is relevant, as is the context of traditional family (authoritarian Spanish). As these examples indicate, cultural influences are relevant for individuals whether or not they reside within the context of their respective cultures of origin.

As we have discovered, there are pertinent issues to consider in the holistic helping/treatment of persons with ties to other cultures. Life experience examples, such as those presented, portray a rich and varied world heritage of cultural perspective from which we gain a greater understanding of our diverse humanity; its essential experiences, its variances in relating to the world in which we live. Hopefully, exposure to the life experiences herein presented will attune the reader to a greater awareness of and sensitivity to the genuine realities of cultural difference, be they what they may, and in so doing, render recognition more readily apparent as they are naturally encountered. To presume to know the meaning of a spirit/mind/body phenomenon without comprehending its embeddedness in contextual background; the relevant cultural conditions; is short-sighted. The assumption of an holistic approach to the matter of spirit/mind/body healing entails expanding our view; allowing awareness of nuances of meaning, relative differences in subjective experiences, and variable interpretations of experience to nonjudgmentally enter our perceptual field of inquiry.

With respect to contexts of culture, there exist, within primary cultures, a variety of subcultures with their own distinct dialects, languages, and perspectives. As Robert Bringhurst, in his book, *The Tree of Meaning* relates, there are a multiplicity of indigenous peoples with languages all their own.[34] In speaking of the diversity, Bringhurst shares his concerns about the accumulating loss of peoples and languages the world over. In his words,

Why does it matter? It matters because a language is a lifeform, like a species of plant or animal. Once extinct, it is gone forever. And as each one dies the intellectual gene pool of the human species shrinks. The big, discontinuous brain to which we all in our way contribute, and on which we all depend, loses a part of itself that it cannot rebuild.

---

[34] Bringhurst, Robert. *The Tree of Meaning: Language, Mind and Ecology.* Counterpoint Press: Berkeley, California, 2008.

It is true, of course, that languages, like plant and animal species, are dying all the time. But in a healthy forest or lake or ocean or grassland, constant replacement also occurs. In a healthy system there will be long-term change and there will be seasonal variations, but neither the total number of species nor the overall biomass nor the aggregate richness of the gene pool will suffer steep and steady decline. In the global forest of language, over the past three centuries, chronic depletion is precisely what we have seen. The number of living languages has been continuously shrinking. So has the intellectual gene pool—the word hoard and grammar hoard and story hoard of the earth. As for the intellectual biomass, I do not claim to know. We could measure it, I think, as the number of stories per year that are told, adjusted for vividness, length, complexity, and ecological attention. Unadjusted, it is probably increasing like the harvest of Christmas trees and nutritionless potatoes and the production of sliced white bread.

A story is an assemblage, you could say, of intellectual chromosomes. Each time a story is told and heard, something like fertilization occurs. But real perpetuation and renewal, as we know, are not achieved by fertilization alone. Gestation and birth and upbringing and maturation are all parts of the process. The accumulation of wisdom is a part of the process, not performed by individuals so much as by whole ecologies. Stories need those too.

Translation, of course, is a hurdle. But it can be crossed, unlike the painted wall of a paraphrase or the blank wall of silence and denial. The labor and pleasure of crossing it should be shared, I think, as widely as possible. But it shouldn't be thrust on the storytellers themselves.

Mythtellers tell their stories to those who are listening. They also tell their stories to themselves. That is hard to do in a foreign language. When you ask a mythteller to tell you a story in your language rather than hers, the mythteller must talk only to you, not to herself. And then something is missing.[35]

In this perspective of language as a context of human culture, we hear Bringhurst's message of concern; that we have lost more than we realize as human languages have become increasingly extinct over the course of the past three hundred years. His sensitivity enables him to experience the loss as one of vital humanity, of essential pieces of the human puzzle, which, in toto, provide a more complete human intellectual understanding of life. In this example, the cultural context of language (indigenous) is relevant, as is the context of concern (sensitive scholarship). The Bringhurst perspective provides us with another angle with which to view the context of culture; one not only of language, but of the reality of diminishing returns.

Within the realms of dominant cultures, varieties continue to prevail. When we fail to attend to the differences between subcultures of a similar type; for instance subcultures of the same race, ethnicity, or country of origin, we face the potential for doing more harm than good. Within the so-called Cuban community of South Florida, for instance, Drs. Eugenio M. Rothe and Andres Pumariega contend there is considerable diversity.[36] In their study of the Cuban exile community; defined as Cubans who emigrated to the Miami/ Dade County area subsequent to the 1,959 C.E. revolution; they identify four distinct subcultures. Temporal differences play a key role in the diversity they discovered.

The first subculture they identify is comprised of those Cubans who arrived secondary to the revolution. These, according to Rothe and Pumariega, are the non-

[35] Bringhurst, Robert. *The Tree of Meaning*, pp. 30-1.

[36] Rothe, M.D., Eugenio M. and Pumariega, M.D., Andres. "Between Hernando Cortez And Lot's Wife: Adaptation And Mental Health Of The Cuban Exiles In The United States", In *PSYCHLINE: Journal of Hispanic American Psychiatry*, Vol. 4(5), 2005, pp. 35-40.

acculturateds; Cubans whose culture of orientation is that of pre-revolutionary Cuba. The second subculture is comprised of what they refer to as the Miami Cubans, based in Little Havana, whose culture of orientation is that of Cuban Miami. The third subculture they identify as the Cuban equivalent of the American yuppie, referring to them as Yucas (young, urban Cuban-Americans); the American-born children of Cuban-born parents, whose culture of orientation is climbing the American ladder of success. The fourth subculture Rothe and Pumariega refer to as the Dialoguers; the more recent arrivals, who desire a normalization of the diplomatic relationship between America and Cuba; and whose culture of orientation is that of the communist country they left behind.

Thus, from the Rothe and Pumariega study, we find that the cultural context of Exile (Cuban) is relevant, as is the cultural context of Time Period (pre-1,959, post-1,959, second generation, and recent arrival). These findings are consistent with cross-cultural research findings regarding attitudes and orientations among other, non-exiled, groups that have immigrated to America. In this respect, the identifiably distinct subcultural differences can be viewed as part of a temporal process; of groups differentially acculturated according to the Zeitgeist of the time.

The example serves to demonstrate that within a broad cultural context, that of the Cuban Exile, there co-exists a complex array of personages, attitudes, and life experiences; more so than one would assume on the basis of hearing the referent, Cuban Exile, alone. Recognition of the subcultures revolving and evolving within the broader cultural context of *Cuban Exile*; an inherently complex culture; adds dimensionality to any understanding of the Cuban cross-cultural experience.

If we fail to take into account important distinctions between subcultures of a broader cultural group, such as those of the Cuban Exile, we may encounter difficulties in our interactions with such individuals, among whom the realities of experience are a matter of emotional sensitivity. The matter of the importance of cultural relativity increases in pertinence and significance when navigating a course of treatment.

Although they are not usually so characterized, from an holistic perspective, groups of persons with distinct experiences may be viewed as comprising subcultures of a kind. Per Merriam-Webster, there is a definition of culture that applies in such instances: *the integrated pattern of human knowledge, belief, and behavior that depends upon man's capacity for learning and transmitting knowledge in succeeding generations.*[37] One such definable subculture consists of persons who have had what are referred to as near-death experiences. In America during the 1990s, the phenomena received considerable attention. While the experience is well-known and well-documented; concerted efforts having been made to study and explain it; there remain divergences in opinion regarding its cause. The recognized experiences which occur as a result of *near-death* are held by some to be of neurological etiology; the belief that they constitute manifestations of bodily death processes; and held by others to be of metaphysical etiology; the belief that they constitute manifestations of spiritual processes. Many of the actual experiences have been documented, by the individuals who had them, as well as by the medical personnel who observed their manifestations. While there is disagreement as to the source of the experience; human biology or metaphysical reality; the supporting evidence that it genuinely occurs has been sufficient to firmly establish its credibility. Subsequent to the near-death experience, a consistent pattern of changes in the attitudes and behaviors of individuals has been noted; indicating a long-term impact upon individual consciousness.

---

[37] *Merriam-Webster's Collegiate Dictionary, 10th ed.* Merriam-Webster, Inc.: Springfield, Massachusetts, 2001, p. 282.

Consistently reported experiences include: the seeing of bright lights, the sensation of being physically drawn into the bright light, the seeing of angels, and the seeing of persons already deceased. Such experiences are sufficiently reported to be considered characteristic. The cultural context of experience (near death) is relevant, as is the context of impact (sensitive consciousness).

The consistent belief on the part of near-death experiencers that what they have witnessed is real parallels the experience of persons who have had other kinds of less-than-usual experiences; it is also the case with psychics and persons who have reported seeing ghosts. In these types of experiences, the belief is attributed to the fact of the experience.

In the respects that near death, psychic, and ghosting experiences happen primarily to individuals; as differentiated from their happening to groups; and the fact that such occurrences span a wide range of experiences, renders the *culture* of such experience a fairly isolated one, that consists primarily of documented cases and knowledge of the existence of the experience. In this respect, individuals who comprise the *culture of experience* are not subject to the same degree of affiliation that is typical of most subcultures.

There is a kind of characteristic isolatedness to these kinds of experiences; a factor that needs to be taken into account, when considering their contextual influence upon the perceptions and presentations of the individual. The well-documented case of Dorothy Eady, is a prime example. Dorothy Eady was born in London, England, in 1,904 CE. At the age of three, she fell down a flight of stairs, and was pronounced dead by her doctor. One hour later, when the doctor returned with the death certificate, he discovered that Dorothy was very much alive, not dead, as he had pronounced. This documented occurrence can be placed in the category of near death experience.

According to Jonathan Cott, in his account, *The Search For Omm Sety*, subsequent to this resuscitation, Dorothy began having recurrent dreams about a huge building with columns, a garden with fruits and flowers, and tall trees in the distance. The dreaming experiences left Dorothy feeling sad, and she was frequently found crying. In response to parental inquiry as to why she was crying, she responded, *I want to go home.* At the age of four, Dorothy was taken by her parents to the British Museum, where they visited the Egyptian galleries. Dorothy was particularly attracted to the mummy room and did not care to leave it. When her mother attempted to pick her up, she grabbed the side of a glass case, and, speaking in the voice of an old woman, said, *Leave me...**these** are my people!*[38]

Instances of past life regression persisted over the course of Dorothy Eady's life. As she reportedly accessed more and more of her past life, Dorothy came to the understanding that she was the reincarnation of an Egyptian priestess-in-training who had committed suicide after becoming pregnant with Pharoah, Sety the First's child. In this, Eady contended that she had committed a taboo act in violation of the ancient Egyptian God, Osiris', rightful domain.[39] She devoted the rest of her life to the cause of making amends for her past life transgression in ancient Egypt; she married an Egyptian, bore a son, obtained work aiding a world-renowned Egyptologist by the name of Selim Hassan, of the Egyptian Antiquities Department, copying what was depicted on the ancient tombs as they were being excavated. Throughout the duration, she experienced visitations by her former Pharoah lover; witnessed once by her mother-in-law,

---

[38] Cott, Jonathan. *The Search For Omm Sety: Reincarnation And Eternal Love.* Doubleday & Company, Inc.: Garden City, New York, 1987, pp.12-13.

[39] Cott, Jonathan. *The Search For Omm Sety: Reincarnation And Eternal Love.* Doubleday & Company, Inc.: New York, 1987.

who mistook him for her own son.[40] The cultural context of experience (past life regression) is relevant, as is the context of emotion (guilty conscience).

Given that one rarely hears about past life regression, it appears to be a relatively isolated occurrence; whether or not it truly is, I don't know. I remember my surprise at learning about a group of people who were reported to have begun having past life regression experiences after they had all gravitated to live in the same small town in the United States. This was reported in the 1990s, although I don't recall the source. As they began to recollect memories of their past lives, they discovered, to their surprise, they had all known each other in their past life. Reportedly, the unconscious gravitation to live in close proximity served as a catalyst for the past life regression experiences. It was as if they had been called upon to remember and share in the remembrance. Clearly, such experiences impact individual perceptions of reality in the present tense. The cultural context of experience (past life regression) is relevant, as is the context of relationship (transcendent).

The validity of alien encounter and abduction experiences has been documented by Pulitzer Prize winner, John E. Mack, who advises sensitivity in responding to reports of such experiences.[41] Persons who have experienced encounters with alien beings comprise a subculture of their own. The cultural context of experience (alien encounter) is relevant, as is the context of relationship (alien). What is interesting is that by virtue of their occurrence; experiences of near death, past life regression, and alien encounter; despite the fact that they constitute unsought experiences, have resulted in the emergence of new subcultures of human experience, with their own phenomenological impacts.

---

[40] Cott, Jonathan. *The Search For Omm Sety: Reincarnation And Eternal Love,* p. 40.

[41] Mack, M.D., John E. *Abduction: Human Encounters With Aliens,* Rev. Ed. Ballantine Books: New York, 1994.

Reflecting upon the universe of cultures and their sets of subcultures, we will note that the world of the addict also constitutes a subculture of its own. As previously indicated, while the holistic inclusion of such a subculture in our definition of cultural context is not traditional, it is nonetheless a pertinent cross-cultural consideration. As was discussed in Chapter 1, the sets comprised by all members of the subcultural experience, are also component constituents of the larger set of all members within the greater culture. As pertains to addiction, the subset of culture comprised by addicts is further divisible into smaller subsets; those of employed addicts, unemployed addicts, housewife/househusband addicts, homeless addicts, criminal addicts; alcoholic addicts, drug addicts, et cetera. Each subset has its own peculiarities of experience. The culture of the addict warrants this attentional designation, or sensitization of view, given its status as an experiential subcultural subset of the total population. The context of culture (addict) is relevant, as is the context of circumstance (variable).

So, too, do the homeless. I owe recognition of the importance of subcultural differences to a Houston homeless man with whom I held a conversation at the behest of a parish priest. While I was serving in the volunteer capacity of preparing bag lunches for Houston's homeless in 1,996 C.E.; the local church distributed the lunches downtown on a weekly basis; one of the parish priests expressed to me his concern that there was a group of homeless persons sheltering on church premises who had refused the offer of transportation to a designated homeless shelter, and were reluctant to discuss the matter.

When I followed up on the priest's suggestion, I discovered that the homeless men to which he referred had moved to a nearby freeway underpass situated close to a gasoline station that allowed them the usage of their bathroom. One of the men, whose name was Stan, was responsive to discussing the problem. He informed me that there were different types of homeless persons; which he identified as alkie (alcoholic), straight (nonalcoholic), crazy (mentally disturbed), and cutthroat (criminal). He attributed the group's reluctance to go to the downtown city shelter to the latter type, whom he attested kept tabs on all of the homeless persons in the downtown area. These, he stated, would cut a person's throat for a quarter; he and his group of friends stayed clear of them out of fear for their lives. Had I not spoken with Stan, I would not have become sensitized to the unperceived reality of his experience. The cultural context of status (homelessness) is relevant, as is the context of skills (survival).

Cross-cultural considerations, in the expanded and more holistic sense, provide the contextual framework for phenomenological comprehensions of consciousness as psychological perceptions at the micro level of the individual, where subcultural experience is most relevant and impactful; as well as the universal framework for phenomenological comprehensions of consciousness as psychological gestalts at the macro level of the larger cultural world. The universe of cultural context as a whole is relevant, as are the contexts of the various subcultures of experience; interactively, their roles are influential, and important to the phenomenological comprehension of experience.

CHAPTER FOUR

The Symptom of Addiction

Having defined holistic perspectives of context, we can proceed to view the appearance of symptoms of illness as signals of opportunity; potential preludes to enhanced awareness and understanding of the individual's deeper needs. These warrant our attention if we aim to holistically heal the person. Understanding the context of the individual person; the spirit/mind/body that he/she is; the context of the culture and subcultures that pertain; the social and personal environments and experiences; prepares us to holistically heal.

The following example is a case in point. I was introduced to a woman from Mexico, whose husband, an MBA, traveled frequently throughout the Caribbean as an employee of an international hotel chain. She was also the mother of three young children. She tended towards the histrionic; excessively concerned with her frequent cold-catching. It proved embarrassing for her. Given the extent of her self-criticism, she appeared to be experiencing the recurrent illnesses as an indication of failure on her part. She asked me, as a psychologist, what I thought about her problem. My sense that she was overextended in her role of primary nurturer led me to suggest that she speak with a psychologist when she returned home to Mexico City. When I happened to run into her some time later, she related that she was still catching a lot of colds, but that she had stopped worrying about it. She had followed up on my suggestion of seeing a psychologist, and he had informed her that her colds were actually good for her, in that they provided her with an opportunity to rest. Instead of becoming hysterical over each new bout of catching a cold, she had begun taking time to nurture herself with rest.

From a perspective of holistic healing, we find in this example an individual whose context of personality, context of motherhood, and context of life circumstances interacted in such a way as to elicit distress in response to the catching of colds. From a perspective of prevention, were this a recent occurrence, in light of what is now known about how colds are caught, she could be cautioned about the effect of cold weather upon nasal membranes. Her frequent visits to a physician ascertained that she was, indeed, suffering from recurrent colds, and provided her with medicinal remedies; with medical treatment. This did nothing however to cure her distress. In holistic terms, she *healed* when her underlying need to know that there was nothing wrong with *her* was satisfied.

To regard the phenomenon of addiction holistically, we may begin with the understanding of illness in context. This will aid in the rendering of comprehensions that are more meaningful. We can take a step backwards; away from the limited focus of our expectations about addicts and addictive families; in order to better perceive addiction as a symptom of something more. As we view the symptoms of dysfunction, imbalance, and inadequacy, we can consider their contextual origins; in biology, family genetics, personality, spirituality, and personal life experience; and we can consider the role of meaning; that is, the existential basis for their original manifestation.

It is the underlying problem to which we must attend in order to *heal* the individual in the holistic sense; to find and address the *something more* that underlies the symptoms we see as manifestations of dis-ease, dys-function, and dis-order. The underlying problem finds source within the contexts of the individual and her/his cultural experience.

When an individual presents with symptoms of addiction, treatment responds with proscribed and prescribed remedies. The usual scenario is one of recidivism; the individual engages in the proscribed and prescribed treatments, drops out or improves, and later returns with the same recurrent symptoms of addiction. As in the case of the woman with the recurrent colds who frequented her physician for treatment each time she caught a cold, the addict repeatedly presents for treatment of her/his recurring illness. Unlike the case of the woman with the recurrent colds, the addict is not *healed* by learning that there is nothing wrong with her/him as a person. Whether or not the individual believes what they are told, they are taught this in treatment; it does nothing to stop the recurrences, and it does not result in their feeling *healed*.

The addict and the treatment professional are often at wits end to solve the malady; cure the real problem; despite their respective well-meaningness. Typically, they face the option of accepting what appears to be the inevitable in order to function without feeling guilty, or they persist in the often futile belief with its resultant frustration that this time will be the last time that treatment is needed. In other words, they either come to accept or continue to challenge the cycle of recurring symptoms. For the addict, recurrent treatment often becomes an alternative *fix*, of the better sort.

There are instances wherein a different kind of approach has been applied. Psychologist Nicholas Cummings, while engaged in the pioneering work of developing treatment protocols for Kaiser Permanente in San Francisco, established a street presence in Haight Ashbury, in the heart of what was then San Francisco's hippie drug culture. He sent trained individuals to distribute step-by-step detoxification kits to hard-core drug users for at-home detoxification. This was a case of providing persons whose personal preference was to avoid institutionalized treatment or who couldn't afford it, with the means by which they could treat themselves with a form of over-the-counter remedy. While such remedy does not *cure* addiction, it serves as an example of creative response to the problem of recidivism and the high costs of recurrent treatment.

To complicate matters, there are two trains of thought on the matter of pharmaceutical intervention as a response to the problem of addiction. Alcoholics Anonymous, the self-help organization, which will be discussed in a later chapter, holds firmly to the belief that the addict in recovery; be they alcohol or narcotic dependent; must abstain from the use of chemicals, including pharmaceuticals, in order for full recovery to occur. The medical community holds firmly to the belief that pharmaceuticals are essential to treatment, and endorses the use of same. With regards to pharmaceutical usage, the positions are diametrically opposed; putting the individual who seeks care simultaneously from both sources; as patients of mine have encountered; in a position of conflict. At a time of personal vulnerability, s/he must decide which route to take. In one instance, I was called to conduct a hospital evaluation of a heroin addict who was being held for detoxification against his will; he had been deemed a danger to himself. Despite the experience of physical agony during the detoxification process, he adamantly refused to be medicated, and had been straight-jacketed. The conflict in this case was one born of fear rather than a difference in beliefs; the individual was not a member of AA and had no interest in recovering from his addiction. Sensitivity to the reality of the person's encounter with such clashes of cultural beliefs is relevant to treatment.

On a voluntary basis, the practice of pharmaceutical intervention in cases of heroin addiction has proven viable in both New York and England. The treatment involves the administration of methadone, a synthetic narcotic, and other such drugs that deter usage by inducing gastrointestinal distress when the individual ingests heroin.

Addicts know that they are addicts. This statement would appear to run counter to the notion of denial; the tendency of the addict to rationalize her/his behavior to others and to themselves. Despite outward denials, consciously or unconsciously, persons know when they have reached the point of addiction. It is not a matter upon which they consciously dwell; preferring to avoid thinking about it, often angering when confronted by others. The knowledge, in the sense of knowing the truth, does not necessarily render them amenable to treatment. At this stage, the matter is one of personal cognizance; it is only for me to know. To intrude upon the privacy of this self-awareness is to violate trust.

Trust is an important consideration when relating with and treating addicts; whether or not the addict feels another person can be trusted is a significant factor in whether or not a relationship will develop and/or continue. At a later stage, if the person has chosen a path of recovery, admittance of addiction to like-kind others takes precedence over admittance to friends and family. Again, the matter is one of trust; who can I most trust?

The addict in recovery, feeling psychologically vulnerable, is more apt to experience like-kind others as a kind of comfort zone. Treatment professionals fall into a similar category of response; that of you're a doctor, I don't have to tell you, you already know the truth. There is a sense of relief in the avoidance of having to take the lead in disclosure; it is one thing for someone who can be safely trusted to know the truth, and quite another to tell the truth to someone who may not be safe to trust.

As recovery continues, if the decision of abstinence has been made, the addict becomes more forthright in admitting her/his addiction to others. At this stage, while the addict becomes more comfortable with the declaration, s/he continues to retain all rights of ownership to the knowledge. The need to possess the knowledge persists; it is *my* knowledge; unless you've been there, you don't understand. At this stage, the need for respect of privacy transforms into the need for respect of experience.

At later stages of recovery, when the likelihood of success in maintaining abstinence becomes a foreseeable reality, the fact that the addict is in recovery becomes a source of pride. Relationship at this point becomes exclusionary in a new way, as the addict begins to lay claim to her/his life as a recovered addict; resulting in the exclusion of others s/he perceives as a threat to the new identity of self. The variable needs and percepts of the addict at different stages of addiction and recovery, which we may regard as symptoms, are clearly relevant to the context of treatment.

The symptomatic picture of addiction is consistent in terms of its physiological and psychological effects. The addicted individual who chooses to abstain from chemical usage, and does so successfully for a considerable period of time, while proud of their continued success at abstinence, knows in her/his heart of hearts that they are not cured of their addiction. More typical than not, the *recovered* addict, while resisting the urge to use substances, or having surpassed this to a point of self-modified behavioral abstinence, has not resolved the underlying cause; that je ne se quois earlier referred to as the *something more* underlying the illness. The fact that symptoms of anxiety, depression, pain, and/or chronic dissatisfaction often precede the process of addiction, and persist when the point of addiction is reached, is indicative of underlying distress. As the process of recovering from substance use progresses, and the chemical lid that masked them is removed from the body, the initial symptoms of distress re-emerge, much to the chagrin of the abstinent addict.

Without an holistic restoration of the out-of-kilter homeostasis of spirit/mind/body, cure does not occur. The addiction, or propensity to engage in addictive behavior, remains on the back burner of being, available for rekindling under conducive circumstances. As addicts themselves relate, this translates into an act of transgression; that of rationalizing the taking of just one drink, just one syringe, or just one pill; subsequent to a period of sobriety, proceeding from there in a process of becoming unstoppably intoxicated. Binging is not uncommon following a period of sustained sobriety, once sobriety is transgressed.

The longer the duration of abstinence, the greater becomes the realization. The process of knowingness that evolves is akin to that of the intellectual; the more they come to know, the greater the realization of how little they know. As this evolutionary recognition arises, a concomitant sense of humility develops; an intellectual humbling in the face of acknowledged reality. The recovered addict at this stage has achieved a breakthrough in consciousness.

Given that symptoms of addiction occur within the context of culture, we can take note of the relationship. Culturally conducive circumstances are not difficult to find. The realities of modern life themselves are conducive to the development of addiction and its kindling within individual lives. Thus, we find that stress; in the strives to survive and succeed; a concomitant tendency to suppress emotionality; as something that gets in the way of striving; the paradox of America; established to uphold individual freedoms, with industrialization and globalization, has witnessed an emergent disregard for the freedom of the individual; persons have become expendable commodities, jobs are short-lived, lives are torn asunder by the emergent reality which threatens the very freedom of their existence, which freedom has been replaced by the industrially-related encouragement to consume; and the related resulting failure to satisfy the innermost needs of the individual.

The cultural reality is complicated by the fact that industry can no longer afford to provide cradle-to-grave assurances, resulting in the lost security of retirement pensions, and government can no longer afford to provide welfare supports except to the neediest members of society. This new economic reality arises from the problem of overpopulation that international demographers forecasted and warned us about in the mid-1970s; that the burgeoning of the world's population posed a potential catastrophe; unabated, it would eventually result in famine and strife. The worldwide cultural circumstance, we find, is one of struggling to contend with the strain of an increasing human population.

I believe these culturally conducive circumstances to be the *something more* underlying the spirit/mind/body phenomenon of addiction and the high incidence of relapse following treatment. These circumstances of culture, rather than an inadequacy in regimens of treatment, an inadequacy in providers of treatment, or an inadequacy in capacities of individuals are largely responsible. Treatment in the context of a persistently counter-productive environment or a persistently unhealed body cannot work miracles; thus, the change that occurs in treatment is one of improvement rather than cure, circumstantially limited to the cessation of substance use. The loss of freedom and regard for the individual has rendered the context of culture significantly relevant to the matter of addiction.

In addition to the extent reality of conducive culture, genetic factors provide further explanation for the *something more* behind the phenomenon. As research has discovered, inherent biological tendencies within certain groups of peoples affect their responses to substances in such a manner as to render them more prone to addiction. For example, it has been discovered that there is a genetic difference among Asian Americans which affects the rate at which their bodies metabolize alcohol; at less than the processing rate of other groups of people studied. Another example is the discovery of a genetic difference among African American men which affects the rate at which their bodies process nicotine; compared to other racial groups, they have been found to retain greater concentrations of nicotine in the blood; a fact which the American Psychological Association states may contribute to greater difficulty in quitting smoking.[42]

Aside from the context of genetics, there exists the potential for substance use to result in brain damage; creating rigidity in the behavior of the individual. The chronic consumption of alcohol can thus be viewed to be a brain damaging factor that results in the alcoholic pattern of insatiability. There is a parallel between the insatiability of the alcoholic; in the repetitive rigidity of the behavior; and similarly rigid patterns of behavior observed among individuals diagnosed as schizophrenic; indicating that similar areas of the brain may have been affected. A nature (schizophrenia) versus nurture (alcoholism) characterization of the etiology of observed similarities in behavioral rigidity provides hypothesis for comparative study. The observed parallel of behavior across contexts is relevant for consideration.

Given that alterations of brain chemistry, functioning, and structure can occur as a result of chronic drinking, addiction is viewed as a consequence of the habit of heavy consumption. This occurs when the substance use reaches the point of altering the normal body-to-brain messaging function such that the person's brain fails to signal the need to stop drinking. In the respect that alcohol is a central nervous system depressant, the degree of depression of consciousness co-varies with the amount of substance ingested. High levels of ingestion result in greater degrees of mental incapacitation. With chronic usage, the potential increases that changes to the brain may become permanent.

---

[42] American Psychiatric Association, p. 267.

From an holistic perspective, the context of substances and their effects upon the brain are relevant to a consideration of the symptoms of addiction, as is the capacity for the brain to heal itself.

The revolving door of addiction treatment speaks to the lack of long-term success. Whether such recurrence may be permanently altered remains to be seen. Given the dynamics of the current picture, one is justified in the perception that attendance to underlying factors appears to be regarded as a luxury rather than a necessity. This follows on the heels of changes in medical practice over the course of the past fifty or so years that have rendered health care more affordable for the masses; in so doing, medical practice has become more practical, more standardized, and less likely to engage in experimental, exploratory, or analytic processes. In the same way that psychoanalysis has come to be perceived as a luxury of the rich, so too, has long-term health care. While such change does not preclude the possibility of effecting cure, the change has resulted in a redefinition of cure; now normatively defined as the goals of treatment. As regards addiction, the current standard of practice is to treat the symptoms versus the underlying cause. Under such contextual cultural circumstance, there exists a greater likelihood that we will miss, rather than hit upon a long-lasting cure.

Given extent realities of culture, and related extent realities of persons, we face a present-day legacy of distress. Perception of the prevalence of this phenomenon no doubt played a key role in the APA's conduct of national conferences on stress in the late 1990s to promote awareness of the problem throughout the psychology community. The context of the many changes which have occurred in the United States over the course of the past fifty years is relevant to an understanding of the psychological disequilibrium. While the collapse of the World Trade Center on Manhattan Island in 2,001 C.E., engendered considerable distress, it is by no means a solitary source; others will be discussed in a later chapter. In the face of prevalent sources of stress, persons experience disequilibrium. The context of stressful change has resulted in a greater incidence of emotional distress among the national population than existed prior to their onset. An act of aggression against one's country, as in war or terrorist attack, may be perceived as an instance of life's failure to meet basic human needs; in this case, security. The experience plunges one into an existential quandary; What is the meaning of this aggression? Why has God forsaken us? The need to make sense of the senseless, and to resolve it, is powerful; motivated as it is by a natural inclination towards healthy functioning. Denial of the need prolongs the negative psychological effects. From an holistic perspective, the powerful polar impacts upon the spirit/mind/body; the horror that sends one careening backwards, and the search for meaning that propels one forwards; are essential aspects of the experience of disequilibrium.

When one considers the extensiveness of the terrorism, war, and natural disasters that have affected so many persons around the globe, one comes to the realization that something significant is happening. As we attend to the matters of distress and illness, a conscious sensitivity to this global state of imbalance affecting human lives is indicated. We would certainly expect to find a higher-than-normal incidence of generalized anxiety and dysphoria among the general populations that have been directly affected. Any person; consciously or unconsciously; aware of and sensitive to the import of such significant occurrences, may also experience reactions. Therefore, the origins of the symptoms we see may not be as obvious as they may, at first consideration, appear. There is no denying that they occur within the context of a global cultural climate that has become less nurturing. Broadening our scope of view to incorporate all aspects of impact will facilitate more holistic comprehension, in the quest to promote healing.

If we expand our perception of addiction as a disease to *addiction as a phenomenon that occurs within the context of culture*, the reason that preventing and curing addiction is such a struggle becomes apparent. We find that we cannot effectively resolve the problem without addressing the underlying variables. Whether one chooses to call such variables deficiencies, factors, imbalances, impingements, et cetera, is irrelevant; the influences exist and they are multi-varied. We may choose to select a particular factor, or a group of factors, with which to clarify our understanding. We may, for instance, select lifestyle as a factor for consideration; or personality type, or observed or reported idiosyncracies. However we choose to address the matter, it is important that we do so with the understanding that such factors of influence are discrete aspects of the phenomenon as a whole. If we ignore these contextual influences, our efforts to resolve how to effectively deal with the problem of addiction, will inevitably fall short. Standardized protocols provide a useful framework for the conduct of treatment; they do not however guarantee a cure. The potential for ineffectiveness in reaching established treatment goals exists even when a standardized treatment protocol is employed. Other variables; such as amenability, readiness, and therapeutic relationship; come into play.

What we can accomplish by perceiving the phenomenon holistically is a greater understanding, a philosophical base of comprehension from which to proceed in our efforts. Knowing that context is important enables us to evaluate the invisible links between influences and symptoms; it enables us to be more response-adaptive in individualizing our interventions to the idiosyncratic experience of the individual.

Whether what we take note of consists of behavioral, cultural, emotional, genetic, legal, medical, social, or spiritual presentation, the noted symptoms are corollary to the primary symptom of addiction; what we clinically refer to as *the disorder.* How we generically regard the primary symptom of addiction is key to how we will specifically regard the corollary symptoms; to whether or not we address the disorder in idiosyncratically relevant terms that are true to the heart and nature of underlying causes for given individuals.

For example, if we regard sixteen year-old Susie Que's alcoholism as a disease, we will do justice to the biology of the problem, but we may fail to enrich her impoverished home life, or fail to facilitate a redirection of her unactualized need for individuation away from substance use towards something more beneficial. If our aim is holistic healing, we will need to consider how best to address Susie Que's self-development needs; the conflict underlying the manifested disorder of adolescent alcoholism.

In keeping with the holistic perspective that contextual factors of influence are relevant to manifestations of illness, we must then proceed to view the phenomenon of addiction itself, as it manifests among individuals and families, as a symptom as well as an illness. In this general regard of illness as a symptom, we must necessarily look to the broader context of culture to more fully understand the problem. When we focus treatment and prevention efforts on the elimination of manifested symptoms of addiction, without altering the underlying contextual problems of human emotion, physiology, and spirituality, we fail to heal the individual. When we address the phenomenon of addiction as an illness without recognizing its simultaneous status as a symptom reflecting the nature or state of the predominant culture, we fail to understand its true origins, and inevitably fall short of effecting meaningful change in the cultural sense.

From this broader perspective, we find that the recurrent symptom of addiction, in the general sense, constitutes an entrenched problem embedded within a problematic cultural context; a cultural context which aids and abets addiction while simultaneously denigrating the addicted; it constitutes a problem within a problem. Unable to find a permanent solution to the problem of addiction, including through prohibition as will be discussed later, we resorted to blame; resulting in ostracization and denial of treatment. The problem persists despite historical efforts to eliminate it. The current Zeitgeist is diagnostic; oriented towards treatment of the problem. And yet, as we understand from the reality of recidivism, the problem persists. It is interesting and relevant to note that in each of the mentioned cultural postures adopted in the United States towards the problem of addiction, the prevailing cultural belief has been that it was the appropriate moral response.

That these responses are well-meaning in their intentions is unquestionable, however short they have fallen from being effective. One could liken America's responses to the problem of addiction in her midst to that of an aspiring Olympiad-in-training; she continues, through trial and error, to hone her capacities in order that she might gain degrees of mastery that will enable her to contend with the problem.

Short of a magic pill to end cravings, and a miracle to end the mental discombobulation that occurs among hard-core alcoholics, there is little likelihood of a cure in the short-term future. At present, we are faced with choosing between the alternatives of abstinence and recurrent treatment. As part of the process of seeking an appropriate moral response, it is my contention that an holistic approach is philosophically essential, in that it will necessitate culture taking stock of itself.

PART TWO

THE CONTEXT OF CONSUMERISM

CHAPTER FIVE

The Context of Identification

Having established what culture is and how it is relevant to an holistic understanding, we proceed to explore the context of consumerism in a changing world. We begin by acknowledging the reality that the world is in tumult; as the process of change that began in the last century continues, the world finds itself in the inescapable throes of a major developmental crisis. Few of us anticipated its coming. Most of us, focusing, as is the tendency, upon individual lives, did not.

The advent of the age of communication technologies; telephony, televisions, computers, and internet; began the process. For the most part fascinated by these technological wonders, people welcomed them with open arms, open hearts, and closed minds. Little did we realize that telephony would one day change the world. Nor did we anticipate the extensiveness of television's reach. We certainly did not foresee, when the massive first computers were constructed, that computers would one day pave the way for the globalization of economy. By the time the internet was invented, the prior communication technologies were already firmly in place; providing a solid foundation for the figurative icing on the cake of planet Earth. Thus, were we ushered out of the theater of the industrial age and into the theater of the information age.

What began as novelty became customary. In time, we became accustomed to using the new devices. As we also became visually accustomed with persons from around the world, we became more interested in the globalization of economy. It is highly doubtful, for example, that an international space station would have been cooperatively engineered by diverse aeronautics and space administrations were it not for the establishment of the information age. It has become customary to refer to *the global economy*, a reality which didn't exist a few decades ago.

Almost without realizing it, and certainly without adequate preparation, the industrialized nations began to turn in the direction of globalization; and like the movement of massive creatures, their turning had ponderous repercussions. The turning created a marked shift in the nature of their societies; from industrial to information-based. The wild horse of globalization was thus spurred; the impact cataclysmic. Rarely in the ascertained history of this planet has an event with such extensive impact occurred. The Ice Age of the Pleistocene epoch; that lasted from 1.6 million years to 10,000 years B.C.E.; when the first humans appeared was one such event. The Flood; The Deluge as it is referred to in the Bible, that lasted from 2,348 to 2,347 B.C.E. was another. The Resurrection; of Jesus the Christ after his crucifixion; in 30 C.E. was another. In terms of human experience, the impact on consciousness is enormous. The paradigm shift has rocked the foundations of social structures around the planet, leaving people feeling shaken, confused, and conflicted about their collective and respective identities.[43]

The conversion has had a trickle down effect; from the top levels of government and industry, to the lowest levels

---

[43] Alvin and Heidi Toffler. *War and Anti-War: Survival at the Dawn of the 21st Century.* Little, Brown and Company: Boston, MA, 1993.

of society. Organizational structures, policies, and practices have been reconstituted to accomodate the paradigmatic change. In people terms, many of the changes that followed proved confusing. The world watched as corporations around the world merged, downsized, reorganized, bankrupted, and laid off employees in greater numbers than previously experienced. The world watched as government followed suit. Was globalization out of control? Had the world gone crazy? Would the changes that were taking place prove beneficial or disastrous? Those in the know provided repeated assurance through the media that all would end well, that the changes were necessary, that economies would have a better chance of survival as a result of the changes being employed. Stock market analysts nodded their heads in assent. Those with the capacity to do so, opportuned.

While the economies of the world engaged in the process of globalization, striving to stabilize their own sectors from failing, another process began; the globalization of governments. The superpower status of the United States of America began to wane; the global body of the United Nations experienced an increase in power; the international trade treaty, G.A.T.T., was signed in Uruguay; the Christian Coalition was formed to ally Christian churches; a European Union to facilitate trade between European nations was formed; Asia followed suit with the establishment of a consortium of Asian nations; all of which happened in response to the emergent reality of globalization.

While the world rumbled, tumbled, and re-engineered, lives reeled from the impact. Reactions were swift; terrorism waxed, wars erupted, a global set of fraternal twins; cooperation and conflict; was born; simultaneously reeking havoc where none existed. There is no apt analogy to explain the experience of watching the worldwide developments; observation was exhausting, the rapidly occurring events were non-stop. Decision-makers; from the level of government to the level of individual; were challenged in consequence by the need to respond.

As entities responded, decisions rendered were met with mixed reactions. Government celebrated the end of the welfare state; it was replaced with low-wage employment. Unionists fought to retain comprehensive benefits, but eventually lost to the changed reality. Professionals and their practices were consumed by the expediency of temp and online services; rendered available on an as-needed basis at lower cost. The private office was replaced by the clinic and the home office. The time-honored tradition of striving to become a doctor or a lawyer lost its place of importance in the mind of the Reformation. It was replaced by the mantra of small business; boosted by an outpouring of ads and offers via electronic mail, postal mail, and the media. Traditions everywhere were impacted; long-standing manifestations of civilized society that no one ever expected to change, crumbled into a thing of the past.

The changes to society have not only impacted the circumstances of living and of individual lives, they have impacted identity; rendering it more fluid, less stable, impermanent. Whereas, in days recently bygone, a person would be identified throughout her/his lifespan by an established role in life; such regard has become irrelevant to the new society. Roles are interchangeable; regard and identity are consequently de-linked from what used to be considered as *one's role in life*. Life, in this respect, has become more here-and-now oriented. What enabled the elders of society to gain in respect and stature, has become an irrelevancy.

Hence, an unforeseen form of democraticization has occurred. More and more often, we encounter such startling changes as physicians working as realtors and mathematicians working as tutors; occurrences previously considered anomalies. Such changes in societal makeup have confused personal and professional identities in a rather fundamental way. If one is a doctor by education and prior practice, and a realtor by current employment, how does one resolve the identification of one's occupation? A doctor and a realtor would be the logical response; however, the logical response is precluded by the strictures of government reporting forms, such as those of the IRS, which require currency in the documentation of employment status. The result is a growing inconsistency in individual status over time.

Whereas, at the turn of the last century, the primary sources of individual employment instability were attributable to immigrant or criminal status, they can no longer be so attributed; given the effect of a globalized society upon the mainstream of life. Appearance has become irrelevant; whereas, previously one could largely distinguish the career orientation of an individual on the basis of clothing style, this is no longer the case. Media portrayals have good-humoredly poked fun at this truth; in a documentary that depicted a man conducting business from his home office in his pajamas, and a program depicting a mother struggling with constant demands from her children while attempting to work from her home. When status, lifestyle, and appearance cease to be relevant to the context of identity, the question becomes, What then?. As a result of changes in the reality of work and lifestyles, people have become more mobile, and communities less stable. The quixotic nature of such extent reality is reflected in the chaos that many persons in industrialized turned informationalized nations face.

The matter of personal identity is complicated by an internet reality which permits the unregulated purchasing of domains. In 1,999 C.E., when I attended a conference in Houston about doing business on the internet, I learned that it was legal for anyone on the planet to purchase an internet domain in any name, including that of genuine individuals. The advice of the conference presenters was that persons would be well-advised to protect their individual identities by purchasing the rights to domains in their own personal and company names in order to prevent others from doing so. As long as a domainer continues to pay annual registration fees, s/he retains the right to the use of the domain name, even if it constitutes the use of someone else's legitimate personal or company name. The potential for confusion is apparent.

A related context of identification is the area of email accounts; a popular tool for communication in the age of information. An example from personal experience demonstrates the potential hazard that exists for individuals. In 2,006 C.E., I discovered another instance of fraudulent use of my identity; that occurred in 2,005 C.E.. In response, I attempted to establish what I hoped would be a protected group of email accounts; one in each of my names of record. It was a novel solution that I thought would put an end to the problem of identity fraud. What I discovered shocked me. I was denied establishing the accounts by provider restrictions that limited the numbers of accounts permitted to use the same or similar name; e.g., John Doe, John Doe1, John Doe2. The fact of the matter was that too many accounts had already been established in my names of record. Who were these persons holding email accounts in my names of record? Why were they using my names for their accounts instead of their own? When such practice; the legal use of other person's identities, on a first-come, first-served basis; exists, the problem of identity confusion is surpassed by the problem of denial of the individual's right to the use of their own identity. The reality of the situation is undeniably absurd. It would not have become possible were it not for the transition to an information age, and the chaos that such transitions engender.

Thus, we find that the context of a change in world society, and the multiplicity of effects which it has engendered, has had far-reaching impacts upon identity, including ways unforeseen. We are, in many respects, at the mercy of such phenomenal change. We cannot help but be buffeted by the force of these winds of change; once enacted, the process has taken on a life of its own, developing in ways unanticipated, for which the majority of us have been unprepared. Who we are, who and what we will become is as yet a mystery to us all. What can be clearly gleaned is an understanding that such process of change is in effect, that it has tremendous impact upon the nature and course of human life, that persons must struggle to find ways to cope with the chaos of a world in process of becoming something other than what it was. How we do so will have its own influence, its own impact upon the end result; when the order of a newly established normalcy results. Until then, we falter, we flail, we strive, we seek, we plan, we attempt; in short, we learn; what it is we are coping with and how best to cope, from a position of experiencing. The context is one of direct, versus vicarious, experience.

Identification at this stage is variable; a factor that must be reckoned with. Persons, companies, public entities, and governments, in the aftermath of the shakeup, face periods of trial-and-error, as they try and test the possibilities, as yet unsure as to which will provide preferred results. What constitutes preferred result is at question; debatable by diverse interests. At this stage, there are no guarantees, only possibilities. We have already changed in more ways than most people either realize or reflect upon, this being more difficult to perceive while in the process of becoming. Perceived or not, many changes have occurred, some of which may last, some of which may not. The outcome, in part, will depend upon choices of identification.

In the midst of the transitioning; from a known past to an unknown future; the status of resources poses a matter of primary importance. Such concerns are reflected in the following questions. Will there be sufficient resources to sustain the globalization process? By whose hand will such resources be controlled? Will the haves protect and care for the don't haves? Will a third world war emerge in a struggle for world dominion? Who will prevail, what will emerge? These are not trivial questions; they are at the heart of every conflict. While we do not yet know the answers, we bear witness to the evidence of the transpiring.

The process can be confusing; the visions we see compelling and contradictory, the emotions we experience undeniable and frightening. Where do we go from here? Under such circumstance, tolerance has its limits and its abuses. Integrity is challenged by opportunism. Definitions of rational response fluctuate. In analogical reference to the life stage of the adolescent, the world is in a similar developmental crisis; the chaos of conflicting and competitive urges mimicking the chaos of raging hormones, the chaos of confused identity paralleling the chaos of adolescent turmoil, the risk potential for irrational conduct at an all-time high. Could we have foreseen that, in leaving the stability of the established past behind, the world would be thrown into a turmoil reminiscent of adolescence? Wherefore art thou, identity?

Emotions are a relevant context of identification. For normally healthy individuals, when life is stable, emotions are stable. When life is unstable, as it is under conditions of major upheaval, emotions are thrown off balance. A normally healthy individual identifies with normalcy; therefore, when life is no longer normal, and emotions respond to the abnormalcy of life, identity is affected. When persons seek treatment, they seek it as much for their need to reaffirm and reestablish their identity; of normalcy; as they do for relief from their emotional distress. Countless times in my experience patients have remarked, I'm so relieved to know I'm not crazy! The reaffirmation of their sense of their own normalcy is what proved most reassuring; putting the rest of the treatment process into proper context. For the normally unhealthy individual, the response follows a similar parallel; they seek a reaffirmation and reestablishment of the identity they were comfortable with prior to life's upheaval. In such cases, the upheaval may have exacerbated already existing symptoms, and added additional ones. In both cases, the normally healthy and the normally unhealthy individual seek stabilization; of their identities, their symptoms, and their life circumstances. In my experience, oblivion is the only reason an individual does not seek restabilization; the kind of oblivion experienced in states of psychosis, and in conditions of organicity.

As persons struggle to secure themselves in the midst of cultural chaos, they must also struggle with the feelings of helplessness and powerlessness it engenders. It is wise to accept that even when persons attempt to regain a sense of normalcy, normalcy in terms of experience may prove elusive. Particularly affected are persons accustomed to living in the so-called fast lane; they are unprepared for the experience of sudden change that occurs when they face the new reality of younger firings in the service of younger hirings. Regardless of the circumstance, anxiety about an uncertain present and an unknown future is a natural response.

When life is insecure, security concerns predominate. In America, this became evident in the early 2000s when a political uproar over government-managed social security ensued; with Republicans contending that individuals could manage their own social security funds to better advantage, and Democrats contending that government management is a safety net for people who would otherwise be unable to protect themselves during their retirement years. The reactions followed on the heels of the government's announcement that, under the prevailing economic conditions, the social security fund would eventually run out of money. The possibility of losing social security elicited strong reactions from an American public accustomed to having a retirement safety net; for approximately seventy years since its beginnings during the Great Depression. This, too, is a natural response. Other industrialized nations have faced similar challenges.

What we have come to know, without accepting, is that life is not the same as it was before globalization began its series of sweeping changes. We know that lives the world over have been impacted; dramatically so in some cases; without the security of life rafts to rescue them from certain calamity. The climate of cultural change contributes to a general sense of unease; persons wonder what the world will be like forty or fifty years hence. The context of identification is one of uncertainty. It was, therefore, both surprising and not surprising when the magazine, *Psychology Today*, at the beginning of this century of change, reported that over ninety percent (90%) of Americans were depressed. Ninety percent is an enormous portion of the population. This telling fact indicates the significance of the impact of what is happening upon the psychology of persons; the context of change and uncertainty is pervasive. Whether similar national surveys have been conducted elsewhere, I do not know; however, the American report would suggest similar findings among other industrialized nations.

As human beings, we need time to absorb and assimilate change. Changes that occur too rapidly or too dramatically overwhelm our systemic capabilities for assimilation; they bombard the sensibilities and interfere with the capacity to respond effectively. The human capacity for shock absorption is not a mechanical reflex, like that of a car. As animate beings, we consciously experience the full impact of any and all shocks. With respect to responding adaptively to the changes that envelope us, we cannot systemically avoid being shocked. We consequently find ourselves jolted by the unreality of unwanted and unexpected life-changing events. We wake up to the discovery that we are working longer and harder, with fewer rewards. We discover that we are readily expendable; dispensable and disposable like the products we consume. Increasingly, we experience a shorter and shorter shelf life. We come to the shocking realization that life is not as good as we would like it to be. It is a vital truth that we must face rather than deny; a revelation about the context of our world that reflects upon our human identity.

While our human consciousness prevents the avoidance of culture shock, we have a saving grace in the form of a capacity to think; and in so doing, to change the way we think. Our capacity as conscious beings is our primary survival mechanism; without it we would likely extinct like our forebears.

The worldwide cultural climate of accelerated change has intensified the angst of modern life. What Nina Tassi described as a phenomenon of urgency addiction persists in new form. A distorted perception of time deriving from artificially imposed cultural pressures to accomplish what isn't essential and doesn't require doing; identified as an emergent phenomenon among over-achievers; has moved to the world stage.[44] Culturally unrealistic expectations and demands continue to be a source of distress; the sense of having too much to do and not enough time to do it in now affects governments as well as individuals. This cultural condition is exacerbated by the rash of unexpected disasters that have taken their toll on human lives and resources, fostering a sense that time is running out; that civilization does not have the proper solutions in place for recuperation to occur.

The condition of high stress Tassi describes is self-imposed; the result of identification with a cultural mantra that says time is of the essence. The mantra engenders fear in individuals; fear of failure if they don't scramble, even when personal success has been achieved. It is a fear of failing to achieve; security and success; deriving from cultural inputs promoting high performance. Tassi's point is that the phenomenon of response has significantly impacted the quality of individual lives; the emphasis on high performance spurring an unnatural state of overdrive.

---

[44] Nina Tassi. Urgency *Addiction: How to Slow Down Without Sacrificing Success.* Taylor Publishing Co.: Dallas, TX, 1991.

Life has become less secure than it was in the 1990s, to some extent in ways unforeseen. Given that conditions of high stress tend to distort our perceptions, adding a sense of urgency, the problem has likely incremented. Shrinking resources exacerbate the already existing problem, making it more difficult to resolve. As difficult as it is under such circumstances, the wisest action, in coinage terms, is to keep our heads on our shoulders; to reason our way through the mental jumble in order to minimize the effect of distorted perception.

Tassi informs us that the sense of time urgency is unnatural and unhealthy; it calls for a reclarification of what is truly important and essential for our lives. From this modern perspective, there is a cultural problem of identification; the context one of identifying with proscriptions contrary to our own happiness. One may well ask whether what we are doing is essential to our health and well-being, whether the actions we engage in are essential to our welfare. An holistic, and patently Western, perspective would wonder whether we have weighed the value of our identifications; whether the returns on our investment, that is, the identificationing of our selves in this and other manners is worth the risk.

An holistic Eastern perspective would wonder whether we are acting in accordance with the cosmic forces of life and the universal principles of change in the world. From such perspective one may well ask whether we are responding, individually and culturally, in a manner that goes with the flow of life's vicissitudes, in order to avoid being drowned by change. This is the perspective presented in the Chinese classic, the *I Ching* (pronounced Yi King), or *Book of Changes.*[45] The Chinese language character for change is a composite of the symbols for crisis and opportunity. From this ancient perspective, we are poised at a critical turning

---

[45] James Legge (Translator). *I Ching, Book of Changes: The Ancient Chinese Guide to Wisdom and Fortunetelling.* Random House Value Publishing, Inc.: New Jersey, 1996.

point in human history; beset by the rapids of the raging river of change. The question becomes one of response; will we respond to the vagaries by turning crisis into opportunity, and find ways to survive the rapids?

If we choose to identify with wisdom, we will hearken to the truths inherent in these holistic perspectives of East and West. They provide relevant insights; comprehending them enables us to assess the contexts of identification and change in holistically meaningful ways.

From my own experience, the following example demonstrates the paradox; of crisis/opportunity; that the ancient Chinese, as evidenced by their language, comprehended. While acting in the position of crisis director with Medco Behavioral Care Corporation, in San Antonio, Texas, I was faced with the responsibility of responding to crises pertaining to mental health. Although I didn't comprehend it this way at the time, the role provided first-hand experience of the crisis/opportunity paradox. As director in charge of crisis services, the on-call responsibility was twenty-four hours, seven days a week, for a population of over 160,000 insured persons. Reflecting upon the experience from a crisis/opportunity perspective, the steady stream of requests for services posed a challenge of crisis; the raging river of change was threatening to drown lives; the challenge was how to save them from drowning without drowning in the process.

This example of the paradox of crisis/opportunity; how the turning of a crisis; a negative situation of critical incident; into an opportunity; a positive situation of quality care; provides elucidation of its holistic meaning, that therein lies the potential; to succumb or to survive. While the facing of crises constitutes challenge, the perspective with which one does so impacts outcome, in a positive or negative direction. In the positive sense, one is proactive; in the negative, reactive. The context of global culture poses a similar challenge of crisis/opportunity; in this as in other circumstances, it is a perspective of wisdom that is essential to saving lives from being drowned by change; at risk are the lives of the individuals and the lives of the individual cultures. Without wise response, they cannot continue to be viable functioning entities. The modality of wise response holds to an attitude of rescue; providing the opportunity for survival in the midst of the situation of crisis. In psychological parlance, survival in the context of change is a matter of consciousness; of thinking and reframing perspective; in this case, identification; how and with what we identify, in order to ensure the survivability of humans and human cultures.

The changed and changing world faces a dilemma similar to that which I faced as a crisis director; how to respond to a seemingly unending stream of change. Each change or deviation from usual and customary practices and tendencies imposes a strain on coping resources. The strain can be endured with a variety of attitudes; with anger, courage, forbearance, suffering, tolerance, et cetera. The strain can be remediated with a variety of responses; with assistance, caring, networking, provisioning, rescuing, et cetera. Response is a matter of perspective. Coping resources, while the currents of change continue flowing, will experience the undesired strain. How the coping resources are applied will depend upon perspective; the attitudes and approach of those in a position to respond; those affected and those providing.

With respect to cultural identity; in all of its planetary varieties; we may allow ourselves to be buffeted by the unpredictability of life, the way that the stock markets react to changes in corporate circumstances, or we may consciously choose to navigate our way through the winds and waters of change; adjusting our steering to re-align and re-balance; maintaining the homeostasis of our boats of culture, and preventing them from being overturned. As members of the flotilla of boats that constitute the world's cultures, do we want the flotilla to acquire a unified cultural identity, or do we want to retain our distinct identities? Under conditions of globalization, the potential for unification of identity exists. This is evidenced by such global unification trends as the internationalization of communication via the internet, the internationalization of the stock markets, the internationalization of language with the recognition of English as a world standard, the internationalization of production and trade, the internationalization of jobs and services, the unification of Europe with the issuance of a European currency, et cetera. To retain distinct cultural identities while experiencing globalization and engaging in international commerce requires agreement; the flotilla must agree to the terms of distinction; else the sheer size of the flotilla threatens to overwhelm not only the identities of its members, but the identities of all else; the cultures of the nonmembers. Ironically, the globalization of economy that has diminished the hazard potential of another world war, has created a new threat; the threat of world domination. For the industrialized turned informationalized nations that have chosen to join the global flotilla, whose identities have been doubled by the joining; adding an identity of international status to that of their identity of national status; the question is one of integrity; will they allow the flotilla to dominate the planet in order to benefit from the joining? The potential for such outcome consists of two scenarios; benign and malignant despotism. Short of a war to force change upon the flotilla, the responsibility lies with the flotilla itself to prevent such outcome. Will the flotilla adopt a perspective of wisdom that will limit its own power to dominate? Will it ensure the rights of nonmember as well as member nations, and protect both from destructive exploitation? These questions are relevant to the context of identification. From human history, we know that power has the potential to yield corruption; it holds a powerful attraction, serving as a magnet, to the corrupt, who gravitate towards it and utilize it for their own expedience.

Thus, the global flotilla, as a large and powerful entity, has the potential to be so affected.

At this turning point in human history, the potential for world domination exists; of the benign and the malignant kind; as does the potential for the elimination and replacement of cultural identities; of the distinctions between the cultures of the world. From a free association perspective; intended to loosen rigidity of thought, consider the nature of the arcade game of Pacman that was popular in the 1970s. In order to win, competing characters must gobble what is in their path. Consider a second free association that Pac is a euphemism for political action committees. The reader may wish to independently proceed with free association. The free associations stated are sufficient for me to come to the realization that, in a competitive world of strivers, the potential for identities to be consumed and subsumed exists. It behooves the mightiest and most powerful to prevent the elimination of individuated identity; at risk are the quality of life, and the survival of the flotilla itself. The Roman Empire of old collapsed with senatorial notions of democratization; the global flotilla faces similar challenges in the course ahead; in holistic terms, it stands to defeat itself in the context of identification, unless there is a willingness to rethink.

The question of what will constitute acceptable identification is a relevant consideration; for us to ask it of ourselves and to soul-searchingly answer. The full impacts of sudden and dramatic change are not readily discernible; they catch up to us at a later date. When they do, we are better able to reflect upon the circumstance of what happened; realizing then the extent of the costs and benefits that have derived. While human beings are not, as a rule, experts of foresight, we may nonetheless adopt a proactive perspective; scrutinizing potential consequences of possible actions in the face of the significant changes that affect us. This applies most significantly to the matter of identification, and to the various contexts within which we find ourselves.

As the reader will come to realize, to some extent contexts of culture are a choice, and to some extent they are not. The matter of identification is thus all the more relevant, for contexts of culture affect us in ways of which we may not be consciously aware.

The crises of globalization provide opportunities for redetermining our own futures; the crux of the matter is whether or not the re-determinations will lend themselves towards generating the outcomes we desire for our lives, and yield the kinds of identifications we seek. What impinges upon culture, impinges upon individuals. The impingements affect matters of addiction. As the tumult of cultural change affects the emotional health and well-being of individuals, it may spur an increase in incidences of addiction; whether it does will be reflected in assessments of prevalence rates in the future. Given the increase in probability of occurrence, it would be wise to include a consideration of this potential change in the rate of addiction in long-term planning. Culturally speaking, with America in view, major metropolitan areas have served as hangouts for what have been termed skid row alcoholics; dis-employed men and women displaced from the mainstream of life. In the 1990s, following a series of major downsizings of the military, considerable numbers of dis-employed military personnel; men, women, and children; joined the ranks as a new class of jobless and homeless; immortalized on film by at least one televised documentary. In the face of such calamity, with its high potential for despair, alcohol and drugs offer meager respite to world-weary souls. In compensation for the foresight we lack, we would do well to think and plan for a potential increase in occurrences of joblessness, homelessness, and addiction in the future; seeking ways to arrest the downward spiralling of persons into destitution and addiction.

CHAPTER SIX

The Holistic Perception Of Desirability

Quality of life is one of those notions that elicits a lot of reaction; mostly in the way of interpretation, of which there are many. What most people refer to as quality of life fits the fifth definition of quality; *the character in a logical proposition of being affirmative or negative*;[46] the essence of affirmative character varying as expressed opinion. What government refers to as quality of life fits the third definition of quality; *social status:rank*;[47] based upon selected factors, such as air and water quality, proximity to services and shopping facilities, and cost of living index, that are used to identify state-of-living conditions in various locations. The rank is a function of rendered opinion, in the form of selected factors, and varies with time.

Matters of ethics, by nature, are open to reflection. By way of one ethical reaction, it has been stated that life is better when priorities aren't confused by turning instrumental

---

[46] Merriam-Webster, Incorporated. *Merriam-Webster's Collegiate Dictionary, 10th Edition.* Springfield, Massachusetts, USA, p. 952.

[47] Merriam-Webster, Incorporated. *Merriam-Webster's Collegiate Dictionary, 10th Edition,* p. 952.

goods into intrinsic goods; inverting means into ends.[48] The statement derives from a discussion of ethical dilemmas. The contextual situation at hand; consumerist perceptions of desirability; poses this very dilemma. At the surface, it would appear that tolerance for meaningless consumption has increased. Under the surface, it would appear that intolerance for meaningless consumption has increased. The two appear to have increased in tandem. At the surface we find people actively engaging in the consumerist process and declaring it desirable. Under the surface we find people suffering from the consumerist process and bemoaning the ails, without fully understanding their origin. The indicators of physical stress; addiction, chronic fatigue, chronic pain, ill health, and insomnia; and the indicators of emotional stress; angst, anxiety, boredom, depression, and dissatisfaction; are flashing unheeded messages. We pay a steep price when we allow our perceptions of desirability; our thoughts about *what is desirable*; to be controlled; altered, manipulated, and regulated by well-versed cultural propaganda aiming to sell us anything we can be convinced into buying.

The fact that people, generally, have become dependent upon programming instructions for direction; what to buy, what to do, where to go, in order to be happy and successful, poses an additional dilemma. When most persons are euphemistically aboard the same boat, facing the same dilemmas, commiseration provides small comfort, but doesn't solve the problem of what ails us. The ethicist would say that the solution must, of necessity, be an individual one. The politicist would say that the solution must, of necessity, be a social one. The dilemma; of an extent reality that the majority of persons do not perceive consumerist culture as the source of their problem; is compounded by what would

---

[48] Joshua Halberstam. *Everyday Ethics Inspired Solutions to Real-Life Dilemmas*. Penguin Books USA Inc.: New York, 1993, p. 191.

happen if/when they do; disagreement as to response would be emergent, adding contention to confusion.

While it is within the intention of this book to foster holistic perspective, the author includes the caveat that change, including change in perspective, can have unforeseen outcomes. As has been discussed, the lesson of history is instructive; it teaches awareness of such possibility. From an ethical perspective, people are entitled to know the truth about what affects them. From a political perspective, public servants have a responsibility to serve their constituents. From an holistic perspective, the matter is sufficiently significant as to have the potential to rock the boat, with unknown consequences. From a psychological perspective, caution in action and judiciousness in reaction is not only wise, but advisable. From a philosophical perspective, the ethical dilemma we face warrants consideration.

Cultural perceptions of desirability impinge upon the individual. With respect to cultural perceptions of the desirability of consumption, the impact is considerable. Degrees of freedom nonetheless exist for individuals to take control of their lives. Failure to do so may result in experiencing lifestyles that are both consumptive and stressful; lacking in existential quality. In consequence, the individual may engage in trivial pursuits that generate feelings of emptiness rather than fulfillment, finding themselves feeling more frequently sick.

With respect to addiction, the Zeitgeist of consumerism; its cultural encouragements to consume; combined with extremist cultural attitudes about substance use, further combined with a high prevalence of depression and psychological dissatisfaction, fosters a cultural condition conducive to the development of substance abuse and substance dependence. Statistics on the prevalence of addiction are presented in Chapter 12; they provide time-dated pictures of the reality of addiction.

The American National Institute on Alcohol Abuse and Alcoholism, also known by its acronym, NIAAA, concluded that alcohol advertisements and broadcast media programming have been found to encourage a favorable view of alcohol use.[49] This would appear to be consistent with the notion that perceptions of desirability and behavioral consumption coexist. However, the report further concluded that it is almost impossible to conduct a meaningful study to separate this effect of advertising from the many other factors involved in alcohol consumption.[50] Therefore, one may conclude that a perception of desirability exists. One may also inductively reason that perceived desirability may contribute to consumption. One may not, however, attribute causal effect to broadcast ads.

The matter of definitively determining influence upon alcohol consumption, from a scientific perspective, is a logistical quandary. It has proven difficult to clarify the epistemological reality. A causal relationship between broadcast ads and alcohol consumption has not been found and is unlikely to be established. The variables are many, the intervening complicated. As was previously mentioned, in discussion of the role of cognitions; what people think about what happens to them; the variable of thought precludes an absolute attribution of cause to the stimulus. People have a greater ability to think about what they see and hear than do dogs; whether and how they do so is a separate consideration. What the NIAAA research, in effect, demonstrated, is that the route of cause-and-effect is not productive; adding another chapter to the book of knowledge.

The route of co-occurrence yielded a relevant finding, although the finding was specific, and did not generalize.

---

[49] "Correlation of Advertising to Consumption", In Advertising and the Alcohol Industry, *Encyclopedia of Drugs and Alcohol*, vol. 1. Jerome H. Jaffe, M.D. (Ed.). Simon & Schuster MacMillan: New York, 1995, p. 37.

[50] Ibid.

It is nonetheless suggestive; the scientific discernment of relationships is a stringent process, and findings do not always replicate. 1,988 C.E., G. Frank and G. Wilcox found a significant correlation between total advertising expenditures and consumption of wine and distilled spirits; they found no such correlation between advertising and beer consumption.[51]

Given that the aim of this book is to provide a philosophical perspective to the matter, it follows that our discussion is not defined or confined by the stringent parameters of scientific research. We are therefore at liberty to go beyond such process in order to arrive at a more holistic understanding. Granted, arriving at truth is a challenging endeavor, and there are many possible avenues of approach.

Given that the cause-and-effect route yielded the conclusive finding of a desirability factor, but no conclusive relationship to consumption, and the co-occurrence route yielded a conclusive relationship to specific consumption; wine and distilled alcohol, but not beer; indicates a steady progress in scientific comprehension. An analogy of the manner in which a banana is ingested is applicable. In an elementary science class, I viewed a movie that included the X-ray depiction of a man eating a banana. The process was curious; it ran contrary to what I, as a child, expected to see. The bites of chewed banana did not pass directly down the esophagus; they fluctuated up-and-down; before completing the passage. Substituting comprehension for the banana, the analogy indicates the inconsistency; it reflects one of the inconsistencies that comprise the nature of acquisition of knowledge. The reader was exposed to the discussion that progress is not linear or consistent. The findings presented in this chapter support the conclusion.

The reader will now be exposed to unscientific analysis following an indirect route. Getting to the truth may require a shift in perspective; this is comparable to the notion of

---

[51] Ibid.

hitting a brick wall, of running into an immoveable obstacle with the result of getting nowhere fast; of having to seek an alternate route. Despite the conclusion that it is almost impossible to conduct a meaningful study to separate the encouragement of favorable attitude towards alcohol use as an effect of advertising from the multitude of other factors involved in alcohol consumption, it is nonetheless possible to indirectly establish a relationship, through behavior analysis and logical reasoning. Pursuing this avenue of approach, the reader will be presented with an analysis of the behavior of alcoholic beverage companies; that explores what they perceive to be effective means for incrementing sales of their beverage products.

Our analysis begins with the finding that over a billion dollars per year is spent in the print and broadcast medias to advertise alcoholic products. An additional billion dollars is estimated to be spent on other advertising and promotional programs. In 1,992 C.E., this amounted to 2 billion dollars worth of advertising purchased by alcoholic beverage companies with the intention of generating sales; retail sales of alcoholic beverages by American companies in the year of the advertising campaigns amounted to 95.1 billion dollars.[52] The fact that alcoholic beverage companies spent such a considerable sum on advertising indicates an expectation that doing so will generate sales. Logically reasoned, this translates into: If we advertise, then we generate sales. They advertised and generated income from sales; at a ratio of 1:49; the advertising cost them 2% of the total income from sales. Logic supports the premise that if they advertise, they generate sales.

It is realistic to presume, given the long-established identities of the companies, that reputation was a significant factor in generating sales. The role of advertising in such case is to maintain a visible presence in the public mind; remember this or that product when you go to buy. While

---

[52] Ibid., pp. 36-7.

one cannot scientifically attribute the purchases to the cause of advertising, one can perceive, from the perspective of the alcoholic beverage companies, that the 2 billion dollars in advertising costs were well spent.

Our analysis continues with the comparative finding that General Motors, at the time, the world's largest corporation, committed to spending between $500 to $750 million dollars in televison ads for the year 1,990 C.E. This investment, which preceded the cited alcoholic beverage companies' advertising expenditure by two years, was the largest advertising commitment in the history of television.[53] While this figure pertains exclusively to television; the total GM advertising budget would have been considerably greater; it suggests that another type of company; an automotive company; also believes in the power of advertising to generate sales. If large corporations believe in the power of advertising to generate sales, then sales are generated after they advertise, are they wrong in their belief? The logical conclusion is that they are correct in their belief.

Our analysis indicates that we can logically, albeit unscientifically, conclude that advertising generates sales. It also concludes that other variables, such as longevity and reputation, enter into the equation. If an alcoholic beverage is purchased, can we logically presume that it will be consumed? Logic says that this is so. If the nature of purchasing is usage of what is purchased, then purchasing results in usage. Via the indirect route, our analysis yields the conclusion that we may reasonably contend that advertising leads to sales, and sales/purchases lead to usage/consumption. It stands to reason.

While government has demonstrated that establishing a cause-and-effect relationship is next to impossible, this does not mean that we have to throw the baby of rationality out with the research bath water. If advertising weren't instrumental

---

[53] Michael O'Higgins and John Downes. *Beating The Dow*, HarperCollins Publishers Inc.: New York, 1992, p. 99.

to sales, would the alcoholic beverage industry funnel so much of its money for this purpose? The logic of reason stands against this kind of fallacious thinking. Therefore, one can reasonably conclude that advertising does, in fact, contribute to product purchase and use; in confirmation of public perception.

Our analysis proceeds with a brief overview; a picture; of substance advertising and consumption. Keeping in mind the variable of the individual; the propensity of the person to use substances, and the sole decision-making authority vested in individual persons; which constitutes a separate contributing factor to substance consumption, we analyze the reality.

We find that tobacco companies spend more than 3.2 billion dollars annually to advertise and promote cigarettes and other tobacco products, and generate 40 billion dollars a year in sales[54]. The ratio of advertising expense to sales income is greater for tobacco products than for alcoholic beverage products; 1:13 versus 1:49; indicating a greater sales yield for the alcoholic beverage industry. As will be presented in Chapter 12, the nationwide prevalence of alcohol consumption is greater than that of tobacco, which supports the NIAAA conclusion regarding a positive public perception of alcohol use; it also supports our identification of the role of the individual.

With respect to tobacco, we find, according to encyclopedic report, that advertising aids in the recruitment of new smokers. One would presume, by logical inference, that the existence of a facilitation effect would apply in like manner to any and all advertising of substances, although this has not been verified. This may, in part, explain government-sponsored negative advertising campaigns promoting a negative perception of illicit substance use;

---

[54] "Advertising and Tobacco Use", *Encyclopedia of Drugs and Alcohol, Vol. 1.* Jerome H. Jaffe, M.D. (Ed.). Simon & Schuster MacMillan, Inc.: New York, 1995, p. 44.

conducted in hope of achieving a negative facilitation effect. According to the encyclopedic report, almost all smokers start smoking before the age of 21; most before the age of 18; resulting in the conclusion that tobacco companies need to recruit more than 3,000 new young smokers every day to replace those who die or otherwise stop smoking.[55] The report contends the existence of a relationship between advertising and tobacco use, with increases in advertising expenditures presented as supporting evidence. Accordingly, expenditures for tobacco ads increased from 361 million dollars in 1,970 C.E. to 3,200 million dollars in 1,990 C.E.[56] Additional promotional expenditures are reported to have increased from 25% of total tobacco marketing dollars in 1,975 C.E., to more than 60% in 1,990 C.E.[57] Thus, we find the contention among the medical community that substance use and advertising are interrelated. We may conclude that it is believed that advertising affects the perception of desirability with regards to usage of substances. We may also conclude that substance product companies believe advertising will promote sales of their products.

The National Household Survey on Drug Abuse, conducted in 1,993 C.E., found that 49.6% of total reported substance use consisted of alcohol, followed by cigarettes at 24.2%, marijuana at 4.3%, smokeless tobacco at 2.9%, and cocaine at 0.6%. Consumption of alcohol and tobacco, the most advertised, surpassed that of other substances.[58] We may infer that the rate of consumption of marijuana and cocaine would increase were they allowed to be publicly advertised, which would instigate a change in public perceptions of

---

[55] Ibid.

[56] Ibid., p. 46.

[57] Ibid.

[58] Table No. 218. "Use of Selected Drugs by Age of User: 1993", In "Drug Use", *Encyclopedia of Drugs and Alcohol*, vol. 1. Jerome H. Jaffe, M.D. (Ed.). Simon & Schuster MacMillan: New York, 1995, p. 137.

their undesirability. The use of marijuana is legal in some United States locations, with specific restrictions for medical as well as recreational use; however, public advertising of the availability of marijuana for sale does not exist, for reasons unknown by this author. Our analysis indicates we may attribute the picture of consumption presented to the fact of advertising, to the fact of cultural acceptance, to governmental policies, and to individual decision-making.

The purpose of marketing is to convince us to consume; that to do so is desirable. The marketing industry's well-financed efforts to convince us have proven remarkably successful. Differences in perceived acceptability nonetheless exist; there are cultures that prohibit advertising in the form of television commercials, and limit the venues of advertising, thereby encouraging persons to seek purchase information directly from store and street vendors. Such cottage industry or small business orientation caters to local populations; the difference is based on a preference for small rather than big business, not on anti-consumption philosophy. Indeed, despite the prevalence of marketing's impact upon consumer behavior, word-of-mouth continues to be a factor in individual choice of proprietor, physician, et cetera; persons tend to trust the personal testimonials of others' satisfaction with the goods and services they obtain. The acquisition of reputation; good or bad; affects customer base. In this respect, we may view word-of-mouth as a form of advertising based upon personal experience; it falls outside of the realm of mass media. It, too, convinces consumption, although on a considerably smaller scale.

Given the human propensity; the social nature which renders us open to influence; we find that perceptions of desirability are malleable, open to the influence of others. The famous case involving the heiress, Patty Hearst, who was abducted by the terrorist Symbionese Liberation Party in the 1970s, provides an extreme example. Influenced by her kidnappers under conditions conducive to psychological vulnerability, she *voluntarily* participated in a terrorist group action. She was tried and found innocent, based upon a recognition of influential process. We know from experience that such influence is not only possible, but that it has been deliberately employed for purposes of manipulation.

Given the reality of our own human susceptibility to influence, it is all the more relevant to consider our perceptions of what is and what is not desirable. We may evaluate our notions of desirability for veracity; that is, to what extent they are true or untrue; and for goodness of fit; that is, to what extent they reflect our true nature---do they fit who we are or do they fit who we have been socialized to become? The matter is one not readily discernible; it is the reason for many a mid-life crisis, when the adult self strives to overcome the influence of childhood conditioning and cultural socialization; sorting through relevancies and irrelevancies to arrive at a more meaningful personal perspective.

Comprehending the reality, discerning what is relevant to oneself, and preparing for personal decision-making requires that we ask the right questions; asking the wrong questions will lead one astray. We may ask of ourselves such questions as the following. Are we consuming what we genuinely find desirable? Are we consuming in a manner consistent with our true nature? Would adopting a different pattern of consumption prove more desirable; that is, more consistent with who we are by nature; and result in our feeling better about ourselves and life in general? These questions are relevant considerations; they symbolize seeking to face the genuine reality of ourselves. For persons seeking to overcome addiction, this involves a change in approach; one that honestly asks and honestly answers; including facing the potential truth that addictive consumption has become nature. The questions appeal directly to the rational ego; they bypass the pleading distractions of the irrational id, they bypass the critical admonitions of the castigating superego; they enable us to access the part of our personality that can tell us the truth, the part with the capacity for comprehension and discernment.

In close, we conclude that to gain a holistic perception of desirability necessitates understanding; of culture, of conditioning and socialization, of self and nature. We may, at this point in our journey of philosophical perspective, consider the relevance of wisdom.

Joshua Halberstam tells us that wisdom is the ability to make distinctions.[59] This indicates that wisdom is a function of the ego. Therefore, by asking the right questions of the ego within ourselves, we may learn to live wisely. Halberstam writes that morality is not primarily about duties and following rules that tell us what to do and what not to do; it is primarily about moral sensitivity. The pivotal moral imperative is not to *do* the right thing, but to *be* the right thing. Accordingly, says Halberstam, if you have a decent character, if you care about intelligence, honesty, and compassion, you'll do the right thing as a matter of course.[60]

The realities of life being what they are, wisdom has proven to be the path of the few rather than the many. Halberstam's points clarify the reason there is so much confusion and contention concerning and discerning right and/from wrong; it is not the path of wisdom. While questions of right and wrong fit the landscape of justice, they do not fit the landscape of wisdom. In this, they have been misapplied. We may rightly infer that the historical advice given unto the early Christians in the midst of the anti-Christian response, that of *turn the other cheek*, constitute words of wisdom. In effect, they indicate a position of wise response; nonjudgmental nonengagement in the service of being.

---

[59] Halberstam, p. 191.

[60] Ibid., p. xvi.

Human culture being what it confusingly is, it is not easy to know the right thing; what it is or what to do. Given the reality, Halberstam's statement makes sense of the need to rise above the matter of right and wrong, the matter of rules for and against, in order to arrive at considered wisdom; the state, as he states it, of being the right thing. We may well ask whether our perceptions of desirability reflect rightful being.

CHAPTER SEVEN

The Historical Perspective

The identity of Western culture changed during the era of industrialization. Prior to this, it was primarily family-oriented; consisting of a variety of family subsistence endeavors; single family services like neighborhood barber shops, bankers, boarding houses, gas stations, legal offices, and newspaper offices; single family stores like neighborhood butcher shops, clothing stores, hardware stores, produce markets, and restaurants; and single family farms like the one depicted in the American television program, *Lassie*. Those not engaged in family business endeavors worked for government; city halls, constables, courthouses, libraries, schools. This was the way of Americana; it was the pattern of life across the country. Life was oriented towards family subsistence; individual families affirming a niche within the pattern, like pieces of an American quilt.

The family-oriented subsistence tradition was the way of the world in Western civilization; the pattern of life in Europe and America; until industrialization. The change in identity from familial to industrial rocked the civilized world in much the same way that it is currently being rocked. The pattern of life changed; work transformed into employment, handmade transformed into manufactured, local transformed into national. Families suffered; quality of life took a nosedive. This is the change that occurred *prior* to the Great Depression that subsequently affected much of Western civilization.

The role of the family was replaced by the role of industry. In consequence, attitudes changed; families ceased to be the controlling interests in the lives of individuals, the authority transferred to the industrial employers. Hence, began the deterioration of family life, resulting in a new legal industry governing divorce, custody rights, et cetera. Family disputes, to be privately resolved, were transformed into legal disputes, to be publicly resolved. The climate of privacy that was second nature to the family-oriented way of life; that one's affairs were one's own, that one's home was one's castle; was replaced by a climate of publicity. The change in climate altered the course of life.

What followed in the wake of industrialization was a new way of life; a life of consumption. Industrialization led to the mass production of goods, which led to the mass consumption of what was produced. In the era of industrialization, supply was the driver, creating new demands for industrialized goods and services.

This was the era that invented the conveyor belt assembly line; whereby persons in factories were assigned piecemeal duties; the lineup of employees adding individual portions to the assemblage of whatever product was being mass produced. It was also an age of child labor; legal restrictions pertaining to childhood employment did not exist at the time. Families displaced by the turn towards industrialization converted themselves and their children into viable economic resources by switching to factory work. It was not unusual for able-bodied family members to be simultaneously employed in a given factory. Farm families sent members that were unnecessary to the upkeep of the family farm to the cities to work in the new factories. Work life became factory-oriented; a new trend of factory towns emerged. Within these towns, conditions were harsh; the hours of work were long, the pay scale was low, the close quartering resulted in frequent outbreaks of illness, the lifespans of the factory workers were foreshortened.

Throughout the Western world, economies converted to industrialization. Life, it would seem, turns on a dime. Enterprising individuals opportuned by establishing catering businesses; catering to the wants, needs, and pocketbooks of the overwrought factory workers. Drinking and prostitution establishments abounded. Factory towns became rowdy. In America, the notoriety of the wild, wild West pioneer days was replaced by the notoriety of the wild, wild East factory days. At this significant turn of economy, smaller in scale than that of the turn in the last century, persons similarly scrambled to survive; the hardships were many.

With the conversion, emerged a culture of consumption, and the invocation to consume. What has come to be called capitalist economy originated as industrialization; a process of manufacturing. The opportunism that followed; the result of opportunists attracted to the power of manufacturing to generate economy; instilled a perpetual push towards consumption to fuel the industrial economy. At the outset, the numbers of persons who derived significant financial benefits from industrialization were few. The impact of the Great Depression's collapse of fortunes, was a democratization of economic circumstances in the 1930s. The numbers of persons who benefitted financially from industrialization increased over time; with the consequence that economies of consumption entrenched and expanded. The discovery that large scales of economy could provide economic support to large numbers of people, ensured the pattern of consumption would continue.

The current reality is one of constant bombardment by advertising to encourage buying; another word for consumption. Over the course of a life, one becomes so accustomed to the barage of advertising and the enticements to buy, that it becomes a fact of life; a kind of second nature.

Maria Artiz, Ph.D.

In truth, one could liken such process to brainwashing; a form of repetitive programming to consume. No matter where one turns, the medium of advertising persists in conveying its message of buy and consume. Westerners hold a particular disregard for communism; it is an historic attitude of aversion inspired by political differences between countries, and a determination to maintain a separate independence of status. The irony is that despite the fact that Western civilizations are capitalist, not communist, they nonetheless function in a similar manner; both engage in various forms of mental programming to ensure the continuance of culture. Whether one lives in a capitalist or a communist country, one experiences invocations that are consistent with the preservation of the cultural orientation.

The human response to cultural programming to consume is akin to the experience of velocitizing; one becomes accustomed to acting in the proscribed manner of consuming in the same way that one becomes accustomed to driving at highway speeds; slowing down requires conscious effort. From this one can see that in the same manner that people are consciously able to slow their speed of driving when they exit a freeway, they are able to consciously slow down their rate of consumption, if they so choose. What makes this less, rather than more, likely is that there are no road signs for our journeys through life that so advise us. People are accustomed to being given directions; road signs are a perfect example of this. From the signs along roadways, we know where to turn, when to go, when to stop, where to exit, how fast to drive, et cetera. We have no such road signs to guide us in making life decisions, regardless of our respective cultural orientations. This puts the burden of responsibility upon the individual to choose her/his own path in life. The reality is that most persons don't give much thought to the matter, the easiest path being the path of least resistance; which amounts to going with the flow of the commonplace. The perception involved in identifying with the path of least resistance; also known as the cultural proscription, is that one cannot go wrong so long as one does what everyone else is doing. In one respect, this is true; one will find a greater degree of acceptance and experience a greater degree of social comfort. In another respect, it is not true; one may fail to find one's true path in life, and miss out on the opportunity. Cultures of all kinds proscribe what are considered to be desirable conditions for living; chapters seven through ten are devoted to discussion specific to the culture of consumption. Having discussed the reasons, the reader will encounter discussion of the realities of becoming accustomed to living in a consumption-oriented society; the historical context that has rendered current patterns of living second nature; as commonplace as eating, breathing or sleeping.

The process of immersion; of being immersed; in cultures of consumptive living distracts us from awareness of other cultural realities and alternate possibilities. Immersed in our patterns of consumption, we may become so habituated to them that we fail to be aware that other possibilities exist. To use another driving metaphor, it is akin to the experience of traversing familiar territory in a state of mental automatic; accustomed to the drive, we pay only cursory attention, not needing to be more attentive. The fact that human beings function this way makes life easier because we are not constantly being pressed into attentive service; it frees us to think about other things. This is the reality of the human experience of familiarity; it is the prime reason why people resist change; it results in the attitude of *Why change anything? I'm comfortable the way I am.* This reality of human nature lends itself to cultural immersion. Once immersed, we lose observational perspective; the point-of-view of self-observation; we are distracted from other considerations by our habituation to what is familiar.

Consumption, carried to extremes, is consonant with addictive behavior. It is for this reason that attending to the reality of the call to consume is relevant to the matter of addiction. Overindulgence can lead to distress; excessive drinking may lead to a hangover, and consistent engagement in excessive drinking may lead to dependence. The call to consume encourages the purchase of alcoholic beverages. Once purchased, persons will find that they either like or don't like alcoholic beverages. Some, with repeated exposure, will acquire a taste for them. The majority of those who drink will experience alcoholic beverages as an aspect of living a good and pleasurable life; like the eating of a satisfying meal. Human nature is such that we respond to food and drink as experiences of nourishment; our experience of early infancy ensures this. Various aspects of oral gratification are psychologically consonant with mother love; they figuratively make us feel warm and nurtured on the inside, just like when we were babies. A significant minority of those who drink will eventually experience enslavement; their lives will become chained to the bottle, forever dependent. The odds of dependence favor those who were inadequately nurtured as infants, and those who take drinking to the extreme.

Understanding the quantitative element pertaining to individuals, we may look to society in order to get a better picture of the consumption phenomenon. Perceptions of reality can be deceiving. For instance, the familiarity level which tendencies us towards accommodation of consumption, lends the impression that we have always been living this way. It may certainly seem that way.

In point of fact, consumptive living is a relatively recent state of affairs that became possible with industrialization, but didn't actually arrive, in the fullness of impact sense, until the 1900s. In America, following on the heels of the industrial success of the mid- to late 1800s, the Roaring Twenties marched flamboyantly in with a show; one that mirrored the new American purchasing power, and lauded excess in consumption, as a manner of enjoying the fruits of American industry. Paralleling the experience of the 1700s and 1800s in Europe; Americans began acquiring more money, became exposed to more and newer goods, and developed a larger appetite. In consequence, a new cultural phenomenon was born; that of the consummate shopper.

From 1,909 to the end of 1,929 C.E., a span of 20 years, American consumption of commodities and services increased 180%. By the end of 1,919 C.E., the year that marked the onset of the golden age, consumption had increased 81.4% over 1,914 C.E. levels; a span of only five years.[61] The 1920s witnessed a responsive surge in new patent issues and mass-produced goods. If Americans wanted more goods, industry would provide them, en masse. What remained was for industry to devise a new method for encouraging people around the country to consume all of the newly patented commodities.

Ann Douglas, in her chronicle, *Terrible Honesty*, portrays the emergence of mass culture in America as a big business venture spawned in the 1920s by the golden age of advertising[62]. According to Douglas, this charging horse was spurred by the production and sale of attention; i.e., advertising, which subsequently became its own big business venture. The spur of advertising, says Douglas, was inspired by the writings of the Austrian neurologist, Sigmund Freud; his findings found a following in New York, rapidly rendering him a vicarious mentor to the development of Madison Avenue; the haven of New York advertising. Freud's nephew, Edward Bernays, went on to become the leading adman of the day and was eventually dubbed the Father of Public Relations; his practices were based upon

---

[61] Series G 470-494. "Personal Consumption Expenditures, by Type of Product: 1909 to 1929", In "Consumer Income and Expenditures", *Historical Statistics of the United States: Colonial Times to 1970. Part 1.* United States Department of Commerce, Bureau of the Census, p. 320.

[62] Ann Douglas. *Terrible Honesty: Mongrel Manhattan in the 1920s.* Farrar, Strauss and Giroux : New York, NY, 1995.

the principles shared by his uncle, who went on to become the Father of Psychiatry. As Douglas states, it was Bernays who orchestrated the commercialization of American culture through the popularizing of Freud's thought. Freud's definition of the analyst-patient relationship is what, according to Douglas, gave advertisers wooing clients their model and their cue.[63]

From a perspective of appetite, the Douglas chronicle depicts Americans as newly hungry; for goods and for service. While Freud inspired doctors to provide patients with psychoanalysis regarding their problems and motivations, Bernays inspired admen to provide shoppers with advertising regarding products and usages. The advent of mass marketing coincided with the emergence of mass production; it was the means by which the message of new goods was publicly proclaimed.

Thus and so the age of the media was born. From the chronicle we learn the results: a proliferation of book clubs, best-sellers, radio, record charts, and movies. The effect was such that by 1,930 C.E., Americans owned a radio and a record player at a ratio of one to three (1:3), and went to the movies once a week or more at a ratio of three to four (3:4). Douglas makes clear the point that advertising's reach was wide-spread; the media ensured it by providing the information vehicle.[64] The information age was in process of becoming. With it, a culture of consumption was engineered and edified. This was no small feat.

From a psychiatric perspective, it was Freud's notion of the unconscious as a competing triad of perspectives; a childish id, an adult ego, and a parental superego; that inspired new ways of thinking about human needs and wants; creating a ripple effect throughout the Western world. From a perspective of context, what transpired was the application of this knowledge from the context of medicine

---

[63] Douglas, p. 34.

[64] Douglas, p. 21.

to the context of business; the psychiatric theory about the unconscious workings of the human mind developed for the purpose of healing was applied to the purpose of promoting sales by appealing to newly understood psychological needs of the individual. In this respect, the vicarious impact of Freud's theory upon American business is significant. By historical American standards, rudimentary principles of psychology have become an integral part of business. The psychologizing of consumption eventually resulted in a proliferation of relevant literature for use by business persons in training. The practice of the traveling salesman; already well-established before the onset of the American Revolution; changed. The practice of seeking interested buyers transformed into the practice of motivating people; converting them into spur-of-the-moment buyers.

Citing America as an example of what happened in the Western world, we find that consumerism became firmly established in the 20th century. It bloomed in the 1920s, then faded in the Depression years; 1,930 through 1,933 C.E.; when consumption declined by 43%[65] The post-Depression years experienced a rebound. From 1,934 to 1,945 C.E., consumption climbed 161%, to the tune of 119, 701 million dollars.[66] When contrasted with the 28,814 million dollars Americans spent in 1,909 C.E., the revolutionary shift to a culture of consumption is evident, despite an economic depression and a world war.

Over the course of the century, the rate of spending continued to rise. The baby boom years; 1,946 through 1,955 C.E.; resulted in a 203% increase in the level of consumption; the spike in birth rate indicating an expansion

[65] Series G 416-469. "Personal Consumption Expenditures, by Type of Product: 1929 to 1970", In Section G: "Consumer Income and Expenditures", *Historical Statistics of the United States: Colonial Times to 1970. Part 1.* United States Department of Commerce, Bureau of the Census, p. 319.

[66] United States Department of Commerce, pp. 318-9.

of the population of American consumers. By the end of the baby boom period, consumption reached a record 254,381 million dollars.[67] After 1,956 C.E., increases in the rate of consumption steadied to an annual average rate of 6.1%. In 1,970 C.E., American consumption registered at 617,644 million dollars; more than double the 1,956 C.E. level.[68] During the sixty-one year historical period from 1,909 to 1,970 C.E., the level of consumption in America increased by 2,044%. The majority of that growth; 1,863%; occurred during the years from 1,929 to 1,970 C.E.[69] It was spurred by the related rise in disposable personal income; a 608.4 billion dollar or 730% increase;[70] and the continuing influence of mass marketing.

We may attribute the mechanism for this phenomenal growth in economy to industrialization, which transformed the way in which goods were produced and enabled them to be produced in mass quantities at more publicly affordable prices. We may attribute the impetus to mass media marketing, for its effectiveness in getting the message to the potential consumer. We may attribute the inspiration to the Freud family, for their remarkable insights.

Towards the end of the 20th century, the process of industrialization was complete, and the process of informationalization was well underway. The mercurial appeal of mass media began to make itself visible on the internet highway in the 1990s. Given the short duration of time that elapsed before mass media advertising effected consumer purchasing in the early 1900s, it is not surprising that the internet has become such a popular venue. The

---

[67] Ibid., pp. 317-8.

[68] Ibid., pp. 316-7.

[69] Ibid., pp. 316-20.

[70] Series F 262-286. "Personal Income and Outlay: 1929 to 1970-Con". In "National Income and Wealth", *Historical Statistics of the United States: Colonial Times to 1970. Part 1.* United States Department of Commerce, Bureau of the Census, p. 242.

power of such resonating medias is their capacity to magnify communication. There is no doubt but that the internet has had a significant hand in spurring globalization; through the near instantaneous transmission of information. While books and newspapers continue to be sources for leisurely and intensive study, the rapid transmit medias of radio, television, film, and internet appeal to a want-it-now sensibility; one that has emerged from their creation. In this regard, planet Earth experienced considerable transition from the creation of such medias.

In retrospect, the 20th century witnessed a combination of defining events that had the power to propel prosperity. It was a turning point in cultural history, when culture and economy became consumptive, and cultural identity was transformed. The general sense of individual beingness changed from one of self-subsistence to one of consumer subsistence.

CHAPTER EIGHT

The Nature of Consumption

The perpetual call to consume predisposes us to engage in consumption. Call it motivation to enjoy the fruits of bounty, maintain au courant status, be an avid consumer; it all boils down to the simple fact that we are encouraged and become predisposed to consume more than what we need for the sake of survival. We are conditioned to consume beyond what is practical, necessary, or essential. The refrain, *I don't really know why I bought it; I don't really need it, I'm not sure I even want it, I just felt like I needed to buy it, I'll probably just give it away,* is characteristic of consumptive culture. The constancy with which advertising barrages the psyche is a form of psychological conditioning or mindwashing that persuades us to buy and use an increasing diversity of goods and services, to replace previous purchases with new, improved, updated, and redesigned versions or models, to try out what's new, and to purchase what isn't needed or wanted. When this sort of thing happens as a result of deceptive manipulation by an unethical salesperson, it is referred to as being conned; when it happens as a result of honest manipulation by ethical entities, it is referred to as being pitched. What is notable within cultures of consumption is the pervasiveness of the pitch; business relies upon it for marketing, consumers rely upon it for guidance; the world of economy rotates on the dissemination of information.

The fact that such consumables as food and drink, by our nature, require continuous consumption lends a ready-made cyclic quality to the reality that we no longer grow our own food or ferment our own drink. The nature of major life events lends another cyclic quality that involves purchases pertaining to births, education, marriages, divorces, deaths, et cetera; events which are regulated by societal law. We rarely engage in home births, home schooling, home marriages, home divorces with over-the-counter legal forms, and home burials. In present reality, there exists a high degree of dependency upon cultural dictates; the rules of law which determine what we can and cannot do; which preponderantly favor public versus private options.

There are numerous instances of products pertaining to modern devices which contribute to cyclic consumption. Battery-operated devices require replacement batteries, lighting devices require replacement bulbs, motor vehicles require replacement parts, et cetera. These products have cyclic propensities, by virtue of the fact that their working parts require frequent replacement. Other products, like appliances, gadgets, and tools, require cyclic repurchasing on the basis of the estimated life of the product. Much of what is purchased eventually wears down or becomes obsolete, ensuring a recurrence of consumption. Cameras, cell phones, computers, radios, and televisions are prime examples. Over relatively short periods of time, improvements in design, function, and utility have a tendency to incapacitate the usefulness and desirability of prior models, rendering the purchase of these products cyclic. In fact, the recycling industry developed in response to the reality that so many consumer products regularly require replacement. Cyclic commodities and cyclic consumption are an established reality; such is the nature of consumption in the information age.

We may understand from this reality that there are two factors in operation. First, is the psychological urge to consume which, aided and abetted by advertising, beckons us to engage in continuous consumption. Second, is the fact that extent technologies wear out routinely or render themselves outdated by new technological developments, encouraging us to engage in cyclic consumption.

As has been previously stated, the societal message of encouragement to consume, which is a cultural constant, has a mental conditioning effect. It functions in the manner of parenting. The repetitive cultural message to consume fosters the belief that we need to consume and keep consuming in order to be accepted; if you are a regular and routine shopper, you are A-Okay. If you aren't, then something is wrong; either with you or the way you are living; you are Not Okay. This cultural messaging functions the way parental messaging functions; in children, beliefs of unworthiness are instilled through repetitive condemnation; in persons-at-large, beliefs of social disapproval are instilled through repetitive messages contrary to the individual's true nature. A primary example of this phenomenon of effect, upon which considerable research has been conducted, is the conditioning of image in media and advertising, such that female and male children are socialized to *look the part* or feel inferior. In the 1970s and 1980s, there were a number of publicly expressed popular concerns regarding the skinny model standard in use by advertisers, with calls for a change in the public image, due to the high incidence of anorexia which had derived. There is no denying that such conditioning has an effect, it influences behavior in various respects; with regards to acquired appearances (clothing, hair, and makeup styles), desires (conceptions of attractiveness, conceptions of needs and wants, desired products), et cetera. It is an experienced fact of life.

Such cultural conditioning; in the form of advertised messages; is ever-present. However, the individual actually sees, hears, or notices the messages intermittently; on a passing bus or taxi, on billboards, in magazines and newspapers, on television, et cetera. Without intending it, the early admen not only applied Freudian principles, they also applied Pavlovian principles, thereby strengthening the impact of their advertising. The Russian physiologist, Ivan Petrovich Pavlov, in his studies of animal behavior, accidently discovered the relationship between stimulus and behavior. In his dog training experiments, he noted that dogs responded to the cue that it was time to be fed by salivating. With further experimentation, Pavlov demonstrated that animal behavior was influenced by stimuli; both positive and negative. He termed the process operant conditioning; establishing a new scientific paradigm. Subsequent investigation yielded the finding that animal behavior is more strongly influenced by intermittent exposure to the conditioning stimulus. What this means, with respect to the cultural conditioning of consumption, is that persons intermittently exposed to ads are more likely to be influenced by them than those who constantly view them; indicating that admen are perhaps the least influenced by their own ads. Curiously, the early admen of Manhattan started a cultural conditioning process of which they were unaware; with respect to potential for awareness, they were the least likely to realize the truth.

Principles of behavioral conditioning are employed in a variety of applications and are now a familiar practice. They are utilized in animal training of all kinds, including dog obedience classes and behavior modification techniques with children in schools. An example from personal experience illustrates how familiar behavioral conditioning is to us, regardless of whether or not we perceive it as such. Having studied Pavlovian principles as an undergraduate, I realized, after the fact, how I had unknowingly conditioned my pets' behavior. When electric can openers became available, I purchased one, and used it to open cans of pet food. The cats became conditioned to the stimulus, and subsequently responded to the sound of the can opener, whether or not the food being opened pertained to them. The same thing happened when I opened and poured from a bag that issued a sound similar to that of bags of cat food being opened and poured. The realization underscored the reality of behavioral conditioning, outside of the domain of experimental study conditions, where it was to be expected.

If my cats could so readily be conditioned, I reasoned, so could other animals, including people. Others had obviously been thinking along the same line, because behavioral psychology was well underway. It was no accident that I pursued graduate training in cognitive-behavioral psychology; I was intrigued by a growing understanding. I remember realizing, when my daughter was a toddler that I was the cause of what was considered undesirable behavior; she developed the periodic habit of waking up during the night to join me at the kitchen table where she would find me at work on the electric typewriter. It was a positive experience of moments privately shared that went against the grain of standard child-rearing practices whereby parents are encouraged to get their children in the habit of going to bed and staying in bed for the night. I enjoyed those moments as much as she did, so I allowed it instead of carting her right back upstairs to bed, knowing full well that I wasn't following proscribed methods; I was taking a practicum in child therapy at the time. I understand the reason for the existence of the adage, *Do as I say, not as I do.*

As members of cultures employing conditioning strategies, we are, in many ways that we think about, and some that we don't, socialized to behave in manners consistent. The curiosity of it all can be viewed from an historical perspective of observation; wherein one is able to compare, contrast, and notice changes that have occurred; across times and places. We have changed ever so much and ever so many times that the historical is illustrative of our changeling nature. What is currently the norm wasn't previously the case, and probably won't be the case in the future. Sometimes the change involves a revisiting, sometimes a transitioning, sometimes a reactioning, sometimes a happening resulting from something new and unexpected, as what occurred with the evolutionary onset of consumption conditioning.

The nature of consumption is such that we are behaviorally trained to be at the ready for new, better, and additional purchases. This is the essence of marketing's current impact upon consumer spending patterns. The marketing industry employs a keen understanding of behavioral psychology in getting people to behave consumptively. From experience, marketers have learned that sex and status have sales appeal. By pairing goods and services with sexiness, endorsements, and images of famous people, marketers tip the odds in favor of purchase. Competition for sales intensifies the use of strategies for getting people to buy; employing behavioral conditioning through advertising (conditioned stimuli) and cognitive conditioning through pitch (persuasion). The outcome is a proliferation of ads, sales techniques, and training programs, designed to promote sales; success in achieving pre-established sales goals, and effectiveness in achieving pre-established customer relations goals. Worldwide expansion of population is not the primary reason why so many trained salespersons now exist; they are essential assets to industry.

Behaviorally speaking, we are not only conditioned to purchase and purchase continuously, over time, the conditioning has become more skillful; it has acquired the status of a technical science, with a creative arts component, designed to ensnare buyers. Buyers are the sturgeon that need to be caught in order to extract the caviar of money from the net of marketing. Towards this end, we are conditioned to consume for the sake of consuming, encouraged to buy specific products and services, and taught to emulate as role models those who possess in greater quantity. The notion of keeping up with the Joneses, in effect prior to industrialization among the moneyed class, emerged as a significant psychological motivator after World War II.

Regardless of how much or what is acquired, with the exception of the person who has the most and the person who has the best, there will always be others who have more and better. This sets the stage for the childlike id to dominate with desire. In psychodynamic terms, it is the id, the child within, who wants without regard to reason, that urges us to buy at the expense of adult rationality. The id causes one to ignore the incurring of unmanageable debt; a prevalent problem among credit card customers. It is not surprising, given a culture of economy that encourages limitless buying, that so many encounter the problem of unmanageable debt. The burden, while self-imposed, is a byproduct of the cultural context, which appeals unabashedly to our psychological id; encouraging continued consumption in the face of mounting and seemingly insurmountable debts.

I recall the case of a woman who presented with the self-avowed problem of being a shopaholic. Regardless of the store she visited, regardless of her current financial resources, she could not refrain from purchasing, as she stated it, *something.* She was frightened, depressed, and considerably in debt. The matter was not one of lack of resources; she was adequately employed, with the means by which to make installment payments. The problem was one of compulsion; she felt compelled to buy, against her own rational sense that to do so was foolish. At the time she presented for treatment, she was experiencing a profound inner struggle between her id, her ego, and her superego; her irrational id and her castigating superego were tormenting her rational ego, which was struggling to maintain a semblance of sanity. Over time, she was able to come to terms with the struggle, consciously resolve what needed to be resolved, and discontinue treatment. Her case was one of the most poignant I have ever encountered.

The nature of the reality is that the more we consume, the more we want to consume; the more we pay close attention to what goods and services we and others are consuming. As social animals, our human tendency is to watch others of our own kind; this is biological destiny; it was designed to enhance survivability, as a form of watching out for one another. Over time, the natural tendency has been exploited; for spying and competition. If we remove the variable of population, we may additionally attribute the pace of consumption to human tendency; the comparison of self to others, culturally facilitated by television programs, magazine ads, and other forms of communication which, as part and parcel of the information age fuel comparisons; and to human industry; which produces products and services and applies psychological principles of behavior and motivation. Both variables have been used to foster competition.

From the analysis herein presented, it becomes evident that consumption, under prevailing cultural conditions; current cultural attitudes, access to products and services, dissemination of information, and available resources for purchasing; has become a self-perpetuating condition. A cycle of consumption, and the potential for addictive consumption, is thereby in process.

The advent of consumerism has not only dramatically altered the *level* of consumption, it has dramatically altered the *nature* of consumption. It resulted in a qualitative shift in cultural patterns of consumption. While the rate of consumption relative to income has remained relatively stable over time, what has changed and keeps changing is the nature of that consumption; that is, what is consumed.[71]

---

[71] George Thomas Kurian, Series F 17-30. "Per Capita Income and Product for Selected Items in Current Prices: 1929 to 1991", In Section F, *Datapedia of the United States: 1790 to 2000.* Bernan Press: Lanham, MD, 1994, p. 90.

Maria Artiz, Ph.D.

The picture of consumption today is very different from the picture of consumption in 1,929 C.E.

Citing America as an example, the picture of consumerism shows that Americans spend the majority of their disposable income on goods and services designed to make life more comfortable. What this results in is a high concentration of spending on goods and services that yield comfort; beauty, beverage, clothing, entertainment, food, health, reading material, recreation, transportation, vacation, et cetera. The array of possibilities for purchase is far greater today than it was in 1,929 C.E., as are the numbers of persons able to afford them.

Industry responds to the changing needs and wants of population cohorts. In consequence, there have developed what are termed target populations for marketing purposes. The elderly, the baby boomer, the generation X, et cetera, are designations designed to indicate a target population. The designations are publicly disseminated and incorporated; they become a viable part of social identity. Thus, we may view the nature of consumption on a categorical basis. For example, the elderly are a primary target population for medical and retirement services; the baby boomer for health and vacation services; the generation X for family and entertainment services, the generation Y for child and home services, and so on.

Culture-wide, places of consumption have acquired a beckoning aura; movie theater, restaurant, and shopping mall locations attract people seeking relatively inexpensive outings; they serve as places of affordable leisurely pursuit. Given the orientation to comfort, it comes as no surprise that food and drink are available to theatergoers, that gum, tobacco, and newpapers are available to restaurant-goers, that services and snacks are available to mall-goers. Such features were not part of the pre-industrialization picture; they were more isolated, concentrated in drinking establishments; bars, saloons, and the like. The orientational change towards consumerism transformed the cultural landscape.

To a significant extent, culture has shifted from consumption in the service of survival; from the purchasing of basic goods and services essential to survival, to consumption in the service of comfort. This constitutes a paradigm shift in consumption; from means to end; wherein consumerism becomes an end in itself, a source of pleasure additional to the need to survive. The characteristic of shopping has changed in consequence; from necessity to lifestyle.

This paradigm shift, as previously discussed, has led to changes in perceptions, including those regarding identity. From the perspective of characteristic, we may note historical changes in the cultural nature of America. In colonial times, persons viewed themselves as living primarily for God; in service to his will. In industrial times, persons viewed themselves as living primarily for survival; in service to work. In post-World War II times, persons viewed themselves as living primarily for family; in service to family life. In present times, persons view themselves as living primarily for the here-and-now; in service to comfort. There has been a dramatic shift in the characteristic of the cultural nature; the nature of attitudes and orientations towards life and its purpose. The current characteristic attitude is a contributing factor to the prevalence and pervasiveness of dissatisfaction in modern societies, where the gap between reality and desire is strikingly self-evident.

An obvious corollary of this change in cultural nature to living for the here-and-now is the change in the behavior of shopping; there is a concomitant psychologic perspect that shopping is a good and satisfying condition of life of which one ought to make full and satisfying use in the present; an attitude of availing oneself of opportunities in the present, and letting the future take care of itself. Culturally, this attitude has become second nature.

The cultural context of consumerism sets the stage for all manner of consumption, including excessive consumption harmful to the individual self. In a very real sense, cultural consumption as a standard, fosters addiction. Considerations of an holistic nature in assessing and administering to the phenomenon of addiction must take into account this reality of cultural context; the consumerism that encourages the id to give vent to its desires. This is a point unconsidered in historical efforts to address and remedy problems of addiction. While treatment tends towards the medical, the psychologic, and the religious in nature, the point of the relevance of context is philosophic. Its relevance is preeminent; an overriding understanding; its rightful place warranted by its philosophical nature.

PART THREE

THE CONTEXT OF MIND/BODY

CHAPTER NINE

The Context of Heritage

In discoursing the spirit/mind/body phenomenon of addiction, we next consider the context of heritage; the historical precedent; of perspectives, prescribes and proscribes. It is a long and varied history, with ancient origins, modern manifests, fluctuating circumstances and reactions. As the reader will soon discover, the phenomenon of addiction predates the historic record; transmitted knowledge of its existence in pre-history was subsequently recorded, enabling us to more fully appreciate its lengthy relationship to human experience. We begin with consideration of terminology, progress to a review of the ancient past, consider the recent past, then proceed to discourse the present. The path is a long and winding one; our vicarious voyage a means of gaining familiarity with the complexity of our human experience, and an appreciation for the reality of the human heritage of substance use.

Addiction, as a linguistic referent to drug dependence, has a relatively recent history. The term *addiction* was originally used in sixteenth century Europe to designate the state of being legally bound or given over; literally, as in bondage of a servant to a master or, figuratively, as in being habitually given over to some practice or habit. In both applications of the term, it implied a loss of liberty of action.[72] Linguistically, the terminology of addiction originated as an indication of slavery, of the state of being enslaved; the manifest of the enslavement was irrelevant to the semantics of the term. From this, we find that the present-day notion of addiction stems from the co-occurrence, in European consciousness, of slavery and habitual practices; and the recognition of a parallel process of characteristic.

A similar state of affairs occurred in the 1990s; with the co-occurrence, in American consciousness, of substance dependence and obsessional craving; and a similar recognition of parallel process of characteristic, that resulted in the labeling of a new variety of "addictions"; among them food, love, sex, and shopping. The manner in which the word usage expanded in the 20th century is consistent with the manner in which the word usage expanded in the 16th century. The application of the concept of addiction to drug use did not occur until the beginning of the twentieth century, a full four centuries after the word was introduced.

Official definitions of addiction and substance dependence have a similarly short and variable history. In 1,957 C.E., the World Health Organization Expert Committee (later renamed the WHO Expert Committee on Drug Dependence) defined addiction as a state of periodic or chronic intoxication produced by the repeated consumption of a drug (natural or synthetic)...[73] In addition to defining addiction on the basis of its pharmacologic impact on the central nervous system, and its impact on social behavior, the Committee distinguished between addiction and habituation. In 1,973 C.E., the WHO Expert Committee revised its definitions and concepts, and instituted the use of the term, *dependence*[74],

---

[72] Kalant, Harold. "Addiction: Concepts and Definitions", *Encyclopedia of Drugs and Alcohol, Vol.1* Jerome H. Jaffe (Ed.), Simon & Schuster MacMillan: New York, 1995, p. 20.

[73] Kalant, p. 20.

[74] Ibid., p. 21.

distinguishing between the historic, and figurative, notion of addiction as a psychological habit, and the modern, and literal, notion of addiction as a physical habit, deriving from addictive properties of ingested substances.

Usage of the term *drug* varies, but is consistent in terms of defining it as the source of a causal effect; this applies to pharmacologic drugs as well as to illicit substances. The applicable dictionary definition of drug is *a substance that causes addiction or habituation*[75]. In *The Encyclopedia of Drug Abuse*, O'Brien et al. state that a drug is *any substance either organic or manmade that creates a change—a change that is either emotional, mental, physical, or psychological.*[76] In linguistic terms; of modern word definition and word usage; we find that cause and effect are the primary considerations regarding addiction, drugs, and substance dependence.

As the reader will soon discover, hindsight yields the revelation that human perception of the spirit/mind/body phenomenon of addiction has a fickle history. Seen through the eye of the beholder, we, as the human observers of life, vascillate in time with respect to our definitions of addiction, as well as to our attitudes regarding it. We will find that drug use has been variously regarded within human cultures as sacred, commonplace, medicinal, nutritious, socially disruptive, socially cohesive, morally offensive, and morally irrelevant, pendant upon the particular sociocultural and historical context. The context of human heritage pertaining to substance use is as varied as the cultures of humanity, and as fickle as the fads of history; as such, since its introduction, it has become an enduring heritage analogous to that of clothing and hairstyles, which, since their inception, vary by culture and by time.

---

[75] Robert O'Brien, Sidney Cohen, M.D., Glen Evans, and James Fine, M.D., "The History of Drugs and Man", *The Encyclopedia of Drug Abuse*, 2nd ed. Facts on File, Inc.: New York, 1992, p. ix.

[76] O'Brien et al., p. ix.

   The context of historical drug use is, by nature, complex, as researchers have observed. O'Brien et al. note that throughout recorded history, drugs have been used for both medicinal and religious purposes. They report that both uses; for the enhancement of physical well-being, and for heightened religious and metaphysical experiences; are closely related to drug use for its own sake. They contend that since drug use has always included recreational intoxication and self-induced relief from psychic pain and emotional malady, distinctions between usages are difficult, and often arbitrarily imposed by a particular culture, religion or social group.[77] We find that the complexity of the nature of drug usage is its interrelatedness; multiple uses for multiple purposes with multiple effects.

   Dwight B. Heath, in *Alcohol: History of Drinking*, explains the reason for alcohol's enduring importance. In his words, *the key to the importance of alcohol in history is that, from its presumed inception when bacteria first consumed plant cells an estimated 1.5 billion years ago, it has become so deeply embedded in human societies that it affects so many aspects of human life; from religion to economics, to age, to sex, to politics.* We find that it is the extent to which alcohol use has become entrenched in human society which has assured it a place of importance in human history.

   Heath also notes the complex relationship between cultural attitudes and substance use; *that a single chemical compound, used or sometimes emphatically avoided by a single species, has resulted in such a complex array of customs, attitudes, beliefs, values, and effects.* States Heath, *the complexity of the responses to alcohol throughout history has resulted in a relationship that demonstrates both unity and diversity in the ways people think about and treat alcohol.*[78] We find that

---

[77]   O'Brien et al., "The History of Drugs and Man, p. ix.

[78]   Heath, Dwight B. "Alcohol: History of Drinking", *Encyclopedia of Drugs and Alcohol, vol. 1.* Jerome H. Jaffe, M.D. (Ed.). Simon & Schuster MacMillan: New York, 1995, p. 70.

alcohol usage, an integral aspect of human cultural context, has historically experienced a controversy of opinions.

The complex historical relationship between cultural perceptions and alcohol use is paralleled by similar complex historical relationships between cultural perceptions and use of other substances that have been characterized as drugs. We find that there is a difference pertaining to alcohol's acceptance. We may conjecture that the difference in social acceptance between alcohol and other substances derives from the fact of alcohol's referencing in the Bible, undisputably one of the most important works of literature in human history, and undeniably one of the most well-read. The impact is paradoxical; at the forefront of consciousness, alcohol consumption is witnessed to have both positive and negative potential. For example, the irreverent consumption portrayed in Sodom and Gomorrah contrasts with the reverent consumption portrayed in meetings of Jesus of Nazareth and his disciples. We find that our conjecture is sufficient to explain the greater degree of acceptance, as well as the historic, and ongoing, controversy.

Our vision pertaining to addiction, lacking in comprehension of our human heritage of substance use, is myopic; our response reactive; like that of a boa constrictor strangling its prey; without regard for cultural and religious differences, including our own variances over time. What is most striking, apart from the durability of substance use throughout history, is the comparative tendency in modern times towards a constriction of difference; such tendency made visible by the overview of the history of addiction. Upon reflection, we appear to be tended towards a greater degree of sameness than has previously been the case. The effect of the globalization of culture has previously been noted. Such tendency may be the underlying factor in the phenomenon of vanishing indigenous cultures noted by Robert Bringhurst, discussed in Chapter 3.

With respect to addiction, we seem to have become less rather than more tolerant; this is true with respect to drug usages now defined as illicit. At the same time, we have become more rather than less tolerant; this is true with respect to drug usages now defined as pharmacologic. The reality is that our codes of acceptable conduct have become newly circumscribed. In truth, when one considers the extensiveness of pharmacologic and over-the-counter drug use, in combination with other forms of recreational, religious, and medicinal usage, we are more predominantly drug-using than non-drug-using, at a far greater rate than at any prior point in human historical time. So much so that one may well wonder whether the notion of drug as panacea has become hardwired in our brains; as a form of instinctive knowing in the service of survival; like the fight or flight tendency attributed to prehistoric survival experience.

The rootedness of what we now refer to as substance use in human history is evidenced by the fact that the use of intoxicants predates the use of language.[79] The earliest evidence is found in early creation mythologies transmitted through oral tradition that were later recorded in written form. O'Brien and Chafetz describe the pre-Christian creation myth of Gilgamesh which was recorded by the ancient Babylonians, in which grape vines commemorate the death and subsequent transformation of benevolent gods who died in the battle between the powers of good and evil for control of the Earth. According to the myth, the powers of good eventually overcame the powers of evil, and grape vines grow from the earth out of the sacrificial blood of the benevolent gods.[80] In the context of this ancient mythology, wine is accorded a symbolic importance; a tribute to the benevolent deities from whose lifeblood the mother plant

---

[79] Robert O'Brien and Morris Chafetz, M.D., "Introduction: History of Alcohol and Man", *The Encyclopedia of Alcoholism, 2nd ed.* Facts on File, Inc.: New York, 1991, p. xi..

[80] Ibid.

sprung; it persists in various religious cultural traditions today.

According to scholars, there are hints of possible evidence in the Judaic creation myth of Genesis; in which Adam and Eve are warned by God not to eat the fruit of the tree of knowledge of good and evil, or they will die. They ignore the warning, eat the fruit, learn of the existence of good and evil, and are subsequently expelled by God from the Garden of Eden, to slave for their survival without ease-of-life provisioning. According to O'Brien and Chafetz, the tree of knowledge described in Genesis has been equated by many scholars with a grape vine.[81] In this legendary context, Adam and Eve, the first man and first woman created to inhabit the Earth in the Garden of Eden, below the heavens of the Gods, violated the world of the Gods by accessing forbidden knowledge. The symbolism represents the impertinence of Man against God, and God's decision to ensure Man will not access the world of the Gods. While the tree of knowledge represents a specific supernatural tree, the contention that the tree was a grape vine suggests the existence of a relationship; in conscious or unconscious belief; between the consumption of grapes/wine and human impertinence.

According to O'Brien and Chavetz, the Bible is the single most successful temperance document in history, with more than 150 references to alcohol.[82] They contend that while alcohol is deeply rooted in Jewish culture, and maintains an important role in religious celebrations, the Hebrews as a people are relatively free of alcoholism, believed attributable to their attending to the warnings about excess found in the Old Testament, of which Genesis is part. We find consistency between the modern preoccupation with good and evil and its parallel in the Old Testament; the paradox

---

[81] O'Brien and Chafetz, M.D., p. xi.

[82] Ibid., p. xii.

of negative and positive potential; with alcohol representing a dual capacity.

Evidence of a relationship between cultural perceptions of medicinal value and drug usage dates back to the earliest records. O'Brien et al. relate that the earliest known records of drug use concern the plants that were discovered to have medicinal effects on the body or mind. Accordingly, they find that the usage of these plant-derived substances in early history is inseparable from the early history of medicine.[83]

Records from Asia Minor in 5,000 B.C.E. document the use of a *joy plant*, hypothesized to be the poppy plant from which opium derives, that was used for medicinal sedation.[84] Chinese records show that in 2,727 B.C.E., the hemp plant, Cannabis sativa, commonly known as marijuana, was brewed as a medicinal tea.[85] Circa 1,500 B.C.E., the ancient Egyptians used opium elixirs to sedate patients for skull surgery.[86]

In Classical times, plant-based alcohol was used as a disinfectant and was thought to strengthen the blood, stimulate milk production in nursing mothers, and relieve a variety of ailments.[87] In 400 B.C.E., we similarly find Hippocrates using opium as an ingredient in medicines[88], and in 164 C.E., Galen touting the medical benefits of eating opium.[89]

Towards the end of the 13th century, two elderly chemists from Montpellier, Switzerland, brewed a distilled alcohol

---

[83] O'Brien et al., "The History of Drugs and Man", p. ix.

[84] Ibid.

[85] Ibid.

[86] Ibid.

[87] Herman H. Sampson, and Nancy L. Sutherland. "Psychological Consequences of Chronic Abuse", *Encyclopedia of Drugs and Alcohol, Vol. 1*, Jerome H. Jaffe (Ed.), Simon & Schuster MacMillan: New York, 1995, p. 80.

[88] O'Brien et al., "The History of Drugs and Man", p. x.

[89] Ibid.

and called it *aqua vitae,* or water of immortality. Their claim resulted in the spread of the belief that distilled alcohol had cure-all medicinal powers throughout Europe during the Middle Ages.[90] The German physician, Hieronymus Brunschwig, claimed distilled alcohol had the medicinal benefits of curing colds, baldness, deafness, and jaundice, in addition to providing courage and a good memory.[91] O'Brien and Chavetz relate that this faith in alcohol as a panacea for all ills led to the practice, by European religious orders of the Middle Ages, of dispensing drinks to weary travelers; portrayed by the tale of the St. Bernard that rescues snowbound travelers from certain death with a flask of brandy.[92]

The English word tobacco derives from the Spanish word tabaco, which is presumed to have derived from the Taino Indians of the Carribbean. It was Christopher Columbus who first discovered the Tainos smoking rolled tobacco leaves when he discovered the West Indies in 1,492 C.E.[93] Tobacco was proclaimed to have great medicinal potential[94] when it was introduced in France in 1,560 C.E. by Jacques Nicot, after whom the term nicotine derives.

Opium, in the liquid form of laudanum, was held to be a medical panacea by Paracelsus, a Swiss alchemist, when he introduced it in 1,541 C.E.[95] During the Civil War in America, morphine, an opium derivative, was routinely administered as a medical treatment to injured soldiers and their distressed families. Reports indicate this practice

[90] O'Brien and Chafetz, M.D., "Introduction: History of Alcohol and Man," p. xiv.

[91] Ibid.

[92] Ibid.

[93] Webster's New Collegiate Dictionary, p. 1217.

[94] O'Brien et al., "The History of Drugs and Man", p. xii.

[95] O'Brien et al., "The History of Drugs and Man", p. xiii.

resulted in an estimated 400,000 cases of morphine addiction among American Army veterans and their families.[96]

Early human drug use was also closely related to geographic availability. O'Brien et al. inform us that the discovery of drug properties varied in accordance with the local vegetation.[97] Thus, coffee berries, cultivated from Arabian trees, were used to make caffeinated beverages.[98] The Incas in South America chewed locally-growing coca leaves for increased energy, suppressed appetite, and short-term euphoria, believed by the authors to have served as an aid to endurance in a rigorously harsh mountain environment.[99] The Mexican Aztecs used hallucinogens, like peyote and psilocybin, found to occur in locally growing cactus and mushrooms.[100] The indigenous cultures of Mexico and Peru produced multipurpose wines and beers from geographically available plants; cactus, maize, and manioc.[101] Ethyl alcohol, or ethanol, the naturally occurring byproduct of fermentation, was variously produced and consumed from local fruit and grain sources throughout the known world.[102]

Cultural exchange through conquest and trade eliminated the restriction of geographic availability, and resulted in increased exposure to different drug sources, customs and technologies. In this way, first century Romans learned about opium during their conquest of the eastern Mediterranean.[103] Knowledge of hashish cultivation, and the process of wine distillation discovered by the Arabian alchemist, Geber, in the

---

[96] O'Brien et al., "The History of Drugs and Man", p. xv.

[97] O'Brien et al., "The History of Drugs and Man", p. xi.

[98] O'Brien et al., "The History of Drugs and Man", p. xii.

[99] O'Brien et al., "The History of Drugs and Man", p. xi.

[100] O'Brien et al.,"The History of Drugs and Man", p. xi-xii.

[101] Heath, "Alcohol: History of Drinking, p. 73.

[102] Heath, "Alcohol: History of Drinking", p. 70.

[103] O'Brien et al., "The History of Drugs and Man", p. x.

eighth century, spread to Europe in the eleventh and twelfth centuries via Crusaders returning from battle with Moslems in the Holy Land.[104] The Crusaders also transported sirah grapes from Persia that were used to plant the now famous vineyards of the French river valleys.[105] Opium and cannabis, originally cultivated in Asia, spread to Europe with Marco Polo.[106] Cannabis, which had become an integral part of the culture of India by 400 C.E., was first introduced in 2,000 B.C.E.[107] Coffee, from the Middle East, spread to Europe in the sixteenth and seventeenth centuries.[108] South American coffee, now the most heavily cultivated coffee in the world, was originally introduced by English traders.[109]

In terms of sociohistoric impact, O'Brien et al. tell us that it was the meeting of the Old and New Worlds that resulted in the most significant exchange of drugs in recorded history. Europe's discovery of the Americas in the 1400s resulted in drug culture exchanges that altered drug use patterns worldwide. European explorers introduced distilled alcohol to the Americas, creating a substantial new market for alcohol production and consumption. Indigenous North American cultures varied in their responses to alcohol. Some Native American groups developed heavy drinking styles, while others drank moderately, and some groups banned alcohol completely.[110]

Per Dwight Heath, countries competed to gain a trading advantage in selling liquor to the Native American groups of North America. Although many tribes purchased the liquor, the Hopi and Zuni tribes never accepted it, and there were

---

[104] O'Brien and Chafetz, M.D., "Introduction: History of Alcohol and Man", p. xiv.

[105] Ibid.

[106] O'Brien et al., "The History of Drugs and Man", p. xi.

[107] O'Brien et al., "The History of Drugs and Man", p. ix-x.

[108] O'Brien et al., "The History of Drugs and Man", p. xii.

[109] Ibid.

[110] Ibid.

differences in drinking patterns between the tribes.[111] The introduction of distilled alcohol facilitated the devise of the African slave trade by the British to finance West Indian sugar used by New England colonialists in the production of rum. At the outbreak of the American Revolution against England, rum production was discontinued, and Americans switched to the production and consumption of whiskey made from locally grown corn and rye.

Across the ocean in Europe, we are told that the introduction of cocaine from South America, hallucinogens from Central America, and tobacco from North America, was given the same welcome given to the receipts of parrots, gold, and furs.[112] These drugs were rapidly incorporated into European cultures. Smoking, especially, became popular for what were touted to be its stimulating and tranquilizing effects.[113] The tobacco trade that developed was highly successful, and led to the distribution of tobacco to other parts of the world.

According to O'Brien et al., in every culture in which tobacco was introduced, its usage became commonplace.[114] In their view, the universal appeal of smoking is accounted for by the addictive quality of nicotine and the conditioning effect of thousands of "hits" to the brain.[115] In light of what we have learned about the ancient and longstanding entrenchment of alcohol in human society, it appears that tobacco, in modern times, has experienced the same reception and pattern of entrenchment. The same could be said for coffee and tea. Thus, alcohol, coffee, tea, and tobacco have evidenced a kind of universal appeal over that of other introduced substances.

---

[111] Ibid.

[112] Heath, "Alcohol: History of Drinking", p. 73.

[113] Ibid.

[114] O'Brien et al., "The History of Drugs and Man", p. xiii.

[115] Ibid.

The fraternal twin developments of colonialization, which provided industrialists with ready access to new markets, indigenous labor, and natural resources; and industrialization, which provided consumers with ready access to mass-produced goods, altered traditional consumption patterns, and facilitated the proliferation and consumption of commercially-produced drug commodities in both the Old and New Worlds. By the mid- to late-1790s, increases in the consumption of distilled alcohol were evidenced among the general populations of England, North America, Sweden, and Russia. In 1700s industrialized London, dismal working conditions, severe unemployment, and cheap liquor, engendered an epidemic of gin consumption, especially among poor and working-class women.[116] In Russia and Sweden, monopolies were established within their governmental boundaries to prevent outsiders from profiting from the massive alcohol consumption that ensued from the ready availability of mass-produced alcohol.[117]

Aggressive trade practices resulted in the proliferation of opium use in China, England, and the United States in the 19th century. In China, consumption flourished after the introduction of opium smoking. The Manchu dynasty was repeatedly unsuccessful in its efforts to stop opium trafficking by the English East India Company. In 1,776 C.E., China made opium a capital offense. In 1,839 C.E., the Chinese government prohibited importation. As a result, the Opium Wars erupted. The first Opium War lasted from 1,839-42 C.E., with England's defeat of China, and resulted in a forced acceptance of English opium imports. The second Opium War began in 1,856 C.E., ending with the Treaty of Tientsin in 1,858 C.E., and China's forced acceptance of high opium tariffs.

In England, opium use reached epidemic proportions; the outcome of widespread availability of over-the-counter

---

[116] Heath, "Alcohol: History of Drinking", p. 73

[117] Ibid.

elixirs among the poor and working classes. Among the affluent, recreational opium smoking was common.[118] In the United States, opium-based elixirs were patented as medicines and popularized through magazine ads and direct mail sales.[119] In both England and America, the marketing and sale of opium elixirs as medicines for children, resulted in frequent incidences of childhood addiction, and death secondary to opioid dependence.[120]

Throughout history, epidemics of drug use have spawned corresponding reactions of moral outrage, and legal restriction or prohibition. In ancient Babylonia, circa 1,700 B.C.E., the Code of Hammurabi restricted drinking to public drinking houses, and established laws for the execution of offenders.[121] Across the globe, the Chinese government of Emperor Chung K'iang demonstrated disapproval of immoderate drinking by executing drunkards.[122] In ancient Persia, the religious ban on drug use within Islamic culture, developed in reaction to the excessive drug practices of the Persian aristocracy.[123] The deterioration of the Greek Symposium into drunken Roman orgies led to a temporary ban by the Roman Senate in 186 B.C.E.[124] In 81 C.E., half of Rome's vineyards were destroyed by order of Emperor Domitian, and the Senate prohibited the planting of new vines until 276 C.E.[125]

In 1,226 C.E., Switzerland implemented closing-time laws for drinking establishments. The practice was followed

---

[118] O'Brien et al., "The History of Drugs and Man", p. xiii.

[119] O'Brien et al., "The History of Drugs and Man", p. xiv.

[120] Ibid.

[121] O'Brien and Chafetz, M.D., "Introduction: History of Alcohol and Man", p. xii.

[122] Ibid.

[123] Ibid.

[124] O'Brien and Chafetz, M.D., "Introduction: History of Alcohol and Man," p. xiv.

[125] Ibid.

by England in 1,285 C.E., and Scotland in 1,436 C.E.[126] Germany banned the sale of alcoholic beverages on Sundays and holy days[127], and the order of St. Christopher was founded in Germany in 1,517 C.E., to reduce excessive drinking.[128] In 1,603 C.E., alarmed by perceived incidences of addiction, Japan prohibited tobacco smoking. In England, James I in 1,604 C.E. and Sir Francis Bacon in 1,623 C.E. both decried the addictive nature of tobacco.[129]

The Puritans of the Protestant Reformation in Europe evolved in moral reaction to the alcoholic excesses of the industrialized period. They viewed intoxication as a moral offense; yet favored the regular drinking of beer, and consumption of liquor for what they believed were its warming, social, and curative properties.[130] In 1,785 C.E. America, Benjamin Rush, a physician and signer of the Declaration of Independence, started an educational campaign against the health effects of long-term heavy drinking.[131]

In the 1800s, The American Temperance Society, mushroomed into an umbrella organization with over 1,000 religious affiliate groups across the rural United States, petitioning state governments to prohibit the sale of alcohol.[132]Their efforts culminated in the passage of the Eighteenth Amendment to the Constitution, which enacted a nationwide prohibition on beverages with alcohol content of more than five-tenths of a percent, beginning in 1,919 C.E. and lasting until its repeal in 1,933 C.E.[133]

---

[126] O'Brien and Chafetz, M.D., "Introduction: History of Alcohol and Man", p. xv.

[127] Ibid.

[128] Ibid.

[129] O'Brien et al., "The History of Drugs and Man", p. xii.

[130] Heath, "Alcohol: History of Drinking", p. 73.

[131] O'Brien and Chafetz, M.D., "Introduction: History of Alcohol and Man", p. xvii.

[132] Ibid.

[133] Ibid.

Historically, the successful entrenchment of new drug cultures has been accompanied by promotional toutings of their medicinal, spiritual, and recreational benefits. Upon successful introduction, with increase in cultural consumption, excess usage and the sociocultural costs of addiction become apparent. We then find evidence of cultural disenchantment, and efforts within cultures to control or restrict drug usage. Efforts to curtail or control culturally-entrenched drug usage utilizing punitive legislation or moral condemnation targeted at drug users, have historically failed. The failure of the Prohibition of alcohol in the United States is a prime example.

According to O'Brien and Chafetz, heavy drinkers were unaffected by the Prohibition because of the enormous quantity of illegal production that replaced the regulated and taxed trade. Moderate drinkers, denied the social outlet of the saloons, subsequently disregarded the law when fashionable speakeasies emerged as substitute drinking establishments. The Prohibition served to entrench the attitudes of the teetotalers, who believed that alcoholism was a sin and that alcoholics should be denied medical treatment.[134] When the Prohibition failed to achieve its stated aim of national moderation, the moral approach was deemed inadequate. O'Brien and Chafetz report that the discrediting of the moral approach to solving alcohol problems opened the door to the alternative approach of scientific investigation of the issues surrounding alcohol consumption.[135]

In reviewing the historical context of heritage, we find an historical pattern of multiple drug use, a predominant pattern of religious tolerance and caution regarding excess, a pattern of government restriction reactions to excess consumption, a persistence of usage, a chameleon-like quality to drug usage, and a general lack of comprehension of the conflicted human relationship. The complexity of the heritage is least

---

[134] Ibid.

[135] Ibid.

attributable to cultural differences, and most attributable to the push-pull between human nature; the inclination to use drugs; and the societal nature; the inclination to control behavior, and thereby, drug usage. In between least and most, there are varying degrees of complexity, and among these resides the interrelated purposes of usage. The long-standing duration of the historical pattern indicates that it represents a reliable picture of the human engagement with substance use.

In turning our attention to the present, we begin with a discourse on tobacco. The matter of addiction pertaining to tobacco products has received considerable governmental and media attention in recent years, following from an official reclassification in America. By the same token that investors are advised to stay apprised of changes in the law which may affect investing, we find that changes in official classifications have similar ramifications. The paradigm shift from a moral to a scientific approach to substance usage altered perceptions.

In the 1980s, the American Psychiatric Association changed its classification of substance dependence pertaining to tobacco. Whereas, in 1,980 C.E., physical dependence from smoking was attributed to tobacco, in 1,987 C.E., it was attributed instead to nicotine, an ingredient of tobacco.[136] In 1,981 C.E., the Merriam-Webster Corporation that publishes dictionaries, defined nicotine as *a poisonous alkaloid C10H14N2 that is the chief active principle of tobacco and is used as an insecticide.* It is still so defined today.[137]

---

[136] Robert L. Spitzer, M.D., and Janet B. W. Williams, D.S.W., "Appendix D: Annotated Comparative Listing of DSM-III and DSM-III-R", In *Diagnostic and Statistical Manual of Mental Disorders (3rd Edition-Revised): DSM-III-R*. American Psychiatric Association: Washington, D.C., 1987 pp. 416 and 419.

[137] *Webster's New Collegiate Dictionary*, p. 768; and *Merriam-Webster's Collegiate Dictionary. 11th ed.* Frederick C. Mish (Ed.). Merriam-Webster, Inc.: MA, 2003, p. 836.

Whereas, in 1,932 C.E., the government position on substance use was prohibition, with moral intolerance; in 1,933 C.E., the government position on substance use was restriction, with scientific tolerance. It remains so after 78 years of scientific investigation. As is the natural case with science, the classification of mental disorders can be viewed as a work in progress. Per June Sprock and Roger K. Blashfield, resolving the serious problems associated with classification will not be a trivial undertaking.[138]

According to the *Diagnostic and Statistical Manual, the DSM IV-TR (Text Revision), 4th ed.,* published in 2,000 C.E., some of the generic dependence criteria do not appear to apply to nicotine, whereas others require further explanation.[139] Further explication of this is that in the diagnosis of nicotine dependence, diagnosis does not meet the established criteria of tolerance for classification as substance dependence, according to diagnostic standards.[140]

Dependence is to be distinguished from habitual use, and there is controversy regarding the appropriateness of classifying nicotine as a drug capable of causing dependence. This is true given that other tobacco substances, such as pipe-smoking, cigar-smoking, and chewing tobacco, which also contain nicotine, historically were not so classified, and nicotine does not typically cause intoxication. Beginning with the 2,000 C.E. version of the DSM IV-TR, however, diagnoses of nicotine dependence and withdrawal were

[138] June Sprock and Roger K. Blashfield, "Classification and Nosology: The History of American Classification Systems of Psychopathology", In Michel Hersen, Alan E. Kazdin, and Alan S. Bellack, (Eds.) *The Clinical Psychology Handbook*, Pergamon Press, Inc.: New York, 1983, p. 304.

[139] American Psychiatric Association. "305.1 Nicotine Dependence", In "Substance-Related Disorders", *Diagnostic and Statistical Manual IV-TR, 4th ed.* Michael B. First et al. (Eds.). APA: Washington, D.C., 2000, p. 264.

[140] APA, p. 263.

applied to all forms of tobacco use; including cigarettes, chewing tobacco, snuff, pipes, and cigars, and to prescription medications containing nicotine, such as nicotine gum and nicotine patches. The caveat is that the relative ability of these products to produce dependence or induce withdrawal is associated with the rapidity characteristic of the route of administration; that is, smoked over oral over transdermal; and the nicotine content of the product.[141]

Governmental restrictions are responsible for consumer product labels, including those found on packages of tobacco products. To put the paradigm shift into context, the scientific approach adopted by government is not restricted to the matter of substance use, it applies to all matters of interest to government. Thus, the identification and labeling of product ingredients, cautions, et cetera, by industry came into effect in response to government standards and requirements based on the new scientific approach. We find that in the history of the manufacturing and distribution of cigarettes, America has gone the gamut from no warning messages on cigarette packages regarding the effects of smoking on health, to a warning message from the Surgeon General of the United States of America that *Cigarette smoking may be hazardous to your health*, to a revised warning message declaring *Quitting smoking now greatly reduces serious risks to your health*, to the most recent warning message that states, *Cigarette smoke contains carbon monoxide*. Variations of these messages appear on other forms of tobacco products.

American government's decision to adopt the approach of science has led to considerable changes across governmental venues. Such decision has had a hand in spurring changes to manufacturing processes of all kinds; including the production of tobacco products. What we find in the modern American context of heritage is an orientation to study; to consider, to assess, to evaluate; the generation of

---

[141] Ibid.

information with an eye towards assisting the governmental decision-making process, consistent with a scientific orientation. The shift in orientation has altered the realm of higher education; through funding by government to provide research of interest to government, thereby influencing courses of study. With respect to the phenomenon of addiction, the modern pattern of study is consistent with the course of modern science; the approach is primarily one of assessment. The results of pertinent assessments are relayed to decision-makers for decisions pertaining to funding, law, policy, further research, standards, treatment, et cetera.

The state of the science pertaining to tobacco is a work in progress. Nicotine has been established to be a poisonous alkaloid. Carbon monoxide has been established to be a toxicity factor in cigarette smoking. The predominant focus is on products and product ingredients; the regulatory domain of government. As studies progress, and knowledge pertaining accumulates, replicates, and refines, a more definitive picture of the reality of tobacco will emerge.

As pertains to the classification of addiction, the reality is complex, confusing, and at times inconsistent. The categorization of nicotine dependence as a mental disorder fits this description. The reasons are several. First, it doesn't fit the intoxication criteria of the term dependence. Second, properties of physical addiction haven't been proven; addiction is diagnosed on the basis of compulsive behavior, and development of tolerance to initial reactions of nausea and dizziness with first use.[142] Third, there are differences in practitioner opinions.

The matter of classifying tobacco product dependence as a mental disorder is complicated by the government-mandate for clinical codes for treatment documentation, provider compensation, governmental and industry gate-keeping and statistical tabulation purposes; matters of utility.

---

[142] Ibid.

The fundamental issue of whether nicotine dependence constitutes a mental disorder is debatable; dependence has not been definitively determined, many compulsive behaviors exist which are not so classified, and the stigmatic effects of such identification warrant consideration. This is a relevant matter, given that a rather stringent social stigma for smoking has developed in response to the change in classification. It is also relevant that the inclusion in diagnostic classification supports medical treatment and insurance compensation. The Hippocratic oath of do no harm, established in 1,747 C.E.[143], provides basis for consideration of whether the stigmatization created by such classification may be causing more harm than help.

Clarifications, useful for the purpose of rendering a differential diagnosis; in the assessment of whether tobacco use constitutes a habit or an addiction; have been forthcoming. According to the *AMA Complete Medical Encyclopedia*, published in 2,003 C.E., addiction is a behavior pursued not for the pleasure or gain it provides but as a way of satisfying a physical or deep-seated psychological compulsion.[144] Accordingly, AMA states that the addiction dominates the person's life and becomes his or her principal activity or pursuit, often at a high personal cost in terms of family, work, school, financial success, and career.

We find that the matter of classifying substance use as a habit or an addiction requires discernment and judgment, in addition to agreement regarding semantics. The concept of insanity proposed by Bill Wilson; reviewed later in this chapter; is a case in point. Wilson distinguishes between the drunk and the insanely drunk, in his explication of the alcoholic. Agreement is assured in cases of addiction that meet the Wilson criteria; that is, substance use

---

[143] *Webster's New Collegiate Dictionary*, p. 548.

[144] American Medical Association. *Complete Medical Encyclopedia*. Jerrold B. Leikin, M.D. and Martin S. Lipsky, M.D. (Eds.). Random House Reference: New York, 2003, p. 116.

that involves a measure of insanity; of losing touch with reality. Such is not the case with all heavy drinkers or with heavy smokers, just as it was not the case with the opium-smoking Sherlock Holmes. It is also not the case with most compulsions, although it is sometimes the case. There is an additional inconsistency in the classification of dependence; prescription and nonprescription drugs that may have withdrawal effects are typically not diagnosed as causing dependence. A further matter that pertains is that of treatment orientation, and the relevance of diagnosis to nonmedical treatment modalities. For example, treatment programs specifically oriented towards the psychological management of compulsive behaviors, will demonstrate a greater tendency to diagnose addiction versus habit, than might a sole practitioner.

Differential diagnosis is clearly relevant. The matter of mental disorder classification is clear-cut in cases which involve breaks with reality, justifiable in cases which involve sought-after treatment, and otherwise a matter of clinical judgment.

As Sprock and Blashfield report, a major persistent difficulty in the field of psychopathology is how to define the boundaries of mental disorders and normality. They cite Korchin's 1,976 C.E. report that the increasing number of problems being dealt with by mental health professionals has further blurred the distinction between normal and abnormal.[145] Per Sprock and Blashfield, Szasz in 1,961 C.E., and Korchin in 1,976 C.E., have both argued against a distinction between normal and abnormal behavior; Szasz contending that there is no qualitative difference between illness and health; rather different degrees in problems in living, and Korchin contending that the distinction between normal and abnormal is needless. They further cite Kendall's 1,975 C.E. contention that the low reliability of psychiatric diagnoses occurs because the syndromes merge into one

---

[145] Ibid., p. 300.

another without natural boundaries, and most patients fit the criteria of several diagnoses while few clearly fit into one category. As Sprock and Blashfield assess, a classification system needs to be flexible in responding to empirical findings and evolving theoretical positions.[146]

Given that nicotine has been identified as a poisonous alkaloid used in the manufacture of insecticides raises the possibility of an unrecognized paradox; a potential utility. Nicotine, administered in sufficiently high concentrations, has poisonous consequences for insects. Given this, it may also be the case that it has a similar impact upon other forms of organic parasites, such as bacteria. If this is the case, then nicotine ingestion may have the side effect of counteracting parasitic infestation; serving a medicinal purpose in killing unwanted bacterias and germs. Nicot's contention in the 1700s that tobacco has medicinal value may yet prove true.

The role of chemicals in manufacturing processes is another relevant consideration; particularly as pertains to the process of washing. For example, coffee manufacturers have discovered they are able to vary the acidity of coffee bean products through changes in bean-washing processes. The potential exists for improvements in tobacco manufacturing processes. The scientific Zeitgeist raises questions that will take time to adequately answer. In this scientific regard, the context of modern heritage is evolutionary.

The context of modern heritage pertaining to attitudes towards substance use tends towards the reactionary. In America, the historical period that followed the Prohibition witnessed the favoring of heavy drinking and heavy smoking; a tolerance for excess. This may be viewed, in part, as a reaction to the end of the days of prohibition, and, in part, as a reaction to the end of the days of World War II. In recent decades, a resurgence in religious fundamentalism and a resurgence in political extremism have resulted in revisited

---

[146] Ibid., p. 304.

reactions of intolerance. In the course of one century, America has experienced four reactionary swings of the pendulum; two alternating periods of social tolerance: the Roaring Twenties and Post-World War II; two alternating periods of social intolerance: the Prohibition and the Christian Coalition movement of the late 1980s and early 1990s. We find that attitude is a chameleon; it changes in response to changes in the environment.

In 1,939 C.E., when Bill Wilson's story first appeared in print, his co-founded Alcoholics Anonymous organization held the position that there was a difference between hard drinkers, problem drinkers, and what Wilson called real alcoholics, who are more or less always insanely drunk.[147] The relevance of this distinction is its capacity to elucidate the sea change in attitudes towards alcoholism and other forms of substance use since the beginning of the last century; a change which has shifted towards catch-all categorization. The present has borne witness to a proliferation of treatments for addiction; benzodiazepines; valium and xanax; crack cocaine, food, gambling, hallucinogens, heroin, love, sex, shopping, and smoking among them. Every form of compulsive behavior has become grist for the treatment mill. To an extent, this change in attitude may be attributed to the swinging of the public opinion pendulum. To an extent, it indicates cultural acclimation to the notion of addiction. To an extent, it speaks to the change towards a more compulsive cultural reality. The modern attitude of generalizing addiction may or may not reflect physical dependency; it does, however, reflect recognition of a more common pattern of compulsive behavior.

Historically, the usage of drugs has been lauded, reviled, and accepted in human society in accordance

---

[147] Wilson, Bill. "Bill's Story", In *Alcoholics Anonymous: The Story of How Many Thousands of Men and Women Have Recovered from Alcoholism. 3rd Ed.* Alcoholics Anonymous World Services, Inc.: New York, 1976, p. 20.

with public, governmental, medical, and religious opinion; it is undoubtedly a fickle heritage. From a philosophical perspective, we approach the matter of understanding. Towards this end, we consider the following points regarding truisms. The book, How Do You Know It's True?, posits that our knowledge is based on probability not certainty, such that each increase in knowledge is a closer approximation to the truth, but not the truth itself, and that in accepting this truism, we acknowledge the reality that a century from now our great-great-grandchildren may look back on today's world and regard it with the same pity and condescension that we now regard the Middle Ages.[148] The point made by David and Marymae Klein regarding condescension; the tendency to regard what came before us as inferior; is relevant to our consideration.

We have arrived at the understanding that knowledge of ourselves is aided by hindsight, muddled by difficulty perceiving ourselves clearly in the present, and lacking in foresight. In this regard, history provides the underpinnings for current and future comprehensions. The tendency towards condescension of the past alerts us to the absence of an historical self-awareness; a tendency towards a disjointed self-perspective. It is a point philosophically well-taken. The tendencies to disregard historical context; perceiving the matter as one of then versus now; failure to put the present into perspective; perceiving the matter as one of a modern point in time; and lack of vision of the future; perceiving the matter as one of linear progression; encumber holistic understanding.

Historical perspective provides us with pertinent insights key to understanding the relationship between humanity and addiction. First, we find that commerce has played a significant role. Intercultural drug commerce has facilitated

---

[148] David Klein and Marymae E. Klein. How Do You Know It's True?: Sifting Sense From Nonsense. Charles Scribner's Sons : New York, 1984, p. 164.

transcultural drug consumption has facilitated drug addiction. While novelty of experience has, in many cases, been a factor, it is not independent of commerce. The relationship is crucial to substance availability. Second, we find that manifest culture and addiction are interrelated phenomena. The nature of the interrelationship is complex and variable. Third, we find that addiction is encouraged by extremism; by the co-existence of social extremes: hedonism and fundamentalism; and discouraged by moderation. The pattern is historically consistent; suggesting the relationship is a constant; one of relativity.

The pronouncements of history; the arbitrary contextually-relevant attitudes and beliefs regarding substance use and addiction; are sufficiently fickle that differentiating fact from fiction, discerning what is rational from what is irrational, determining what is culturally derived and what is not, in assessing the context of heritage is complicated by the historical pattern of inconsistency. We find that human nature, across the time span of human existence, is a consistent variable. Arriving at a point of refined perspective regarding the matter of addiction; one that provides a more complete understanding of substances, effects, and related phenomena, necessarily entails consideration of the human nature.

CHAPTER TEN

The Prevalence of Addiction

Addiction is a pervasive and characteristic phenomenon in modern culture. The modern prevalence of addiction, unsurpassed in human history, is a legacy of intra-global commerce, population expansion, and consumptive culture. The unprecedented commercial accessibility of a wide array of addictive substances across the population spectrum provides the opportunity for usage. This being the case, the caveat of buyer beware applies as well to the purchase and use of potentially addictive substances as it does to any other purchasable commodity. In conclusion of this section, we consider the prevalence of substance use, citing America as example.

Overall Prevalence.
    The overall prevalence of drug use in the United States is presented in Table 1.[149] The rates presented are based upon United States government classifications of alcohol, cigarettes, marijuana, smokeless tobacco, and cocaine as drugs. Alcohol had the highest frequency of total population

---

[149] Table No. 218. "Use of Selected Drugs by Age of User: 1993", In "Drug Use", *Encyclopedia of Addiction*, vol. 3, p. 137.

use at 50%, followed by cigarettes at 24%, marijuana at 4%, smokeless tobacco at 3%, and cocaine at 1%.

Prevalence by Age.

Alcohol use begins early and increases with age, stabilizing at the age of 35, close to the 50% national drinking rate. As Table 1 shows, the prevalence of alcohol use was 18% among 12-17 year olds, 59% among 18-25 year olds, 63% among 26-34 year olds, and 49% among those aged 35 and older.

Cigarette smoking similarly begins early and increases with age, stabilizing at age 35, close to the national smoking rate of 25%. The prevalence of cigarette smoking was 10% among 12-17 year olds, 29% among 18-25 year olds, 30% among 26-34 year olds, and 24% among those aged 35 and older.

In contrast to alcohol and cigarettes, the prevalence of marijuana use is low at 4%. Five percent of 12-17 year olds, 11% of 18-25 year olds, 7% of 26-34 year olds, and 2% of those 35 and older used marijuana.

National prevalence of smokeless tobacco use is 3%; with 2% of 12-17 year olds, 6% of 18-25 year olds, 4% of 26-34 year olds, and 2% of those 35 and older who used it.

Cocaine had the lowest national prevalence of use at 1%. Less than 1% of 12-17 year olds, 2% of 18-25 year olds, 1% of 26-34 year olds, and less than 1% of those aged 35 and older used cocaine.

Table 1.
Prevalence of Drug Use in the United States: 1995

	12-17 yo	18-25 yo	26-34 yo	35+ yo	Total
Alcohol	18%	59%	63%	49%	50%
Cigarettes	10%	29%	30%	24%	24%
Marijuana	5%	11%	7%	2%	4%
Tobacco(SL)	2%	6%	4%	2%	3%
Cocaine	<1%	2%	1%	<1%	1%

Key: SL=smokeless; yo=year olds

Maria Artiz, Ph.D.

Table 2.
Prevalence of U.S. Drug Use by Sex and Age

	12-17 yo	18-25 yo	26-34 yo	35+ yo	Total
	Female/Male	Female/Male	Female/Male	Female/Male	Female/Male
Alcohol	18% v. 18%	54% v. 65%	56% v. 70%	40% v. 59%	43% v. 57%
Cigarettes	10% v. 09%	27% v. 31%	29% v. 31%	21% v. 27%	22% v. 26%
Marijuana	04% v.06%	06% v. 17%	05% v. 09%	01% v. 03%	03% v. 06%
Tobacco (SL) (chew)	NA v. 04%	<1% v. 13%	<1% v. 09%	<1% v. 04%	<1% v. 06%
Cocaine	<1% v. <1%	01% v. 02%	<1% v. 02%	<1% v. 01%	<1% v. 01%

Prevalence by Sex.

The prevalence of drug use in the United States by sex and age is presented in Table 2. The prevalence of drug use was higher among males than females. As Table 2 shows, males had a higher rate of alcohol use (57% vs. 43%), a higher rate of cigarette smoking (26% vs. 22%), a higher rate of marijuana use (6% vs. 3%), a higher rate of smokeless tobacco use (6% vs. <1%), and a higher rate of cocaine use (1% vs. <1%).

Men are more likely than women to be heavy drinkers, and to be involved in drinking-related accidents.[150] Of the estimated 15 million alcohol-abusing or alcohol-dependent individuals in the United States, fewer than one-third are women.[151]Women who use drugs are more likely to have partners who use drugs.[152]

Among both men and women, marijuana is the most frequently used illicit drug. The majority of heroin users are men. Women have a higher consumption of prescription tranquilizers, sleeping pills, and over-the-counter drugs.[153] With regard to cigarette use, once smoking is initiated women are less likely to quit than men, and when they do quit women are more likely than men to relapse.[154]

Prevalence by Sex and Age.

Among 12-17 year olds, the prevalence of alcohol use at 18% was the same for females and males. Cigarette prevalence was higher among teenage females; 10% versus

---

[150] Robbins, Cynthia. "Women and Substance Abuse," *Encyclopedia of Drugs and Alcohol, vol. 3*, Jerome H. Jaffe (Ed.), Simon & Schuster MacMillan: New York, 1995, p. 1289.

[151] Robbins, p. 1289.

[152] Schneiderman, Joyce. F. "Gender and Complications of Substance Abuse", *Encyclopedia of Drugs and Alcohol, vol. 2*, Jerome H. Jaffe (Ed.), Simon & Schuster MacMillan: New York, 1995, p. 527.

[153] Robbins, "Women and Substance Abuse", p. 1289.

[154] Ibid.

9% for males. Marijuana use was higher among teenage males; 6% versus 4%. Smokeless tobacco use was higher among teenage males, although exact figures for females were not available. Cocaine use was slightly higher among males.

Among 18-25 year olds, the prevalence of drug use was higher among males than females. Alcohol prevalence was 65% for males vs. 54% for females. Male cigarette use was higher (31% vs. 27%), male marijuana use was higher (17% vs. 6%), male smokeless tobacco use was higher (13% vs. <1%), and male cocaine use was higher (2% vs. 1%).

Among 26-34 year olds, the prevalence of drug use was highest among males. Males had a higher prevalence of alcohol use (70% vs. 56%), cigarette use (31% vs. 29%), marijuana use (9% vs. 5%), smokeless tobacco use (9% vs. <1%), and cocaine use (2% vs. <1%) than females.

In the 35 and older group, prevalence of drug use was higher among males than females. Males had a higher prevalence of alcohol use (59% vs. 40%), cigarette use (27% vs. 21%), marijuana use (3% vs. 1%), smokeless tobacco use (4% vs. <1%), and cocaine use (1% vs. <1%).

Prevalence by Race/Ethnicity.

The prevalence of drug use in the United States by race and ethnicity is presented in Table 3, utilizing the major government-defined categories. The prevalence of alcohol use is higher among Whites (52.7%) than among Hispanics (45.6%) or Blacks (37.6%). The prevalence of cigarette use is also higher among Whites (24.7%) than among Blacks (23.4%) or Hispanics (21.2%). The prevalence of marijuana use is higher among Blacks (5.6%) than among Hispanics (4.7%) or Whites (4.2%). The prevalence of smokeless tobacco use is higher among Whites (3.5%) than among Blacks (1.5%) or Hispanics (1.1%). The prevalence of cocaine use is higher among Blacks (1.3%) than among Hispanics (1.1%) or Whites (0.5%).

Table 3.
Prevalence of U.S. Drug Use by Race/Ethnicity

	White	Hispanic	Black	Total
Alcohol	52.7%	45.6%	37.6%	49.6%
Cigarettes	24.7%	21.2%	23.4%	24.2%
Marijuana	04.2%	04.7%	05.6%	04.3%
Tobacco (SL)	03.5%	01.1%	01.5%	02.9%
Cocaine	00.5%	01.1%	01.3%	00.6%

Maria Artiz, Ph.D.

Table 4.
Prevalence of U.S. Drug Use by Geographic Region

	Northeast	Midwest	South	West
Alcohol	54.1%	48.6%	44.9%	54.2%
Cigarettes	25.4%	24.3%	24.3%	22.7%
Marijuana	04.2%	03.5%	04.3%	05.5%
Tobacco (SL)	02.2%	03.0%	03.9%	02.0%
Cocaine	00.7%	00.5%	00.6%	00.8%

Key: SL=smokeless

Prevalence by Geographic Region.

The prevalence of drug use in the United States by geographic region is presented in Table 4. Alcohol use was more prevalent in the West (54.2%) and the Northeast (54.1%), than in the Midwest (48.6%) or the South (44.9%). The prevalence of cigarette use was highest in the Northeast (25.4%), followed by the Midwest (24.3%) and South (24.3%), and the West (22.7%). Marijuana use was more prevalent in the West (5.5%), followed by the South (4.3%), the Northeast (4.2%), and the Midwest (3.5%). Smokeless tobacco use was more prevalent in the South (3.9%) and Midwest (3.0%), than in the Northeast (2.2%), and West (2.0%). The prevalence of cocaine use was approximately the same across regions, with variance of only tenths of a percentage point; West (0.8%), Northeast (0.7%), South (0.6%), and Midwest (0.5%).

Table 5. Overall Drug Use in the United States: A Time Comparison

	12-17 yo	18-25 yo	26-34 yo*	35+ yo	Total
Alcohol	1995: 18% 2003: 18%	1995: 59% 2003: 61%	1995: 63% 2003: 53%	1995: 49% 2003: NA	1995: 50% 2003: 50%
Cigarettes	1995: 10% 2003: 12%	1995: 29% 2003: 40%	1995: 30% 2003: 25%	1995: 24% 2003: NA	1995: 24% 2003: 25%
Marijuana	1995: 05%	1995: 11%	1995: 07%	1995: 02%	1995: 04% 2003: 06%
Cocaine	1995: <01%	1995: 02%	1995: 01%	1995: <01%	1995: 01% 2003: 01%

Key: SL=smokeless; yo=year olds; *25+ for 2003 rates.

Prevalence by Time.

A comparison of substance use prevalence from 1,995 to 2,003 C.E. is presented in Table 5. Overall, rates of substance usage are consistent, with slight increases in the use of cigarettes and marijuana. Alcohol use remained unchanged at 50%, cigarette use increased by 1% (25% vs. 24%), marijuana use increased by 2% (6% vs. 4%), and cocaine use remained unchanged at 1%.

Among 12-17 year olds, the rate of alcohol use remained the same (18%) and the rate of cigarette usage increased (12% vs. 10%). Among 18-25 year olds, the rate of alcohol use increased (61% vs. 59%) and the rate of cigarette use increased (40% vs. 29%). Collapsing the age groups of 26-34 year olds and 35 and older for the sake of data comparison, into the category of 25 and older, the rate of alcohol use decreased (53% vs. 56%) and the rate of cigarette use decreased (25% vs. 27%).

Prevalence of Addiction

An estimated 22 million Americans (approximately 13% of the total population) were classified with substance dependence or abuse in 2,003 C.E. This figure includes 9% of the population of youth, aged 12 or older. Of the 22 million, 3 million (14%) were classified with dependence on or abuse of both alcohol and illicit drugs, 4 million (18%) were dependent on or abused illicit drugs but not alcohol, and 15 million (68%) were dependent on or abused alcohol but not illicit drugs.[155] We find that 1 in 8 Americans were classified with a form of substance dependence or abuse.

According to the National Survey on Drug Use and Health, heavy alcohol use comprised 7% of total usage and binge alcohol use comprised 23%; a total of 30% of the

---

[155] *TIME Almanac*, "Overview of Drug Use in the United States"; Source: Substance Abuse and Mental Health Services Administration, In "Health and Nutrition", TIME, Inc.: New York, New York, 2006, p.560.

Maria Artiz, Ph.D.

50% of overall alcohol consumption in 2,003 C.E.[156] In 2,002 C.E., 31% of college students met criteria for a diagnosis of alcohol abuse, and 6% met criteria for a diagnosis of alcohol dependence.[157] These figures represent an assessment of alcohol dependence versus formal classification for treatment purposes. Accordingly, approximately one-fourth (1/4) of the total adult population in 2,003 C.E. and approximately one-seventeenth (1/17) of the total college age population in 2,002 C.E. met criteria for a diagnosis of alcohol dependence. We find that 1 in 4 Americans and 1 in 6 college students meet criteria for alcohol dependence or abuse.

Alcohol and the Nation.

Half of the American population reportedly consumes alcohol; rendering it the most prevalently used drug. In 1,995 C.E., 6.6 billion gallons of alcoholic beverages were consumed. Nationally, the use and abuse of ethanol is a recognized public health problem.[158]

Alcohol and the Elderly.

Among the elderly, alcohol abuse is a significant factor in the reduction of what gerontologists refer to as health span.[159] It is reported that about 6% of the elderly are heavy drinkers. Among sixty year olds, 5 to 12% of men, and 1 to

---

[156] *TIME Almanac.*, "Alcohol Use in the Past Month, by Characteristics, 2003"; Source: SAMHSA, Office of Applied Studies, National Survey on Drug Use and Health, 2002 and 2003, In "Health and Nutrition", TIME, Inc.: New York, New York, 2006, p.561.

[157] *TIME Almanac*, "A Snapshot of Annual High-Risk College Drinking Consequences"; Source: National Institute on Alcohol Abuse and Alcoholism, In "Health and Nutrition", TIME, Inc.: New York, New York, 2006, p. 561.

[158] Madhu R. Korrapati, and Robert E. Vestal, "Aging, Drugs, and Alcohol", *Encyclopedia of Drugs and Alcohol, vol. 1*, Jerome H. Jaffe, M.D. (Ed.). Simon & Schuster MacMillan: New York, 1995, p. 51.

[159] O'Brien et al., "Introduction : History of Alcohol and Man", p. xv.

2% of women have been reported to be problem drinkers.[160] Among sixty-five to seventy-four year olds, 42.5% reported using some amount of alcohol.[161] After age seventy-five, this figure drops to 30%.[162] According to statistics, the rate of alcohol use among the elderly is approximately one-third of the elderly population; this compares with a rate of approximately one-half of the middle-aged population. Whether this difference between age cohorts constitutes a change in drinking behavior with age, or whether it represents a difference in population cohorts is not determinable from prevalence rate data.

Pharmacokinetics, the process by which drugs are absorbed, distributed, metabolized, and excreted, changes with age.[163] The result is that older persons process alcohol and other drugs differently than younger persons. This change is exacerbated by multiple drug interactions. High rates of alcohol use, prescription drug use, and polypharmacy; the use of multiple drug regimens; pose significant risks to the health spans of the elderly.

Alcohol and Accidents.

Alcohol, in combination with other substances, is the most frequent cause of emergency room episodes tracked by the Drug Abuse Warning Network (DAWN).[164] Alcohol is a primary factor in approximately one-fourth of all accidents in the United States. Alcohol accounts for 50% of motor vehicle traffic accidents; 35% of accidents caused by submersion, suffocation, and foreign bodies, 25% of accidental falls, 25% of accidents caused by fire, 25% of accidents due to natural and environmental factors, 20% of water transport accidents, 20% of other road vehicle accidents, 10% of

---

[160] Korrapati and Vestal, "Aging, Drugs, and Alcohol", pp. 51-2.

[161] Korrapati and Vestal, "Aging, Drugs, and Alcohol", p. 52.

[162] Ibid., p. 51.

[163] Ibid.

[164] Ibid., p. 52.

railway accidents, 10% of air and space accidents, and 25% of all other accidents.[165] According to a report in 1,985 C.E., the economic cost of alcohol abuse was projected to rise from $116.9 billion in 1,983 C.E. to $150 billion by 1,995 C.E., primarily due to lost employment and reduced productivity.[166] Only $15 billion or 12.8% of this cost was attributable to treatment.[167]

Tobacco and the Nation.

The United States government estimate is that 46 million adults, or approximately 25% of the total adult population in the U.S. smoke cigarettes.[168] According to the Centers for Disease Control (CDC), the overall smoking prevalence among adults has been consistently maintained at approximately a 25% level since 1,990 C.E.[169] The rate of adult smoking was higher among men than among women at 24 versus 22 million. The highest prevalence of smoking was found among those with the least education and those living below the poverty level.[170] Among juveniles, it is estimated that 6 million teenagers, and 100,000 children under the age of 13 smoke cigarettes.[171] CDC data indicate that the percentage of students in grades 9 through 12 who smoke increased from 27.5% in 1,991 C.E. to 34.8% in 1,995 C.E.[172]

---

[165] Robbins, "Women and Substance Abuse", p. 1290.

[166] O'Brien and Chafetz, M.D., Table, "Estimated Number of Deaths Attributable to Alcohol: United States, 1980. *The Encyclopedia of Alcoholism*, Facts on File, Inc.: New York, 1991, p. 151.

[167] O"Brien and Chafetz, M.D., "Economic Impact", p. 98.

[168] Ibid.

[169] Carl E. Bartecchi, Thomas D. MacKenzie, and Robert W. Schrier. "The Global Tobacco Epidemic", *Scientific American*, May 1995, p. 46.

[170] Ibid.

[171] Ibid.

[172] Ibid.

Tobacco is reported to be the #1 leading cause of preventable death in the United States.[173] In 1,990 C.E., 19% of total deaths from preventable causes were attributed to tobacco consumption.[174]

Tobacco and Unit Pricing.

With respect to prevalence, industry unit pricing has been cited as a factor in the incidence of tobacco usage. Bartecchi et al., noting in an article entitled, *The Global Tobacco Epidemic*, that the average intake of cigarettes per person per year increased from 40 in 1,880 C.E. to 12, 854 in 1,977 C.E.,[175] contended that the popularity of discount brands has made cigarettes cheaper and more accessible.[176] From a free market perspective, the indication is that consumer demand for cheaper tobacco products led to an increase in sales and consumption. Accordingly, discount cigarette brands increased their market share from 10% in 1,987 C.E. to 36% in 1,993 C.E. They report that manufacturers earn about 5 cents profit per package of discounted cigarettes, and 55 cents per package of name-brand cigarettes. Given the increase in market share for discounted cigarettes, and resultant price cuts by major brands in 1,993 C.E., Bartecchi et al. predicted the possibility of an increase in smoking prevalence in the U.S., especially among young and poor populations for whom price is important, if price cuts sustained.

Since the report in 1,995 C.E., cigarette prices have increased; in many cases doubling; in response to a rash of federal government lawsuits in the late 1990s against the tobacco industry predicted by O'Higgins and Downes in 1,992 C.E., who stated that the threat of adverse litigation

---

[173] Ibid.

[174] Factoid. CNN Headline News, May 23, 1996.

[175] Bartecchi et al., p. 46.

[176] Ibid.

hangs over the cigarette industry like a sword of Damocles.[177] While the prediction of adverse litigation proved accurate, the prediction of expected outcome in smoking prevalence did not materialize; despite unexpected significant increases in unit pricing, cigarette consumption remained stable overall, and increased among youthful populations. Government deterrence, in the form of a more rigorous enforcement of *carding* practices; requiring identification checks of legal age eligibility for purchase of tobacco products by vendors as a requisite for licensing; has had a similar lack of impact. We find that a demand and supply relationship exists between consumer demand and sales of tobacco products. We also find that while discount brands are popular, the unavailability of discounted tobacco products does not deter consumption. We further find that government regulation does not deter usage; as indicated by prevalence rates for underaged users.

Tobacco and Globalization.
There are six major transnational tobacco companies. Three are based in the United States and three are based in the United Kingdom. Phillip Morris, listed in the U.S. on the Dow Jones Industrial Average, had $50 billion in sales and $4.9 billion in profits in 1,992 C.E., making it the highest-ranking corporate earner for the year. Nearly half of its profits were generated from cigarette sales.

The globalization of the cigarette trade is evidenced by an increase in exports; from 8% in 1,984 C.E. to 30% in 1,994 C.E.[178] This increase in tobacco product exportation did not go unnoticed at the Seventh World Conference on Tobacco and Health in 1,990 C.E., where concern was registered that it was unconscionable for transnational tobacco companies to be peddling their poison product to less developed countries

[177] O'Higgins, Michael and Downes, John. *Beating the Dow. 1992 Edition.* HarperCollins Publishers: New York, 1992, p. 130.

[178] Bartecchi et al., p. 44.

by pressuring and forcing market openings.[179] According to the report, the dearth of government regulation of tobacco products produced for consumption in the United States was exceeded only by the absence of U.S. government regulation on advertising and content labeling of tobacco products produced for export to developing nations. Tougher U.S. regulations have since been enacted; by government and industry; in response to the concerns, with no discernible detrimental effect upon consumption of U.S. tobacco exports. We find that the globalization of industry; the establishment of an international business presence; incurs international notice and response, with beneficial impact on regulatory practices, and no effect on product consumption.

Illicit Drug Use.

The overall prevalence of illicit drug use in the United States is lower than the overall prevalence of legal drug use. Illicit drug use accounts for less than one percent (<1%) of preventable deaths.[180] At every age, men are more likely to use illicit drugs than women, at a rate of 19% versus 8%.[181] Men are also far more likely than women to be arrested for possessing or selling illicit drugs. In 1,992 C.E., the Federal Bureau of Investigation reported that only 16% of those arrested for drug-abuse violations were women.[182]

Marijuana is the most frequently used illicit drug; with 16% of men and 6% of women reporting use. Cocaine use has decreased since the mid-1980s, and is rare compared with marijuana use.[183] Use of cocaine is most common in the young adult age group of 18 to 34.[184] Among 18 to 34 year olds, 1.7% of men and 1.4% of women reported current

---

[179] Ibid, p. 46.

[180] Ibid.

[181] Ibid.

[182] Bartecchi et al., p. 48.

[183] Bartecchi et al., p. 46.

[184] Bartecchi et al., p. 50.

Maria Artiz, Ph.D.

use.[185] Female and male youths, aged 12 to 16, were equally likely to report cocaine use in the past month at a low rate of 0.4%.[186] In 1,993 C.E., only about one in one thousand Americans, a ratio of 1:1000, aged 12 and older, reported using heroin during the past year.[187] The majority of reported heroin users were men.[188]

Prescription Drug Abuse and Polypharmacy.

The use and abuse of prescription drugs and over-the-counter medications has increased steadily in recent decades, and is considered a serious national and international trend. An international survey at the beginning of the 1980s, showed that tranquilizers and sedatives of any type had been used at some time during the previous year by 15.9% of adults in France, 12.9% of adults in the U.S., 11.2% of adults in the United Kingdom, and 7.4% of adults in the Netherlands.[189] Survey results showed that 5% of all French adults, 3.1% of all United Kingdom adults, 1.8% of all United States adults, and 1.7% of all Netherlands adults, are persistent long-term users.[190]

According to Malcolm H. Lader, the rate of repeat prescriptions for tranquilizers, one of the most commonly abused prescription medications, has increased steadily since about 1,970 C.E.[191] Lader reports that the benzodiazepines were initially hailed as wonder drugs, and consequently were widely prescribed for extended periods of time, but have since been shown to have definite risks as

---

[185] Bartecchi et al., pp. 50-1.

[186] Ibid.

[187] Robbins, "Women and Substance Abuse", pp. 1289-90.

[188] Ibid.

[189] Ibid.

[190] Ibid.

[191] Lader, Malcolm H. "Benzodiazepines: Complications", *Encyclopedia of Drugs and Alcohol*, vol. 1, Jerome H. Jaffe, M.D. (Ed.). Simon & Schuster MacMillan: New York, 1995, pp. 158-161.

well as undoubted benefits associated with their use.[192] Not surprisingly, the medical community has expressed concern over the incidence of prescription drug abuse.

Pharmaceutical corporations received a boon in recent years from a shortening of the United States Food and Drug Administration approval processing time, resulting in a more rapid product development-to-market process. The proliferation of pharmaceuticals for public use has led to considerable improvements in overall health and longevity. Statistically, the number of prescriptions dispensed by community pharmacies rose from approximately 363 million in 1,950 C.E. to 1.6 billion in 1,985 C.E.[193]

Polypharmacy, the use of multiple prescription and over-the-counter medications, according to Cynthia A. Robbins, was cited as the most significant safety-related drug issue of the 1990s.[194] Robbins notes that polypharmacy is common among older Americans, who are the recipients of approximately one-third of all prescription medications, although they account for only 13 percent of the population.[195] We find, along with an increase in drug use among elderly populations, a concomitant increase in potential risk.

Robbins contends that much of the medical drug use among the elderly is inappropriate and insufficiently monitored, with the consequence that elderly people experience more than 9 million adverse drug reactions each year, which account for roughly 25% of all adverse drug reactions.[196]

Given that there is an abundance of over-the-counter drugs available for self-medication, a potential for error in timing self-administered dosages, the reality that many

---

[192] Ibid.

[193] Ibid.

[194] Robbins, Cynthia A. "Elderly and Drug Use", *Encyclopedia of Drugs and Alcohol,* vol.2, pp. 448-9.

[195] Ibid.

[196] Ibid.

older persons have multiple health conditions requiring multiple medications often prescribed by more than one physician, a potential for alcohol-related interactions, the reality that individuals are differentially affected by the same medications, then it stands to reason that risk potential is higher among the elderly population. As the numbers of elderly increase in relation to the general population, as a function of greater longevity and the aging of the Baby Boom cohort, related matters of drug abuse and polypharmacy will undoubtedly receive greater attention.

In sum, we find that alcohol, cigarettes, nonprescription drugs, and prescription drugs comprise the most prevalently used substances. Usage ranges from 50% for alcohol, 25% for cigarettes, and 8% for illicit drugs. Rates of addiction (dependence and abuse) are more difficult to assess than rates of substance usage; they occur at a classified rate of 1 in 8. Among the overall population, 9% have been diagnosed for alcohol, 2% for illicit drugs, and 2% for both alcohol and illicit drug dependence or abuse. Actual rates of occurrence are higher.

CHAPTER ELEVEN

The Mind Perspective

Our journey proceeds from the context of heritage of substance use to a consideration of the human variable; with its inconsistencies of belief, perspective, and reaction. These we will identify as perspectives of the human mind. We have established that there is a larger transcultural array of addictive drugs currently available and accessible than at any other time in human history. We have also established that cultural prescriptions and proscriptions regarding drug usage have varied over time both within and across cultures, and exert considerable influence upon substance use behavior. We have concluded that the current reality of substance proliferation and availability is evidence of a cultural propensity towards substance use. We have also concluded that the human element is a primary source of the inconstancy we have encountered. We therefore now consider, from a variety of perspectives, the role of the variable human mind.

We begin by considering the changing human perspective as a form of mindset. According to Merriam-

Webster's Collegiate Dictionary, mind-set is defined as *a mental attitude or inclination* or *a fixed state of mind.*[197]

We know that, for the most part, people prefer pleasure to pain. Given a choice, normal people will choose pleasurable over painful experiences; the case is different for masochistic and sadistic individuals. The choice is also tempered by reason. For example, the decision to engage in dangerous activities for the purpose of defending oneself, one's family, one's country is a choice of experiencing temporary pain in the service of safety and security. Another example is the choice to defer gratification; in the service of achievement, greater long-term reward, et cetera. In this regard, persons defer gratification; the pleasure that derives from having income; when they attend college. Generally speaking, people prefer pleasure to pain, and prefer avoiding delays in gratification.

Historically, as is the case with substance use, the human mindset is a paradox of constancy and variability. The natural, and survival-oriented, tendency is to avoid pain. Human bodies are designed to automatically react to the experience of pain with withdrawal from the source. We know this instantly when we hold a hand too close to a flame, and react by quickly pulling it away. We know this also from the observation of children; when they hurt, they react; with expressions of pain, such as crying, and with expressions of escape from pain, such as seeking parental protection and soothing. Active pain-seeking is not the human norm.

Another natural, and survival-oriented, tendency is to seek pleasure, in the form of sexual intercourse. Human bodies are designed to procreate and perpetuate the human species. We know, from societal experience, the difficulties that may arise, in the form of promiscuity, unwanted

---

[197] *Merriam-Webster's Collegiate Dictionary. 10th ed.* Merriam-Webster, Incorporated: Springfield, Massachusetts, USA, p. 738.

pregnancies, unwed mothers, et cetera. Active pleasure-seeking is the human norm.

In general, the avoidance of pain and the orienting to pleasure is a human characteristic. In behavioral terms, we find that knowledge of this reality is used for the facilitation of society; persons receive the pleasure of recognition for their accomplishments and the pleasure of payment for services rendered; they receive the pain of punishment for their violations. Children receive rewards for good behavior and punishments for bad conduct. While such is the accepted and acceptable case, applied in excessive or extreme manner, reward and punishment are seen to violate notions of acceptability. For example, cases of child and spouse abuse, cases of police and military brutality, and cases of student hazing are currently criticized and condemned.

We may posit that human beings are generally oriented towards pleasure and away from pain. The historical reality of experience pertaining to pleasure and pain is complex and varied. The whims of nature, the whims of culture, the whims of family, and the whims of individuals have yielded an historical reality inconsistent with the human natural desire. We find considerable differences between the actual and the natural. From a perspective of survival, we may reasonably consider that the natural; the avoidance of pain and the orienting to pleasure; is the ideal. In this vein, humanitarianism can be seen as a response oriented towards establishing the ideal of human nature.

Understanding these principles of pain and pleasure facilitates our consideration of the role they play in human behavior. People routinely reward themselves; with activities, purchases, self-congratulatory pats on the back, vacations, et cetera. They also routinely punish themselves; with self-accusations, self-criticisms, self-doubts, self-condemnations, et cetera. We glean from this a recognition of the role that self-reward plays in consumptive behavior, and the role that self-punishment plays in self-condemnation pertaining. In this respect, society has succeeded perhaps too well in its socializing of individuals according to human propensity. Human consciousness has evolved to view life in terms of reward and punishment.

It is thus not surprising, in light of the propensity to seek pleasure and avoid pain, that consumptive living holds such appeal. The pain of debt is eased by partial payments and new purchases. The pain of stress is eased by the ingestion of substances. Natural human aversion and orientation responses have become exaggerated by more demanding lifestyles, greater degrees of stress, and higher rates of illness; difficulties related to living and longevity. The tendency towards medication, including self-medication, is understandable as a reaction to discomfort, pain and suffering.

We have arrived at a juncture where resources and technology have provided us with considerable means of escape. While desire to escape from danger and pain is a natural given, escapism as mindset is an unexpected evolutionary development. We seek to escape displeasure, in whatever form it manifests. The hard-working, self-sacrificing protagonist of the father provider; touted in the entertainment media of half a century ago; has been replaced by the pleasure-seeking escapist in comparative competition with peers; mirroring the change in society.

A further indication of the change in mindset is the modern option of living wills to prevent the mechanical extension of life; a far cry from the days when the thinking was that doctor knows best. The practice of assisted suicide in cases of terminal illness, in order to avoid prolonging suffering towards an inevitable end, is another example. These are indications of shifts in thinking; assertions of personal decision-making versus reliance upon authority; pertaining to avoidance of pain and suffering, that has generated into an intolerance for pain and suffering.

The newly-evolved intolerance for personal pain and suffering drives the use of substances. While other usages; experimental, recreational, and religious; persist, it is the usage related to the avoidance of suffering, which takes precedence in cases of substance abuse and dependence.

We know from history that drug usage has been influenced by the dissemination of incomplete, inconsistent, and patently false information. Instances of such misinformation have derived from both innocent ignorance and deliberate design. At times, knowledge has been unavailable, incomplete, or lacking. This was often the case when newly-introduced substances were involved. We bring this knowledge into a consideration of the recent past and our discourse on mindset.

We know, from our discussion of prescription drug abuse, that the benzodiazepine product, Valium, was introduced in the 20th century as a palliative for anxiety; it was highly popular among physicians and patients. It was later determined to induce drug dependence. Prior to this, we know that thalidomide was routinely administered to housewives in the 1960s to curb appetite for the purpose of weight reduction; it was later determined to cause birth defects; such as the development of extra fingers and toes. These examples demonstrate unintentional ignorance; the manufacturers of thalidomide and Valium did not have advance knowledge of these side effects. Such cases in recent history have spurred stricter regulations pertaining to the testing and release of pharmaceutical drugs. To use a horse-racing metaphor, we find that there is a tendency, when it comes to the alleviation of pain and suffering, to jump the starting gun. We may take comfort from the fact that regulatory reactions have resulted in safer (not guaranteed safe) pharmaceuticals, and take umbrage from the fact that despite our self-perceived sophistication, we have so recently snafued. Rather than condescend the past, we are placed in the position of recognizing the human fallibility and the incompleteness of medical knowledge.

Maria Artiz, Ph.D.

There is a marked degree of historical inconsistency with respect to allowed drug practices. For example, heroin and other opiates were legally used in the United States in the early part of the 19th century. There were, however, sociopolitical and economic differences in the manner in which opiate products were treated. Medicinal products; patented prescription and over-the-counter elixirs; were legal for sale and touted as highly effective cures. Recreational use; in the form of opium smoking; was banned.

O'Brien et al. point out that the grade of opium used for smoking was considerably weaker than that used in the patent medications, but the first was illegalized and the second was legalized.[198] They report that the United States raised the tariff on imported opium for smoking to $10 a pound, and did not raise taxes on the finer grades of opium used in patent medicines. The populations that used these opiates were similarly dichotomous; the domestically grown opium-based medicines were prescribed primarily to white, middle-aged, middle-class housewives as a palliative; the Chinese-grown imported opium was primarily sold to Chinese immigrants, for use in traditional smoking dens. We find two inconsistencies; one, approval of opiates for medical purposes and disapproval for recreational purposes; and two, bans on smoking while permitting importations.

Another case in point is that of the German Bayer Company, which began commercial production of heroin as a cure for opium and morphine addiction in 1,898 C.E. The company stopped its production of heroin in 1,900 C.E. when heroin was discovered to be addictive. After two years of production and sale of heroin, an estimated 250,000 to 1 million Americans had become heroin users.[199] From

---

[198] Robert O'Brien, Sidney Cohen, M.D., Glen Evans, and James Fine, M.D., "History of Heroin", *The Encyclopedia of Drug Abuse*, 2nd ed. Facts on File, Inc.: New York, 1992, p. 143.
[199] Ibid.

these examples we find an historical basis for the American proclivity for pharmaceutical substance use.

In discoursing the perspective of mind, we find that research findings are inconclusive with respect to attributions of subcultural beliefs and practices. While cross-cultural research on substance use has demonstrated differences in rates and practices of substance usage between subcultural groups, caution has been urged regarding the interpretations of these findings. Marsha Lillie-Blanton and Amelia Arria point out that there are difficulties in interpreting findings of differences in drug use between minority and nonminority groups within the U.S. They contend that socially shared environmental conditions, rather than race or ethnic identity, may be responsible for the underlying patterns of drug use.[200] Lillie-Blanton and Arria further report a public health finding that, after holding constant social and neighborhood conditions in a number of studies, little evidence was found that African Americans or Hispanics were more likely to smoke crack or use cocaine.[201]

They note that biological factors may also play a role in determining individual preference for alcohol or particular drugs. Asian Americans, as a group, consume less alcohol than any other racial or ethnic group. This lower drinking rate has been attributed, in part, to the fact that the majority of Asians possess a particular form of an alcohol-metabolizing enzyme whose action results in unpleasant side effects when alcohol is consumed.[202]

Biological factors, in turn, are affected by the context of culture. While there has been a low incidence of alcohol abuse traditionally among Asian-Americans, their use of alcohol is reported to be increasing as a result of assimilation

---

[200] Marsha Lillie-Blanton and Amelia Arria, "Ethnicity and Drugs", *Encyclopedia of Alcohol and Drug Abuse*, p. 473.

[201] Ibid.

[202] Ibid.

and acculturation.[203] Thus, observed differences in substance use between racial and ethnic groups arise from a variety of factors.

Despite the limitations, cross-cultural research studies, in exploring differences in cultural views and patterns of drug use, provide useful information for clarifying relationships between culture, environment, subculture, and manifest usage. We find, in the case of the Asian-American, evidence of the role of culture and socialization in the development of amenabilities to and proclivities for particular types of substance usage. The Chinese immigrant of the early 19th century was culturally-oriented to the Chinese practice of opium smoking versus the American practice of drinking opiate elixirs. In the 20th century, Asian-Americans as a group, have become more oriented to the American cultural context, with a resultant increase in alcohol consumption. We further find, in the case of the American housewife, evidence of the role of culture and socialization in the use of prescribed opiates in the 19th century, and in the use of prescribed anxiolytics in the 20th century.

Comparably little attention has been paid to the contextual role of dominant culture in shaping substance use and addictive behavior; one of the tenets of this book. The role of dominant culture has not been the primary focus of addiction research, cross-cultural research, medical research, or public health studies. To use a photography analogy, research has tended to zoom in on subcultures and subcultural differences. This zoom lens perspective provides a view of what a subcultures look like up close. It does not, in and of itself, provide an inclusive, or for that matter, conclusive, explanation for the picture obtained. Nor does it provide information about what goes on outside of the zoom range, in the context of the larger background.

---

[203] Robert O'Brien and Morris Chafetz, M.D., "Asian Americans", *The Encyclopedia of Alcoholism, 2nd ed.*, Glen Evans (Ed.). Facts on File, Inc.: New York, 1991, p. 38.

This may help explain why efforts to establish profiles of subcultural beliefs that foster moderate drug use; termed *recipes* in the research literature; have found only weak empirical support.[204]

If we view subculture as a circle contained within the larger circle of dominant culture; an overall view of two concentric circles; we can better gauge how the subcultural manifests of addiction fit within the larger cultural universe. We are thus compelled to comprehend how subcultural attitudes, beliefs, and practices are shaped and determined, not only by biologic and subcultural differences, but also by the influences of the mainstream culture within which they reside.

Another perspective of mind pertains to values, in the context of the experience of meaningfulness. It has been suggested that values play an influencing role regarding whether or not people use drugs, whether they use them regularly, whether they become addicted, and whether they remain addicted.[205] Peele contends that people become addicted because of a failure of the values that maintain ordinary life involvements. Noting Peele's perspective, that a failure in values plays a role in eventuating addiction, we consider the perception of Bill Wilson, the co-founder of Alcoholics Anonymous, who stated that there is an element of debauchery in the nature of an alcoholic's manner of drinking; which is incredibly dishonest and selfish. Peele's existential perspective on addiction is consistent with Wilson's perception of the alcoholic. From an existential perspective, the dishonesty and selfishness of the alcoholic described by Wilson may reflect a failure in life's values. To extend the reasoning along existential thinking lines, such failure would

---

[204] Stanton Peele. "Values and Beliefs: Existential Models of Addiction", *Encyclopedia of Drugs and Alcohol,* vol. 3, Jerome H. Jaffe, M.D. (Ed.). Simon & Schuster MacMillan: New York, 1995, p. 1241.

[205] Peele, p. 1242.

be precipitated by existential crisis; that is, a loss of perceived meaning in one's life. When one considers the impacts of major life stresses; including family upheavals, deaths, dis-employments, and divorces; potential sources of existential crisis are abundant. Couple this with the existential crisis potential that exists with violations of interpersonal trust; secondary to cruelty, deception, dishonesty, et cetera; and we find an even greater abundance of potential sources.

The matter of values as a precipitating factor is complicated by the resultant reality of addiction. Once addicted, the emergent reality is one of uncontrollability. According to Wilson, what differentiates the alcoholic; the uncontrollability of his drinking; is as much a mystery to the alcoholic as it is to others. Wilson views the threshold of alcoholism as being the point at which, for an inexplicable reason, an individual suddenly loses control of the ability to self-regulate. From this point forward, the alcoholic loses all control of her or his drinking consumption, and loses all awareness of how much he or she is drinking.[206]

Given this perspective that alcoholics, and we may extrapolate here an application to addicts in general, do not know why they do what they do, and science and medicine have no foolproof remedy, then we find it is not surprising that alcoholism has been historically regarded with an element of disdain; a reaction of disgust to the debauchery, a reaction of fear to the uncontrollability. We find that such responses to alcoholism and other forms of physical addiction to substances are historically consistent with responses to communicable disease, such as autoimmune deficiency syndrome, more commonly referred to as AIDS, and leprosy; and responses to insanity; conditions viewed as best avoided. Societal responses of aversion and/or contempt are an additional perspective of mind which may serve to impose an unwarranted burden upon the afflicted.

---

[206] Wilson, p. 21.

An example from personal experience serves to elucidate the human reaction to what is uncontrollably abnormal. As a program therapist on an open adult unit in a private psychiatric hospital, I was assigned the case of a young married woman from Mexico, admitted during a postpartum psychotic episode. Her psychosis proved unusually resistant to trials of neuroleptic medications. Nursing staff efforts to engage the patient in eating regular meals resulted in subsequent uncontrollable regurgitation. The experience of witnessing the episodes of uncontrollable vomiting; while the patient sat upright, staring, without expression, without comment, without recognition of her own spewing vomit; was akin to watching the 1,973 C.E. movie portrayal; the *Exorcist*; wherein the actress, Linda Blair, plays a possessed woman character, Mercedes McCambridge. To be in the presence of such abnormal behavior is to know the sensation of discomfort that comes from recognition of what is not normal.

When treatment options other than electroshock therapy had been exhausted, the woman's husband, a professional wrestler, opted for early discharge. Approximately three months post-discharge, I read in the newspaper that the woman had been charged with murder in the death of her infant child. The case was one of abnormal, and abnormally unresponsive, behavior. This case example demonstrates the aversiveness of stridently abnormal and uncontrollable behavior, as a referent for comparative purposes in cases where uncontrolled and unnatural behaviors accompany addiction.

Given the reality that the alcoholic and the addict, upon crossing the threshold of addiction, lose capacity for self-control, it is no wonder that addiction has held such a powerful place in the forefront of the human mentality. The spirit/mind/body phenomenon of addiction is a human reality to be reckoned with. Perspectives of mind are variable, conflicted, and complex.

From a spiritual perspective, we find the perception that addiction is precipitated by the striving for a magical solution to life's problems. According to Kurtz and Ketcham, addiction simultaneously represents the ultimate effort to control, the definitive demand for magic, and final failure of spirituality. In their view, addiction is the desperate attempt to fill a spiritual void with a material reality, an attempt to substitute chemical magic for spiritual miracle.[207]

Accordingly, the problem for addicts may be the same as what Joseph Campbell of Harvard University described as the problem for people generally. Campbell contended that we are not well acquainted with the literature of the spirit, that instead we are more interested in the news of the day and the problems of the hour, and that as a result of this distraction, we no longer listen to those who speak of the eternal values that have to do with the centering of our lives.[208] Campbell's view suggests a lack of consciousness secondary to the distractions of modern-day living.

We find that knowledge is not a constant; it changes with time and relevant new learnings. We find that attitudes, beliefs, practices, and values are relevant considerations. We find awareness of the role of consciousness and the mitigating effect of spirit. To more holistically comprehend the complex relationship between the human variable and addiction necessitates going beyond the scientific, with its inherent limitations, in consideration of the spiritual. Exploring the role and impacts of culture and experience on the spirit/mind/body phenomenon of addiction is a complicated pursuit.

This book is predicated on the perspective of philosophy; the pursuit of wisdom through speculation; it constitutes

---

[207] Ernest Kurtz and Katherine Ketcham. *The Spirituality of Imperfection: Modern Wisdom From Classic Stories.* Bantam Books: New York, p. 120.

[208] Campbell, Joseph. *Thou Art That: Transforming Religious Metaphor.* New World Library: Novato, CA, 2001.

reaching for a wiser understanding that extends beyond scientific observation. Transcending the limits of historical belief and certainty to derive new answers and achieve ever closer approximations of truth and reality is a worthy and challenging endeavor. The reader may, nonetheless, experience the process of exposure to such philosophical considerations unsettling.

A variety of cultural and individual attitudes and conditions compel consumption, substance use, and distraction. According to Peele, there is a tendency to view cultural attitudes about drug use and addiction as oddities. To counter the compelling; the complacency of now-sightedness; requires commitment to consideration of what does not come naturally; considering what we think we know from a different perspective.

We find an inherent *opportunity* in this present-day *crisis* of cultural habituation to distraction and pervasive desire for a magical means to the end of our sufferings. The desire for a magical solution, while impractical in the day-to-day living sense, is nonetheless a valid perspective; whether it derives from a childlike innocence or a religious faith in miracles. Like the proverbial experience of the alcoholic, whose life of desperation, drowned in drink, is inexplicably rescued, the possibility exists for society to be inexplicably rescued; the experience profoundly startling, attributable to an act of God. In an instant, crisis may stand upside down on his head, causing us to laugh ourselves into a more conscious, undistracted sensibility that enables recovery.

CHAPTER TWELVE

The Holistic Perception of Body

This chapter continues our exploration of the context of mind and body with an holistic consideration of body. Towards this end, the effects of substance use and addiction on the body are considered. Affective states and body states are addressed, with inclusion of perspectives on the nature of these states.

Addiction is a complex condition which affects the mind, the body, and the emotions. The interrelationship between affective states and body states is a significant factor for our consideration. We find addiction and affect to be causally interrelated; addiction may cause changes in affect, and affect may lead to addictive behavior. According to *The Encyclopedia of Alcoholism*, one of the primary psychological causes of alcoholism is anxiety.[209] Alcohol is commonly consumed as a form of self-medication for the relief of tension and anxiety. From a behavioral science perspective, the anxious individual who drinks readily learns that an immediate effect of drinking is a calming of anxiety.

---

[209] Robert O'Brien and Morris Chafetz, M.D., "Anxiety", *The Encyclopedia of Alcoholism*, 2nd ed., Glen Evans (Ed.). Facts on File, Inc.: New York, 1991, p. 36.

This learning leads to drinking when anxious. From a basic learned response to drink when anxious, alcohol easily becomes a remedy for the management of any and all disturbing feelings.[210]

While anxiety may serve as an affective prompt in some cases, not all people drink when anxious, nor do all anxious people drink or become alcoholic. A prime example of this is people who undergo psychoanalysis, for which the ability to tolerate high levels of anxiety on a years-long basis is a prerequisite. Still, many do. Social factors and other learned responses to stress are part of the equation in determining if an individual turns to alcohol or to some other means of coping under conditions of stress and anxiety.[211] There is evidence to support that social learning is a factor in the substance use behaviors of persons raised in alcoholic environments. In such instances, reliance upon alcohol consumption as a means of coping is a learned response.

The capacity of alcohol to reduce anxiety varies with the individual, the amount of alcohol consumed, and whether or not the person is already an alcoholic or otherwise addicted. The conclusion of one study was that for an alcoholic on a drinking bout, as the loss of central nervous system control progressed, anxiety actually increased and was relieved for only short periods by renewed drinking.[212] We find that anxiety may serve as an emotional prompt to alcohol consumption, and that excessive alcohol intake may prove ineffective in controlling anxiety.

The interactive dynamic between substance use and affect is also evident with respect to depression. Depression is commonly associated with the use of alcohol. Like anxiety, it sometimes serves as a psychological prompt and/or rationalization for alcohol use, and prolonged use similarly results in a recurrence of depressed mood.

---

[210] Ibid.

[211] Ibid.

[212] Ibid.

Maria Artiz, Ph.D.

We find that, in cases of anxiety and depression, self-medicating with alcohol may produce a boomerang effect. Studies with alcoholics show that they tend to become more depressed and hostile after drinking and that drinking actually serves to reduce their feelings of self-worth.[213] While the social drinker may experience a temporary boost in self-confidence, stemming from a depression of social anxiety and inhibition, the alcoholic experiences an increase in feelings of worthlessness with continued drinking, which compounds original problems of anxiety and/or depression. Alcohol, barbiturates, and heroin depress the central nervous system; their use induces states of depressed affective experience. We find, in the interactivity between substance use and affect, the nature of a vicious cycle.

The use of stimulant drugs; amphetamines and methamphetamines, like cocaine and ecstasy; induces intense states of anxiety, followed by mixed anxious and depressed mood states during periods of nonuse. The alternating appearance of anxious, depressed, and mixed mood states with substance use may, in addition to the effects of the baseline mood state of the individual, and the substances used, reflect a relationship between anxiety and depression. Anxiety and depression have been posited to be different aspects of the same affective phenomenon; like flip sides of the same affective coin; heads or tails, up or down. The affective picture is complicated, in that it derives from a variety of factors.

The *Encyclopedia of Drug Abuse* tells us that the majority of chemically dependent people complain that they experience insomnia.[214] Insomnia, an effect of drug dependency, affects mood. Sleep deprivation is known to foster feelings of anxiety and depression. After detoxification

---

[213] Ibid.

[214] Robert O'Brien, Sidney Cohen, M.D., Glen Evans, and James Fine, M.D., "Insomnia", *The Encyclopedia of Drug Abuse*, 2nd ed. Facts on File, Inc.: New York, 1992, p. 151.

and recovery from substance use, insomnia and depression almost always resolve. This is not, however, the case for anxiety, which is a major factor in relapse to resumed substance use following treatment.

Depression has also been shown to be a prompt for tobacco use. It has been reported that individuals with a history of depression are more likely to smoke, perhaps to mask underlying feelings of dysphoria, and that they may develop depression when they try to stop.[215] Vincent Dole suspects that in such cases the depression that results from smoking cessation has been there all along.[216] In the case of the chronically depressive individual, smoking may serve as a form of distraction from the discomfort of dysphoria.

Periods of smoking cessation, like medication holidays, periods of abstinence from caffeine and sugar, and periods of fasting, serve to clear the body and may be accompanied by affective sensitivity, including tearfulness, and lightheadedness. Such reactions are natural responses to body cleansing processes, and do not constitute depression. The fact that veterinary medicine has discovered sensitivity in bowel responses to changes in animal diets; averaging three-to-five days; suggests that people animals experience similar body sensitivities to changes in consumed substances. I recall having once read, from an unremembered source, that you are what you ate three days ago; suggesting a rather rapid effect upon the body from consumed foods and substances. If this is the case, it stands to reason that the body may respond in similar rapid manner to cleansing processes.

According to Dole, a physician and prior administrator of The Methadone Program in New York, the addictive behavior of chronic users of narcotics stems less from

---

[215] Robert O'Brien and Morris Chafetz, M.D., "Addiction", *The Encyclopedia of Alcoholism*, 2nd ed. Facts on File, Inc.: New York, 1991, p. 6.

[216] O'Brien and Chafetz, p. 6.

pleasure seeking than from a need to relieve a recurring discomfort. His finding is that addicts with a history of two or more years of addiction to heroin seemed to be quite willing to sacrifice the occasional euphoria produced by the drug for a continued feeling of normality. Dole posits the same may be true for chronic smokers and chronic drinkers.[217]

Dole's assessments are compatible with the methodology and perspectives of behavioral medicine. His observations of heroin addicts yield insight regarding the cause of such addiction different from the traditionally-held perspective that it is the substance that is responsible for addiction.

Dole points out that physical dependence does not explain the drug-seeking behavior characteristic of addiction. We may extrapolate from this that people can be physically dependent on drugs without being addicted to them, as in the case of drugs such as steroids, prescribed for medicinal purposes, which can give rise to physical dependence without causing a desire for the substance. At the same time, people can be addicted to drugs without being physically dependent upon them, as in the case of the detoxed heroin addict, whose body has been cleared of substances, but who usually relapses. Dole reports that, unfortunately, those definitions that include some concept of psychological dependence are unable to explain the behavior.[218] We find that the factors involved in addiction are multiple and various; they impact upon the course of addiction at various points in time; from onset of usage, to maintenance of usage, to relapse to usage. They include propensities of individuals, properties of substances, and influences of culture.

In holistic consideration of non-normative professional views pertaining to substance use, in this case, what is responsible for the widespread appeal of smoking, we include

---

[217] Ibid.

[218] See also Dole, Vincent P. "Addictive Behavior", *Scientific American* 243, no. 6 (Dec. 1980): 138-154.

the perception of psychologist Jack Traktir. His practice of medical hypnotherapy in the Houston Medical Center was popular among the Houston elite in the 1980s. Called by physicians for consultation in cases where medicine alone was not succeeding, he engaged in a successful practice of hypnotherapy for the reduction of tumors. According to Traktir, tobacco smoking appeals to people because of the smoke. His contention that smoke is the attraction is suggestive of the primordial; like the attraction in watching a flaming candle, or a flaming fire; there may be something inherently appealing in the watching of tobacco smoke. Some time after I became acquainted with Dr. Traktir and his perspective, a smokeless cigarette product appeared on the market; it was later discontinued due to a lack of popularity, perhaps reinforcing Dr. Traktir's contention. His perception speaks to the psychological component of addiction.

In addressing the perception of body, it behooves us to address the potential role of emotional development. In this day and age of functional treatment categories, one does not often hear discussion of oral, anal, and latency stages of psychological development, as was the case in the middle part of the last century. In the recent past, it was second nature for persons in the psychiatry and clinical psychology fields to identify themselves and others as *oral* or *anal* personality types; for some reason, I never heard anyone identify themselves as *latent*. These *personality types* are not emotional disorder classifications. From a psychodynamic perspective, such distinction adds another dimension to the matter of individual propensities. The individual whose emotional development arrests or predominantly leans towards the oral stage, will be inclined to oral consumption; including compulsive eating, drinking, and smoking, as a means of oral gratification. The individual whose emotional development arrests or predominantly leans towards the anal stage, may be inclined to substance usage, as a means of control; over emotions and life.

The individual whose emotional development arrests or predominantly leans towards the latency stage, may be inclined to sexual compulsions and *addiction*, as a means of sexual gratification. Our holistic perception of body includes this perception of personality development, from which we find that the affective experience of the individual as a child impinges upon the individual's propensities as an adult.

Once manifested, addiction activates alternating extremes of affective experience. According to psychologist Nicholas A. Cummings, whereas the normal person dwells in the central living area of the home of emotionality, the addict alternates between the attic and the basement, between elation and depression.[219] The addict, contends Cummings, does not know what normal affect is because he or she does not experience it. During the researching and writing of this book, years after the post-doctoral training I received under Dr. Cummings' tutelage in South San Francisco, California, I comprehended the meaning of his perspective in a new way. I discovered that the bell curve of normalcy could be creatively applied to his house analogy of the affective experience of the addict. In so doing, the hypothetical nonaddicted *normals* would fall in the central, normal range of the curve; while the hypothetical addicted *depressed* would fall in the far left, tail end of the curve along with others currently depressed; and the hypothetical addicted *elateds* would fall in the far right, tail end of the curve along with others currently manic. My hypothetical bell curve presumes that most people are not addicted and are affectively normal; in this regard, it is the normal standard. However, given the finding already discussed that the affective state of Americans is currently considerably more depressed than normal, my bell curve does not apply to the current picture of *normalcy*. It is nonetheless useful

---

[219] Cummings, Nicholas A. *American Biodyne Treatment Manual.* American Biodyne, Inc.: South San Francisco, CA, 1989, Section 10-6.

for a scientific understanding of the abnormalcy of affect being described. From Cummings' perspective, we find that addiction blocks out the central tendency of normal individuals, overriding the limits of normal experience, such that only the extreme tail ends of positive and negative affect are available for experience.

With respect to body affectivity and substance usage, we consider a portrayal from literature that provides a useful example for holistic consideration of the nature of the relationship between the two, in the case of the heroin user. The alternating affectivity of the heroin-addicted state of being is immortalized by Sir Arthur Conan Doyle, in the fictional character of Sherlock Holmes.[220] The brilliant, crime-solving Holmes relaxes regularly by smoking a pipeful of heroin, during which time he ponders the case he is currently attempting to solve. His affective states are portrayed as variable; alternating between bouts of irritability, manic obsession, and fatigue. Sherlock Holmes, in his opium-facilitated eccentricity, exemplifies the self-controlled heroin addict; the equivalent of the employed alcoholic whom no one regards as alcoholic. He indulges, but does not indulge in a manner that is out-of-control; he paces his usage, such that it does not interfere with his crime-solving efforts. From a psychodynamic perspective, the portrayal is indicative of a well-adjusted individual; who, while experiencing the affectivity of the addicted, nonetheless compensates in socially acceptable ways. Opium smoking was both popular and socially acceptable during the time setting of the novel. From this example, we may infer variability in the picture of addiction with respect to personal resources; the varying emotional and intellectual capacities of individuals to compensate for their conditions in a functional manner.

---

[220] Doyle, Sir Arthur Conan. *The original illustrated Sherlock Holmes; 37 short stories plus a complete novel.* Seacaucus, New Jersey:. Castle Books, 1891. Based on *Adventures of Sherlock Holmes.* Strand Magazine, 1891-1893.

Maria Artiz, Ph.D.

From the perspective of psychophysiology, substance-induced altered states of being represent affective experiences different from normal. The use of substances with such capacity, in effect, activates the central nervous system to respond as if the altered reality were true. During the 1960s in America, when hallucinogens were popular, many persons behaved in ways inconsistent with genuine reality because their brains were responding to the false information about what was real. In one well-publicized case, the daughter of talk show host, Art Linkletter, jumped to her death in California, while hallucinating from substance use. Addiction-altered psychophysiology is just that; an altered state of being. As human beings, we have a tendency to believe what our psychophysiology tells us, even when it is wrong.

Consider the analogous historical phenomenon of the Bermuda Triangle. There are documented cases of trained pilots encountering problems with instrumentation; these are essential to flying in the same way that speedometers are essential to driving. In some cases, instrument needles and readings went out of control; swinging back and forth without accurate measurement. In others, the instrument readings changed to false readings. According to at least one report, in cases where the instruments were still indicating, albeit indicating false readings, the pilots tended to accept the feedback of the altered instrumentations as valid, because this is what they are trained to do; trust the instruments, follow the readings. Per at least one verbal report, involving someone who noticed a difference between the readings and the surroundings, secondary to familiarity with the environment of the flight pattern, the decision was made to trust the instrument readings.

This phenomenon, first documented in 1,945 C.E., continues to the present. According to Brian Hicks, in his nonfiction book, *Ghost Ship: The Mysterious True Story Of The Mary Celeste And Her Missing Crew:*

"On the afternoon of December 5, 1945, five Grumman torpedo bombers took off from the naval air station at Fort Lauderdale and banked east over the Atlantic. The planes, called Avengers, flew in tight formation toward the Bahamas, where the crew were scheduled to go through a series of detailed exercises before returning to Florida. It was an advanced lesson in navigation for pilots nearing the end of their apprenticeship. Although World War II had ended just three months earlier, the U.S. military had not become lackadaisical in its training.

The planes had been ordered to fly nearly sixty miles off the coast to the Hen and Chicken Shoals, do some low-level bombing, then change course three more times before returning to base. Even though most of the fourteen men on the five planes were still technically trainees, it wasn't considered a particularly arduous task or difficult flight pattern. It was basically a triangular route.

Flight 19 was supposed to be gone for two hours.

The events of that afternoon would become infamous in part simply because Flight 19's disappearance sparked the largest ocean search and rescue mission to date. The Navy, Coast Guard and scores of private ships combed the Atlantic for five days, but never found a trace of the missing men or their airplanes-- not a piece of debris, a lifeboat, or an oil slick. But the most intriguing thing about Flight 19 was the bizarre radio transmissions between the flighters and the base, the way the pilots sounded so disoriented, and so lost. There's also the fact that a search plane sent to find the men went missing as well, and that no one ever learned exactly what happened. Flight 19 became such a frustrating mystery that some historians and journalists called it the Mary Celeste of aviation."[221]

The conclusion that mysterious forces govern *The Bermuda Triangle* was reached in 1,945 C.E. Subsequent events support the original conclusion. While not all planes (or boats) go missing, some do, and sufficient others experience navigational interference as to warrant continued monitoring.

---

[221] Hicks, Brian. Ghost Ship: *The Mysterious True Story Of The Mary Celeste And Her Missing Crew.* Ballantine Books: New York, New York, 2004, pp. 215-6.

The analogy of the pilot, who, in the face of contradictory evidence, persists in believing the indications of navigational instruments, as s/he is trained to do, is indicative of the human tendency. Given what is known about false respondings to hallucinogens, it stands to reason that the same applies in certain cases of substance use. As human beings, the survival tendency appears to be to trust the hardware equivalent of our human psychophysiology, even when it has been altered and is no longer providing an accurate reading. These are instances of temporary effects upon central nervous system functioning which alter the body's reactions.

We can look to organic brain conditions, such as Alzheimer's, for recognition of similar effect. The individual with Alzheimer's may cease to believe and trust persons whom they believed and trusted prior to the onset of the brain-damaged condition, indicating a similar human responding to psychophysiological instrumentation. We tend to believe what our brains are telling us, even when our brains are no longer properly functioning. This would appear to be a biological survival mechanism, given that we are born to trust our own brains over what others may or may not tell us is true. Given that human beings are predominantly social animals, the reality of experience that we trust what our own brains tell us over what that of others tell us supports the conclusion that the response is biologically related to survival.

There is a fundamental psychophysiological reality, and to some extent unreality, that underlies much of the eccentricities of affect characteristic of the spirit/mind/body phenomenon of addiction. In addition to what we know about the contributants of depression and anxiety to substance use, and the aftermath of substance- and individual-idiosyncratic affective experiences, the altering of human psychophysiology through the ingestion of brain-altering substances results in induced states of being that, while experientially genuine, may or may not reflect genuine reality. The point is relative; given the possibility that substance alteration of psychophysiology may result in an override of preconception and an enhanced awareness; it is not limited to perception of an inaccurate nature. Whether the experience proves beneficial or detrimental, the use of substances in such manner constitutes a synthetic distortion of life experience.

As an indicator, the affect of reality experiences is relevantly reliable; the affect of synthetically-induced experiences, while reliable, may not be relevant to reality; it may mirror a different reality. It may also, as in the case of Sherlock Holmes, provide a window into a world of different perspective that may serve to figuratively shake up stultified patterns of thinking in novel and creative ways.

In addition to a beneficial potential, substance use has the detrimental potential to obfuscate the heart and soul of experience. Extensive and prolonged usage may dull consciousness and thereby, conscious awareness of life. The life that is perceived may be clouded by persistent chemical alteration, persistent cognitive distraction, and bouts of cognitive distortion. In some cases, the line of temporary insanity is crossed, and the addict's mind becomes a realm of permanent insanity; as is the case with alcohol-induced hallucinosis, giving rise to the presentiment that extreme cases of alcoholism symptomatically constitute a form of substance-induced schizophrenia.

The person in addicted state of being may rationalize or intellectualize life; compartmentalizing, rationalizing, and denying reality; avoiding the experience of normal emotionality by holding emotions in check and at bay, preferring to avoid emotionalism and unpleasantness in oneself and others. What we find with addiction is an aversion to and avoidance of experiencing the heart and soulfulness of human life experience; a preference for avoiding or postponing self-reckoning; the coming to terms

195

with the personal truth of oneself and one's reality. It is for this very reason that Alcoholics Anonymous requires members to complete a personal life inventory; as a means of promoting self-awareness. The average way of life does not appeal to the genuine addict; for reasons of over-sensitivity to natural emotions and self-reinforcing experienced aversion reactions. Normal life tends to be experienced as unpleasant.

The strived-for containment of affectivity by the addict serves to curtail the full range of affective experience; so doing enables the addict to experience life as more psychologically manageable. Closing oneself off from experiencing the full range of human emotions is akin to closing one's mind to new learning and closing one's heart to new love. To use a painting analogy, one chooses to rely upon a palate of limited options; selecting fewer paints from which to create the painting of one's life experience. Rationalizing, intellectualizing, and denying, in the service of avoiding emotional experience, serves as a buffer to unmanageable unpleasantness. Clouded consciousness, induced by substance ingestion, further serves this purpose. The impact of this, is a state of existence that is lacking in the fullness that derives from soulfulness and heartfulness; a constricted affectivity and state of consciousness.

In ancient tradition, the term *heart* was synonymous with wholeness; an holistic perception of affectivity. The term affectivity derives from the Latin word *affectus*; which describes, in addition to emotions, the state of openness in which the individual leaves her- or himself vulnerable to the world outside oneself; responsive to being affected by others.[222] This is the original meaning of the use of the term heartfelt.

This is an area of particular import for addicts, whose capacity for relationship tends to be constricted because of this lack of openness of the heart to being emotionally

---

[222] Kurtz and Ketcham, pp. 73-4.

impinged upon. One can't become emotionally intimate if one isn't willing to feel the effects of intimacy. Holding a partner at psychological arm's length prevents the intimacy necessary for an emotionally close relationship. Whether such holding of intimacy at bay is due to fear, aversion, generalized discomfort, or a perceived need for emotional self-defense, it serves to prevent the relationship from going beyond the practical.

In this day and age of cumulative marriages, practicality has become increasingly popular as a justification for marriage; a perceived movement away from prior encumbrances of emotional involvement. One may perhaps better comprehend the experience of the addict by considering the nature of the difference between first and subsequent marriages; wherein one enters subsequent marriages with less vulnerability and less of a willingness to deny one's self in the service of merging identities with another. In the modern era, such merging tends to be perceived as the growing up together that happens between youthful first marriage partners.

In the ancient sense of the word, affectivity is what enables us to be open, not only to being affected by others, but also to being affected by creative impulse, psychic experience, spiritual experience, and the like. Without the necessary prerequisite of openness in affectivity, one cannot experience such connections to the world outside oneself. From this understanding, we find that a closing of the heart may constrict the relationships we have with others as well as the relationships we have with metaphysical experience. Both are forms of constriction to receptive experience. There is an element of ironic perversity in the fact that substance abusers tend to block others from getting too close emotionally with a defensive wall, yet permit substances closer. Holding a heartfelt conversation with one's bottle of beer is safer than holding a heartfelt conversation with someone who may turn psychologically hurtful.

In the extreme sense of constricted living, the person whose life revolves around addiction lives in a state of diminished existence. Like a dimly-lit lamp, the addicted individual is capable of brilliant illumination, of seeing and knowing beyond the confines of constricted existence, yet lacks the luminosity that derives from wholeness and openness. The tragic legacy of addiction, like the tragic legacy of sexual repression, is its light-extinguishing, consciousness-diminishing impact.

Michael Murphy informs us that physicians and contemplatives have known for millennia that most people function in a dissociated way, with divided intentions that inhibit the enjoyment of life and the realization of metanormal capacities.[223] This truth is exemplified by a cultural style which encourages mindless, repetitive activity which may generate a spiritless, automaton form of existence such as the one portrayed in the 1,990 C.E. movie, *Joe versus the Volcano*, featuring the actor, Tom Hanks.

The protagonist, Joe, has a death-like appearance; he works in a dungeon-like warehouse where he perfunctorily performs at a desk surrounded by a roomful of others doing the same thing. His psychosomaticization of his unhappiness leads him to frequent his physician, in a state of perpetual convince that he is dying. On one fateful visit, his physician accidently reads him the prognosis of a terminally ill patient, convincing Joe that he was right all along. Believing he is dying, Joe quits his job, and goes to Hawaii to commit suicide by jumping into a volcano. Instead of dying as expected, he gets spit out of the volcano into the ocean, where, as a castaway living aboard steamer trunks, his vitality is restored. He then faces the truth that he is not going to die. In this movie example, we find a depiction of the kind of dissociated living Michael Murphy describes. One

[223] Murphy, Michael. *The Future of the Body: Explorations Into The Further Evolution of Human Nature*. Jeremy P. Tarcher, Inc.: Los Angeles, CA, 1992, p. 309.

of living the life of an insect; catering to the needs of the hive, functioning as a drone, unconscious to the source of unhappiness; an experience of life that is subhuman in terms of realizable human potential, until, as fate would have it, the protagonist is unexpectedly rescued. While the example is fictional, and being spewed out alive by an exploding volcano is unrealistic, it serves as one visual analogy of living a dissociated life.

With specific regard to addiction, an addict may live a generally dissociated life, and present for detoxification under conditions of clouded consciousness. Post-detoxification, with unclouded consciousness, the individual struggles with sobriety. Soberly facing the truth of living a dissociated and distracted life may or may not follow; in this, the addict has considerable company among the nonaddicted.

Substance abuse and addiction reduce the mind and body's overall level of wellness. They may negatively impact health in the short-run and reduce the lifespan in the long-run. By causing changes to the mind and body that may impair or result in permanent damage to normal bodily and mental functioning, substance abuse facilitates unwellness.

Women's wellness is more quickly impacted by addiction. According to the report, *Gender Differences in the Consequences of Substance Abuse*, it is generally presumed that alcohol and drug abuse will produce more deleterious consequences among women than among men.[224] This follows from the fact that a woman's metabolism differs from a man's. These gender differences in metabolic processes result in women passing higher levels of alcohol into the bloodstream and reaching higher peak blood alcohol concentrations than men.[225] This is exacerbated during the premenstrual period, when a woman's blood alcohol

---

[224] Robbins, "Women and Substance Abuse", p. 1291.
[225] Ibid.

levels measure higher for any given amount of alcohol consumed.[226]

Women are at greater risk of suffering from alcohol-related brain damage, after shorter drinking histories.[227] Sclerosis of the liver, or alcohol-induced liver disease, progresses more rapidly in women than in men.[228] Women diagnosed as alcoholic have very high mortality rates relative to alcoholic men, and relative to women in general.[229]

Deaths from drugs other than alcohol and tobacco are relatively uncommon among women.[230] However, drugs that deposit in body fat, for example, marijuana, appear to clear out of the body more slowly in women than men, resulting in a greater potential for cumulative toxicity in women.[231]

While men's wellness is less quickly impacted by addiction than women's, addiction's impact on men is more often fatal. Men are far more likely than women to die from drug-related causes, at a rate of 71% versus 29%, as a direct consequence of higher consumption rates, higher rates of fatal overdose, and higher rates of accidental injury.[232]

Addiction can also have a negative impact on reproductive functioning for both men and women. Alcohol, tobacco, and illicit drugs, like cocaine and heroin, are all associated with decreased fertility.[233] Alcohol and drug abuse are specifically associated with breast cancer, amenorrhea, failure to ovulate, atrophy of the ovaries, miscarriage, and early menopause in women.[234]

---

[226] Schneiderman, p. 527.

[227] Robbins, p. 1291.

[228] Ibid.

[229] Ibid.

[230] Ibid.

[231] Ibid.

[232] Ibid.

[233] Schneiderman, p. 527.

[234] Robbins, p. 1291.

In men, they are associated with impotence, low testosterone levels, testicular atrophy, breast enlargement, and diminished libido.[235] Cigarette smoking is correlated with earlier onset of menopause.[236] And drug dependency can result in lower newborn birth weights.[237]

While these findings do not confirm a cause and effect relationship between substance use and bodily impairments, they do indicate a cause for caution and concern. Deleterious effects are associated with chronicity of use. Given that malnutrition tends to coincide with sustained addiction, and malnutrition has a potentially negative impact upon reproduction, the likelihood is high that nutrition plays a significant role in associated reproductive impairments.

Addiction has the potential to damage vital brain cells; affecting aspects of mind and body functioning. Two examples from personal experience are illustrative. In the capacity of a program therapist, working with adult psychiatric patients, I met a program therapist working with drug and alcohol patients who had dropped out of medical school secondary to drug addiction. Her prior drug usage had permanently damaged her brain; resulting in impairment of abstract reasoning ability, bouts of mental blankness, also referred to as spacing out, and occasional incongruencies of affect. The diminished mental capacity that resulted from her drug use precluded a return to medical school, but did not preclude successful adjustment to a career as a drug and alcohol counselor; an adjustment facilitated by affinity with the user-seeking-recovery population. This example depicts bodily impairment, in the form of brain damage, resulting from drug abuse, with a subsequently well-adjusted individual.

As a graduate student in clinical psychology, I met a fellow graduate student who had been recently blinded

---

[235] Robbins, pp. 1291-2.

[236] Ibid.

[237] Schneiderman, p. 527.

Maria Artiz, Ph.D.

in consequence of chronic drinking. At the time, I was unaware that alcoholism could result in blindness. Her impairment posed physical as well as mental challenges; of ambulation, learning braille, securing an aide, adjusting to the change of life circumstances, contending with recurrent bouts of depression; while studying to be a counselor. The addiction-induced blindness affected her physicality and her emotionality in medically usual ways, rendering her personally challenged. It also, idiosyncratically, facilitated her development of a greater olfactory acuity; such that she became able to recognize others by their distinctive scents, and determine their moods and mood changes from changes in their scent; rendering her personally enhanced. This unusual capacity is akin to that of the aura reader, who is able to determine mood from visible changes in the colors of the auras which emanate from organic beings. According to the perspective of Michael Murphy, she developed a metanormal capacity in response to a sensory loss. This example depicts bodily impairment, in the form of blindness, resulting from alcohol abuse, in a subsequently well-compensated individual.

These examples reflect potentially severe impacts of substance abuse and addiction upon mind and body functioning. Less severe are the impacts upon mind and body which do not reflect permanent damage. In addition to temporary alterations in bodily functioning and perception; changes to digestive, elimination, vascular, respiratory, visual, auditory, emotive functioning, et cetera; substance abuse impacts cognitive functioning. Thinking may become distorted, rigid, and self-critical; self-recrimination may result in low self-esteem, accompanied by feelings of inadequacy and shame; thoughts may become irrational, paranoid, and persistent.

The cognitive distortions in functioning which co-occur with substance abuse and addiction impact family relationships. Much has been written about the interactional nature of such relationships; which tend to manifest in two types of relationship matches: that of substance user-substance user and that of substance user-codependent.[238] Distorted cognitive functioning is a factor in relationship instability.

The role of cognitions in influencing substance use and abuse has previously been discussed. In addition to influencing substance usage, and the development of a dependency upon substances, the cognitive experience of the substance abuser may influence dependency upon others compatible with sustaining usage. There is a psychological dependency transfer process which may occur during and after recovery, wherein relationship dependency transfers to other recovering individuals or ongoing treatment professionals. Whether such psychological dependency precedes substance abuse or develops with substance abuse is relative to the individual.

The impact of addiction on psychospirituality is like the sound in the forest conundrum. Many of us, growing up, were intellectually challenged to answer the question, *When a tree falls in the forest, and no one is present to hear it, is there sound?* According to Robert Beyer, in the *Encyclopedia of Physics*, sound demands a material medium for its transmission from place to place.[239] This tells us that sound requires a means of travel, such as gas, liquid, or mass. It does not, however, answer the question posed by the conundrum. When the wave of a sound traveling through a medium reaches the ear of an observer, it produces a motion of the eardrum, which in turn moves the little bones in the middle ear, and this movement communicates motion to the hair cells in the cochlea in the inner ear. In this complicated biophysical process which is not yet completely understood, sound is heard.[240]

---

[238] Beattie, Melody. *Codependent No More*. Hazelden: Center City, MN, 1987.

[239] Beyer, Robert T. "Acoustics", In *Encyclopedia of Physics*, 2nd ed. Rita G. Lerner and George L. Trigg (Eds.) VCH Publishers, Inc.: New York, 1991, pp. 13-5.

[240] Beyer, p. 13.

Intellectually reasoned, for the psychophysiological experience of sound to occur, two conditions must be met; first, a transmitting medium must exist to transmit the sound waves, and second, a receptive medium must exist to receive the sound waves. Animals have this physiological hardware capacity of auditory reception. Other forms of life, like insects, detect vibrations with antennaes, and are alerted to movements in a displaced medium, such as air, which constitute sound waves traveling within their environments, but do not experience the psychophysiological phenomenon of sound per se. Without its reception, sound remains unrealized as mechanical energy transmitting in waves of varying frequency, velocity, and intensity through air.

For purpose of comprehension, consider the difference between the hearing abilities of dogs and humans. Dog whistles are acoustically designed for detection at high frequencies of hearing range considered ultrasonic, meaning that they occur above the audible human range. If you or I blow on a dog whistle, we will not hear a sound, even though the sound waves are present. This is because the structure of our human hearing apparatus is such that it can only detect sounds within a specific acoustical range, which is lower in frequency than that of canines. Above and below the human range of detection, no sound is heard. If there is a dog present, however, it will acoustically detect and respond to the whistle. Thus reasoned, sound exists in a psychophysiologically meaningful sense, only if it can be heard. The answer to the conundrum, then, is a paradoxical yes and no. While the mechanical energy of potential sound caused by the fallen tree exists in the physical sense, sound itself does not exist in the acoustical sense, because there is no one around to detect it.

A comparable situation exists with respect to psychospirituality. In order for the experience of psychospiritual awareness to occur, a being capable of its detection must be present. Psychospirituality is the detection of the meaningfulness of existence, in the same way that psychophysiology is the detection of the meaningfulness of sound.

Addiction is a state of fettered awareness characterized by a lack of existential meaningfulness and a lack of psychospiritual receptiveness. Substance abuse may interfere with experiences of meaningfulness and psychospirituality. It may manifest as a symptom, as well as a source, of psychospiritual impoverishment.

Psychospirituality manifests in unfettered consciousness; that is, consciousness that is not addicted or otherwise shackled. The experience of psychospirituality, like the experience of sound, requires a capable receptivity. According to Kurtz and Ketcham, the word *experience* speaks to the wholeness, the fitting together of seeing, feeling, and willing. It is more than just feeling because it involves knowing, and it is more than just seeing because it is knowledge of as well as knowledge about. They posit that experience signifies a kind of hands on grasping to taste the honey of life while trying to simultaneously understand the essence of sweetness. Such experience knows life not as an object to observe, but as a living breathing reality that can be creatively embraced and that fully returns the embrace.[241] We find that in order to experience psychospirituality, one must be simultaneously capable of reception and appreciation; a form of holistic *getting it* akin to the experience of art appreciation.

This understanding of psychospirituality calls to mind reflections; what it means to live the good life. In the same way that the soul is the portal to awareness of ultimate reality and the meaning of existence, conscious experience of life is the portal to the soul. Through consciousness, we permeate the mists of distractedness, and navigate the soulscape.

Given that existential meaningfulness and psychospiritual awareness are areas of known deficiency among addicts, the international self-help organization, Alcoholics Anonymous, adheres to a treatment strategy that incorporates

---

[241] Kurtz and Ketcham, p. 156.

psychospiritual philosophy and practice. Named in 1,939 C.E., the organization began with informal gatherings in New York City in 1,935 C.E. The treatment strategy was established by Bill Wilson, a stockbroker by trade prior to the 1,929 C.E. stock market crash, in consultation with his physician co-founder, Bob Smith. Himself an alcoholic, Wilson contended that the strategy was an efficacious cure for what the medical community of the time considered to be the hopelessness of alcoholism.

Now widely regarded as the AA program, the strategy insists upon the need for a moral inventory, a confession of personality defects, a restitution to those harmed, a practiced helpfulness to others, and the necessity of a belief in and dependence upon God, in whatever form one's personal conception of a higher power than oneself takes shape.[242]

In the recording of his personal story, Wilson relates his initial antipathy towards the thought that there might be a God personal to him and his experience. His story, and his personal resolution of the intellectual impasse, by reframing the notion of God as a creative intelligence, universal mind, or spirit of nature; what he refers to as a form of God-consciousness; which he *could* believe in, facilitated his own recovery from alcoholism, and has aided many other alcoholics struggling with spiritual disbelief to comprehend the notion that there are powers in this universe greater than one's own. It is a treatment strategy which has worked well over the years.

We find that an holistic perception of substance usage and addiction pertaining to body includes a variety of effects and experiences; both temporary and permanent, ranging in scope from the behavioral, the cognitive, the emotional, and the physical to the psychospiritual.

---

[242] Wilson, pp. 1-16.

PART FOUR

THE CONTEXT OF SPIRIT

CHAPTER THIRTEEN

The Context of Spirit

In holistically comprehending the matter of substance abuse and addiction, we have come to the understanding that spirit, or the psychospiritual, plays an important role; through its absence and its presence. We discussed in the last chapter of Part 3, the reality that psychospirituality tends to be lacking in persons who, for whatever reason, become addicted. In addition to biology, culture, and personality, life's circumstances impinge upon the individual's experiences of life.

We know, from experience, that persons despair; most often in response to a significant loss of meaning. To comprehend the impact of such experience, consider the hypothetical situation of an individual who devotes his entire life to a preconceived notion of reality; a view of how things are; which, as a result of changes in the ways of the world, or changes in the person's capacity to perceive, fails him in the end. Imagine the shock, the confusion, the heartache, the discouragement that such reckoning entails; to have devoted one's entire life to something; a cause, a belief, a perception, an effort, et cetera; only to discover that it was or has become meaningless. To a lesser extent, a failed marriage may have a similar impact.

The experience figuratively turns one's world upside down, leaving one feeling at a loss to explain life, and without the assurance of meaningfulness; what one thought was meaningful no longer applies. The result is a void in existential meaning; the kind of meaning that renders life bearable, significant, worth living for, et cetera. Many persons experience such existential loss of meaning in their lives; some to a greater extent than others, some more often than others. One can only wonder at the reasons why creative intelligence of the higher order permits such happenings.

The rabbi, Harold Kushner, addressed this matter when he wrote, *When Bad Things Happen To Good People.*[243] It explores the thinking processes involved in experiencing a bad happening; what it means, why it happened, why it happened to me, et cetera. Like Wilson's story, Rabbi Kushner's story is an exploration of truth based upon personal experience; in his case, the death of his fourteen year-old son secondary to a motorcycle accident. It is a relevant comprehension to the understanding of spiritual dissonance; those times when life yields a blow that literally knocks the wind out of you.

The difference between depression and despair is significant. Depression may lead to despair, and despair may lead to depression. However, they are not synonymous. Depression constitutes a phenomenon of mind/body, whereas despair constitutes a phenomenon of spirit. When spirit fails, life loses its former appeal; the luster is gone, the reality grows dull; and escape from the emptiness of life holds a greater attraction. We find there is then a higher propensity for addiction and suicide.

The meaningfulness of life is a variant not a static; at times it is more meaningful than others. In addition to the potential for disillusionment to negatively impact the sense of all-rightness; that all is as one believes it to be; there exists

---

[243] Kushner, Harold S. *When Bad Things Happen To Good People.* New York: Schocken Books, 1981.

the potential for spirit to positively impact the sensibility, and restore a sense of all-rightness, albeit perhaps differently than before. For this reason, spirit is an important and relevant consideration.

The concept of soul is universally recognized and understood. The soul is understood to be the means of accessing spiritual reality. This concept has persisted throughout the ages in spite of the fact that what is referred to as *ultimate reality* has consistently been reported to be incomprehensible for most people, and linguistically inexplicable for those capable of its perception.[244]

The American philosopher, Aldous Leonard Huxley, has contended that those capable of comprehending the great mystery of life are challenged by the inadequacy of language as a representational tool for conveying the experience to others. Huxley states that theological statements regarding the correspondence between human symbols and divine fact are as true as it is possible for us to make them.[245]

Huxley's commentary is relevant to the experience of contacting spiritual reality. When a preexisting language is nonexistent or limited, conveyance of meaning is impeded. Persons who experience a reality that is unfamiliar; such as spiritual reality; may or may not have available to them the linguistic tools for adequate communication. To make matters worse, the transition between realities alters perception and remembrance. A facilely comprehendible explanation is the alteration of time perception that is experienced when transitioning; in my experience, this occurs with access to spiritual reality as well as with reception from psychic reality. Time loses its relevance in timeless realities, resulting in a necessary adjustment upon reorientation to the everyday reality. This is akin to the refocusing one experiences when entering a dark room from a sunlit outdoors; it takes time

---

[244] Huxley, Aldous. *The Perennial Philosophy.* Ayer Company Publishers, Inc.: Salem, NH, 1945, p. 126.
[245] Ibid, p. 125.

for one's eyes to adjust to the extremeness of the change in lighting. So, too, with transitions into timeless realities; one must adjust to the extremeness of the difference between them, upon arriving and upon returning. This alteration of the perception of time is but one of a myriad of differences one may experience. An apt, although not mirror image, analogy is that of the difference between wake consciousness and dream consciousness. One encounters, in the dream state, images that may or may not make overt sense, sequences that may or may not appear to be related, and either a sense of timing or absence of timing that is different than during wakefulness; there is a kind of disjointedness that makes perfect sense when we dream, yet which becomes confusing when we awake. When we dream, we enter a different state of consciousness. When we access spiritual reality, we similarly enter a different state of consciousness. In the same manner that most people find it difficult to explain, remember, understand, and interpret their dreams to others, people who experience the process of transitioning from a spiritual state to a normal state may encounter difficulty with both the comprehension and the translation of what they have experienced. Spiritual reality has influence upon the consciousness in the same way that dreams have influence upon the subconscious.

In addition to difficulties inherent to the process of awareness of spiritual reality, as Huxley points out, there may be language barriers. If one considers the hypothetical situation of someone beginning a new language and the process that would ensue from this until the language became integrated with social culture, one can better understand the difficulty. In the beginning, only the individual starting the language would know and comprehend it. In time, others would learn the idiosyncracies of the language and begin to speak it; the process would take years to eventuate into what would be termed a formal language. The evolution of language is bidirectional; languages may develop and they may deteriorate. That is, linguists have discovered that, for instance, the English language has deteriorated markedly over time; that, in fact, its transmission and usage across time and place has resulted in a process of deformalization and deterioration of the original language. Language is not a static entity in and of itself, but rather an interactive and reflective means of communication, that adapts with usage and the needs of the users.

All languages have beginnings; the fact that we are generally unaware of their origins; that is, how they started; indicates the lengthy passage of time involved in their development. While we have come to know the terminologies and root word origins of most of the world's recognized languages, we do not know all of the origins in terms of who was responsible for the words that came into being; much of this knowledge having been lost to unrecorded history. With respect to language beginnings, it stands to reason that the development of language pertaining to everyday reality would precede the development of language pertaining to spiritual reality, given that everyday reality is the predominant realm of existence requiring practical means for communication.

One may comprehend the difficulty of communicating in the absence of a formalized language with relevant terminology to convey experience by considering how such absence was recognized by the women's movements in America and England in the 20th century. Following the publication of Betty Friedan's book, in which she identified the problem of women in society as the problem with no name, a language of feminism began to evolve; providing a terminology for communicating the experience.[246] Like Friedan, women around the world soon discovered that they shared a similar experience; a frustration of communication; that resulted from a general absence of identification of the female experience in paternalistic society. From this, such

---

[246] Friedan, Betty. *The Feminine Mystique.* Norton Company, Inc.: New York, 1963.

comprehensions as, *the personal is political*; meaning that women's personal experiences are every bit as relevant and significant as men's authority experiences; emerged, with newfound regard for women in society. A relevant expression of the frustration with the limitations of language for conveying experience is immortalized in a song by Gloria Estefan of The Miami Sound Machine, when she bemoans, *but the words get in the way*"[247]. The import of language is clearly relevant.

John Hick reports in *The Philosophy of Religion*, that the application of language to convey a comparative meaning of religious experience is analogical in nature. He credits this perspective to Baron von Hugel, who compared the apprehension and affirmation of spiritual realities to the hierarchical superiorities inherent in nature. Spiritual realities, which are superior in quality and amount of reality to ourselves, that is, which are greater than ourselves, provide us with, according to Hugel, a sustainable, although unpicturable intimacy. From this analogical perspective, Hugel perceives that man's obscurity to his dog is like God's obscurity to man; the chief difference being the invisibility of God to man. Further, that man is to God as plant is to man; an innately inferior existence which is poor in relation to God's superior life and reality.[248] In Hugel's view, the life of man is as limited in relation to the life of God as the life of a plant is to the life of man; neither plant or man, as inferior forms of existence, are capable of fully knowing the superiority of the other.

In Hugel's religious perspective, we find a comprehension of the inadequacy of a lesser being to fully know a superior being. We may further comprehend this by considering the differences between persons who are intellectually

[247] Estefan, Gloria. *Words get in the way.* Greatest hits. New York: Epic, 1992.

[248] Hick, John. *Philosophy of Religion.* Prentice-Hall, Inc.: New Jersey, 1990, p. 85.

disadvantaged, intellectually normal, and intellectually superior. The lesser advantaged individual will recognize the greater capability of the more advantaged person, but will lack the ability for a complete understanding. Hugel's perspective presumes the existence of a parallel between mortal and immortal realities; such that this difference encountered in mortal reality is mirrored in immortal reality. Correct or not, it provides an intellectually useful percept for understanding what the actual relationship may be.

When one has an out-of-the-ordinary experience, the tendency is to seek an explanatory source. This has been the case historically. Such experiences, when known, have tended to be documented, as aids to human understanding. The documentations of the disciples of Jesus the Christ are important for this reason. We may know from them, vicariously, of unusual human experiences. There are many other such documentations, which, taken together, comprise a body of knowledge significant to the understanding of the metanormal experiences of human beings.

Personal experience in modern times has become more personal and less publicly known, for a variety of reasons. The expansion of the human population is one factor, the diversity of the human population is another factor, and regard for individual right to privacy is another. For these reasons, knowledge of present-day metanormal experiences is limited to reported cases and personal experience. For example, the personal experiences included in this book become part of the public pool of knowledge; otherwise, they would remain private, and not be counted. This fact is relevant to our consideration of experiences with spiritual reality in that what is available for discussion is limited not only by the number of experiencers, but also by the extent to which their experiences are part of the public record.

In light of this consideration, part of what I reflected upon, in the search for explanatory sources for my personal experiences have been included in this book. The fact of experiencing an increasing number of unusual occurrences led me to explore the possible sources. Having known for some time that I was psychic did not fully explain what was happening to me. Having a near-death experience that did not fit the standard description provided partial explanation, given that it is publicly documented that such individuals begin to see life in a new light. Meditations upon the matter resulted in a greater contact with metanormal reality. In these respects, one could attribute source to the supernatural, to God or the omniscience of creative intelligence. With the increase in experiences arose an attendant increase in being noticed by the supernatural, as related in Chapter 2, when spirit beings appeared out of the blue. My interpretation is that the act of contacting what is referred to as the Godhead resulted in a kind of supernatural attention I had not previously experienced.

Further consideration of the matter led to discovery of facts about my family about which I had no prior knowledge. I learned, for example, that not only had my maternal grandmother been psychic, one of my paternal aunts secretly was as well. I also learned that an ancestral Spanish Basque bloodline relative was a first cousin of Janinne Abadie, one of the two young girls to whom the apparition of the Virgin Mary appeared in Lourdes, France, in 1,858 C.E. The second, Marie Bernarde Soubirous, joined a convent; her visions have been documented by the Catholic Church. I considered the possibility of lineage as a factor. To my knowledge, there are no other family records of a vision or other supernatural experience, apart from the psychic, on both sides of the family. Lineage is clearly relevant to psychic receptivity, and may be relevant to spiritual perception.

Finally, I considered the metaphysical fact that I was astrologically born an Aquarian; a sign known for its prophetic, healing, and psychic capacities. Regarding the Aquarian, Linda Joyce states, "You have a well-developed third eye. Your instincts guide you, phantoms instruct you, and there is no place you cannot go. Your vision reaches into the future."[249] The astrological perspective provides parallels to my experience; as a healer, a psychic, and an out-of-the ordinary experiencer. Such influence from the cosmos cannot be disregarded. In sum, I concluded there were a number of sources of influence; contact with supernatural reality, family lineage, and astrology; and that these likely interacted to make my experiences possible. These influences, combined with experience, have served to facilitate my explorations, and have, no doubt, spurred my interest in making this philosophical foray. The relevance of idiosyncratic sources of influence in experiences of the spirit cannot be overstated; this is therefore an important point to consider in evaluating one's own spirituality and life experiences.

The context of spirit, in addition to the matter of soul-spirit communication and comprehension, and individual idiosyncracies of influence, includes differences in soul sensitivity. The matter of soul sensitivity is addressed by John Carmody, in *How To Handle Trouble: A Guide To Peace Of Mind*. Speaking of the situation in America, Carmody states that people don't know what to make of the soul.[250] This, he posits, is the reason why so many individuals make bad decisions. According to Carmody, a good decision flows from a moment, a mood, a disposition of peace,[251] and we act best when our soul is collected, integrated, and whole; whereas bad decisions flow up from an unsettled soul.[252]

If Carmody is correct, and society is experiencing a lack of soul sensitivity, we may well wish to reflect upon

[249] Joyce, Linda. *The Day You Were Born: A Journey to Wholeness through Astrology and Numerology*. Kensington Publishing Corporation: New York, 1998, p. 334.

[250] Carmody, John. *How To Handle Trouble: A Guide To Peace Of Mind*. Ballantine Books: New York, 1993, p. 137.

[251] Carmody, p. 138.

[252] Ibid., pp. 138-9.

the reasons. Given what we have reviewed regarding high levels of stress, cultural pressure, change, and depression, the perception of unsettled states of souls is consistent; indicating a generalized dissonance incompatible with peace of mind. We may also consider such factors as emotional maturity, motivation to learn how to render one's soul more sensitive, and the preponderant ages of manifested souls; a prevalence of younger souls would suggest that the problem stems from soul immaturity. As difficult as it might seem to ascertain this, analysis of population based upon zodiacal positions would provide an approximation that could then be used to gauge the distribution of souls along a continuum of soul maturity. This would serve to clarify the extent to which soul maturity is a relevant consideration.

Deliberative sensitization is a remedial option. Carmody states that reflective, contemplative pauses are necessary to inculcate peace of soul; not only do these allow us to live gracefully with the animal fluidity we ought, they are essential for fully human, healthy, happy living. In this respect, peace of soul is not a luxury, it is an essential.[253] Carmody further contends that we need contemplative techniques because the meaning of our lives is not apparent. In this respect, he says, there is a paradoxical blessing to getting into trouble, in that trouble forces us to face this bedrock fact that the meaning of our lives is unclear to us.[254] Without trouble, he states, we view our lives as making sense, when in fact little about human beings makes any sense.

Carmody contends that the fact that we can't answer such fundamental questions as, *Where did we come from? What caused the big bang? Where are we going? What happens at death?* and *What is a man or woman worth?* is indicative of a strange fundamental reality of our human beingness that is both amusing and frightening. The mysteriousness of human life that Carmody addresses is a reality that has

[253] Ibid., p. 139.
[254] Ibid., p. 4.

kept humanity puzzled throughout the ages. Recognition of this truth is humbling; in light of how much we know about so many other things; the physical world we inhabit, the physical body we are born with; how is it that we know so little about where we came from and where we go? Consciousness has a drawback; awareness of not knowing everything there is to know. Given that the spirit is the means by which we may better know what we individually need to know, and the fact that reflection, contemplation, meditation, and prayer are means by which we may become more acquainted with the spirit, Carmody's advice is both relevant and practical. His belief is that making friends with the mysteriousness is the way to launch oneself on the contemplative path, and on the way to getting a handle on one's worst troubles.[255]

As we struggle to comprehend the mysteries of life, we may consider the relativity of plants to man, as posited by Hugel. Science has demonstrated that, despite not having obvious nervous or sensory organs, and thereby, having a limited capacity for perception relative to animals, plants nonetheless exhibit responsivity to sound, and recoil from; that is, can wither and die; under negative conditions of harsh verbal exposure. This finding has led to the consideration that plants do indeed have a consciousness; albeit a lower level form of consciousness. Given that plants are not only sensitive to the environmental conditions of light, moisture, nutrient, temperature, and wind; but also to the environmental condition of sound indicates a far greater sensitivity than previously realized. One can but wonder that man has for so long been ignorant of and insensitive to the sensitivity of plants; such realization is further humbling. It has been said that the more one knows, the more one comes to realize how little one knows. We find that the realm of consciousness is in many ways itself yet a mystery.

This scientific discovery speaks to the popularized belief regarding the interconnectedness of all living things. We

---

[255] Ibid., pp. 4-5.

are finding that all forms of life have the capacity to both detect other life forms and to affect and be affected by them. Responding to that which is outside of ourselves; in the form of relationships to nature, to others, and to a superior consciousness; that is, to what is alive, whether such affect is directly perceivable or not, enables us to benefit from the available potential influences and influencings of life.

According to Ernest Kurtz and Katherine Ketcham, in *The Spirituality of Imperfection*, the closest approximation of the truth is to be found in the apparent contradiction inherent in paradox, which combines two realities that don't seem to belong together, and thus calls into question our assumptions about seeming. They cite the English essayist, Gilbert Keith Chesterton, who described paradox as truth standing on her head to attract attention.[256] Kurtz and Ketcham contend that paradox is the nature of spirituality because paradox is the nature of human beings.[257]

Efforts to communicate understanding about what is not naturally intuitive, in this case, communication about spiritual reality, are often analogous and paradoxical in nature. Kurtz and Ketcham tell us that according to the Indian, Shankara, in *Viveka-Chudamani* or *The Crest-Jewel of Wisdom*,[258] *when a man follows the way of the world, or the way of the flesh, or the way of tradition, i.e. when he believes in religious rites and the letter of the scriptures as though they were intrinsically sacred, knowledge of reality cannot arise in him.* This is paradoxical in that one is taught through religious rites and religious scriptures about God and supernatural consciousness, yet, to regard the rites and scriptures as intrinsically sacred inhibits access to divine knowledge. This perception goes against the grain of expectation; in this respect, it is very much like the description of paradox itself; truth standing on her head to get our attention. We find in

---

[256] Kurtz and Ketcham, pp. 18-9.

[257] Ibid., p. 18.

[258] Huxley, pp. 6-7.

Shankara the comprehension that Man is not God; therefore, what Man creates pertaining to God may honor God, but cannot be mistaken for God. Such reasoning speaks to the genuineness of the divine, as well as to the fallibility of human beingness.

Shankara's insight is relevant to our holistic understanding. The matter of genuineness may be further addressed in terms of actual versus vicarious experience. Given that direct knowledge of spiritual reality requires individual contact, and is not absorbable from rites and scriptures; a combination of symbolic expressions and accounts of others' experiences and comprehensions; we may follow Shankara's line of reasoning and conclude that to presume engagement in attendant religious activities constitutes contact with God is to confuse the issue. Shankara heeds us to discern the difference.

Religious rites and scriptures provide comfort, knowledge, and guidance; they are not substitutes for personal communication with God. The role of the religious leader has evolved over time; in antiquity, leaders were often those who had received divine guidance and insight and shared these with others; in modern times, leaders have tended towards the roles of the philosopher who interprets, the shepherd who guides, and the teacher who explains.

Shankara interprets Brahman; the Indian conception of the transcendent supernatural divine; stating that caste, creed, family, and lineage do not exist in Brahman; which has no name or form, transcends merit and demerit, is beyond time, space, and the objects of sense experience. In Shankara's words, such is Brahman; he advises meditatation upon this truth within our own consciousness. According to Shankara's interpretation, the superior consciousness that we call Brahman or God or something else, cannot be categorized in the human traditions; the names that we ascribe it do not generate from the superior consciousness itself; naming is irrelevant, as are our names of ourselves to it.

Maria Artiz, Ph.D.

Shankara refers to the Sanskrit formula, *tat tvam asi*, or *that art thou*; the spiritual doctrine that there is an immanent eternal self in the depth of all individual selves that is one with the divine ground or absolute principle of existence. The doctrine contends that it is the end of every human being to discover this truth, and find out who s/he really is.[259] That is, to reach into that part of oneself which is a part of ultimate reality, in order to learn the truth. Deepak Chopra, in his books combining the perspectives of medical healing and Indian spirituality, speaks to this same fundamental reality when he cites the Biblical passage, *Be still, and know that I am God.*[260] Through the silence accessed between thoughts during meditation, says Chopra, we are able to access this universal ground of all creation, which is pure consciousness.

To draw a parallel to the spirituality of Roman Catholicism, the process takes the form of allowing the eternal essence of the spirit; the Holy Ghost; to spring forth, much like a ghostly fountain and fill the soul. In the modern Catholic tradition, the soul is the principle of life in a human being.[261] Since the late 13th century, the predominant notion of soul in Catholic theology is that of Thomas Aquinas, whose thinking followed Aristotle's. In this interpretation, soul is perceived as the pattern of interrelatedness that integrates the many parts and processes of an organism into a functioning whole. In human beings, this integrating or formal element manifests itself not only in the activities that Aquinas referred to as *vegetative*, such as nutrition and growth, or *sensitive*, such as seeing and hearing, but also in the higher-order activities he designated as *intellectual* or *rational*, such as questioning, understanding, deciding, and loving. In Aquinas'

[259] Ibid., pp. 1-2.

[260] Chopra, Deepak. *The Seven Spiritual Laws Of Success*. Amber-Allen Publishing and New World Library: San Rafael, CA, 1994, p. 17.

[261] McBrien, pp. 1210-11.

222

view, the human soul is naturally and intrinsically related to the body; it is not a spiritual captive in a material prison.[262] From this derived the Catholic conception of mind/body as an inseparable entity.

In the American Christian tradition, influenced heavily by the Plymouth brethren, with the characteristic of teaching the truth according to the pure word of the Bible, receiving the divine is a matter of acquiring God within one's spirit; of inviting and receiving God into oneself, separate from the soul with which we psychologically know the world.[263] In this tradition, the human spirit is viewed as the key to experiencing Christ; man is viewed, in accordance with the New Testament passage, 1 Thessalonians 5:23, to be comprised of three parts; the spirit, the soul, and the body. The American Christian tradition holds these to be the three distinct and separate parts of a human being [264] The soul is also viewed as having three distinct parts; the emotion, the mind, and the will.[265] There are key differences between fundamentalist; Biblical passage adherers; and other Christian positions; such as belief that the Spirit of Christ enters into and overtakes the spirit of the individual; as opposed to entering the soul which is seen as a pure psychologic aspect of man; related belief in the experience of being reborn through the inviting of the Spirit of Christ into oneself;[266] related belief in the necessity of destructing the soul at this occurrence; a process called *giving up the soul* to the Spirit of Christ;[267] and belief that the matter of experiencing Christ and God's salvation is absolutely

---

[262] Ibid.

[263] Lee, Witness and Nee, Watchman. *Basic Elements of the Christian Life. Vol. 1.* Living Stream Ministry: Anaheim, CA, 2003, pp. 7-10.

[264] Lee and Nee, p. 37.

[265] Ibid., pp. 38-9.

[266] Ibid., p. 40.

[267] Ibid., p. 42.

different from religion which teaches right and wrong.[268] We find, by way of example, parallels between Christian fundamentalism, Catholicism, and Sanskrit; that spirit is a divine eternal that enters the individual; and a parallel between fundamentalism and Sanskrit that religion and spirituality are not synonymous. Such similarities of belief, and differences in sources and interpretations occur across the span of Christian religious doctrines. Found differences reside in the realm of sources of interpretaton, including bibles and scriptural equivalents; found parallels reside in the realm of experience.

The matter of the differences in interpretation speaks to such variables as: linguistics; translations of original documents from the Arabic, Greek, and Judaic; semantics; ascribed interpretations of meaning to scriptural language, and perceptions based on the semantics; ascribed interpretations of scriptural events; rather than upon differences in experience of spiritual reality. What it speaks to is the difficulty of knowing the truth of antiquity; given the reality of incomplete historical records. For example, discovery of the Dead Sea Scrolls provided scholars with additional knowledge and the means by which to correct prior incorrect translations; altering interpretations of history. To date, not all of the scrolls have been translated. The matter of historical record is clearly fundamental to an understanding of what occurred in biblical times, and it is this, the incomplete historical record, which is most at issue. To comprehend how crucial the issue is, consider the analogous impact upon an individual whose life history was incorrectly told, such that his belief about his family was based upon a false history. The incomplete record of human antiquity renders such falsity possible, to a lesser and to a greater extent, pendant upon the actual discrepancies. This is not a matter of considered opinion or contention, this is a

---

[268] Ibid., p. 43.

matter of not knowing. It is a matter of such importance that it has occupied scholars for centuries.

In addition to the various interpretations of spirit, soul, and spiritual reality found among Christian religions, we find interpretations among individuals and scholars. Chris Rohmann, in *A World Of Ideas*, states that a common distinction between soul and spirit sees the former as the immortal essence of the person, surviving the body's death, and the latter as the animating principle, the spark that distinguishes life from nonlife.[269] According to Rohmann, soul and spirit are understood as the seat of consciousness and the self, although spirit is the more inclusive and expansive term; soul is usually conceived as personal and internal, whereas spirit is universal and transcendent. The soul is distinguished as the immortal essence of the person, and the spirit as the immortal transcendent; one is individual and the other is universal.

Upon one key point interpretive positions converge; that the essence of the divine; be it soul, spirit, or something else; is the source of creation, of salvation, and it is that which has the capability of filling the individual with the power to transcend everyday experience. While there is considerable room for intellectual and religious discourse regarding linguistics and semantics, and the differences may prove confusing to the uninitiated, belief in a transcendent capacity tends to be the norm.

Huxley relates the position of Eckhart, who stated that the more God is in all things, the more he is outside them.[270] From the perspective of spirit, the implication is significant. Using Bill Wilson's terminology of God-consciousness,[271] the greater the extent to which we allow the God-consciousness

---

[269] Rohmann, Chris. "Soul and spirit", In *A World Of Ideas: A Dictionary of Important Theories, Concepts, Beliefs and Thinkers*. The Ballantine Publishing Group: New York, 1999, pp. 372-3.

[270] Huxley, p. 2.

[271] Wilson, p. 13.

to pervade our inner being, the more extensively, according to Eckhart's perception, will this God-consciousness pervade the world; as within, so without. His contention provides additional support for the notion of interconnectedness; that the impact of consciousness is not limited to the body. Given what we have learned about the importance of affectability, I find the term interaffectedness to be a more apt characterization. The matter of affectability, in terms of consciousness, is discussed in Chapter 14.

Consistent with the fact that religions converge in agreement regarding the existence of a spiritual reality greater than ourselves, Aldous Huxley notes that the philosophy of an ultimate reality, which he terms the *perennial philosophy*, exists in various stages of development in all cultures throughout history. We thus find that the belief extends not only across religions, but across cultures as well. According to Huxley, the thing represented by the phrase perennial philosophy is a metaphysic that recognizes a divine reality substantial to the world of things and lives and minds. It is the psychology that finds in the soul something similar to, or even identical with, divine reality. It is the ethic that places man's final end in the knowledge of the immanent and transcendent ground of all being. And it is a thing immemorial and universal.[272]

Huxley reports that the fundamental aspects of the perennial philosophy are present in the lore of primitive peoples in every region of the world, and that the fully developed form is incorporated in every one of the higher religions.[273] Thus, Huxley informs, the concept of a divine reality, found in the soul, knowable only through the fulfillment of certain experiential conditions, is universal to human culture.

Paradoxically, consistent with what Kurtz and Ketcham attribute is a paradoxical human nature, we find a lack of

---

[272] Huxley, p. vii.
[273] Ibid.

universal human experience of this spiritual reality. According to Huxley, who lived from 1,894 C.E. to 1,963 C.E., even when poets and metaphysicians talk about perennial philosophy, it is generally from second hand, not direct, knowledge. Twentieth century fundamentalist contemporaries of Huxley similarly contend that many Christians don't experience the fullness of God because they fail to use their spirit.[274] According to Lee and Nee, we pray, talk, argue, read the Bible, reason, debate, and discuss---mostly by the exercise of our soul, but we fail to exercise our spirit to contact God within it.[275] That we believe in the existence of a divine and ultimate spiritual reality accessible through the soul is attributable to corroborated experiences of transcendents; that is, people who have transcended the bounds of ordinary sensory experience to experience, and thereby know, the extraordinary experience of contacting God, the Godhead, or the Spirit of God. They may or may not be poets and metaphysicians. In truth, transcendents may be a lot like geniuses in that they arise from a background of familial capability, but their unique capacities are not predictably inherited.

At the very least, to expand upon Daniel Goleman, who contends in his book, *Emotional Intelligence*, that intelligence is multivarious; there being such diverse intelligence abilities as the standard notion (usually referred to as IQ or Intelligence Quotient), as well as many others not typically assessed, including what he terms emotional intelligence; transcendents may have a particular form of intelligence, not standardly assessed.[276]

Comprehending the reason for this vast discrepancy is a matter of supposition. From an astrological perspective, one may consider that, with mastery, souls evolve to metaphysical

---

[274] Lee and Nee, p. 41.

[275] Ibid., p. 42.

[276] Goleman, Daniel. *Emotional Intelligence*. Bantam Books: New York, New York, 1995.

states of capability. From a genetic perspective, one may consider that such capacity may run in families. From a religious perspective, one may consider that God or superior intelligence determines which individuals will be so affected. From a scientific perspective, one may consider that persons capable of spiritual transcendence manifest randomly as reflections of the randomness inherent in the universe. From a philosophical perspective, one may consider that, in the way of genius, leadership, et cetera, manifestation of capability is unpredictable.

Huxley provides an additional perspective; that of the deliberate contemplative, who chooses as opposed to being chosen. He informs us somewhat enigmatically that there have been some men and women in every age that have deliberately undertaken to fulfill the only empirical conditions upon which such immediate knowledge can be had. He further attests that a few of these have left first-hand accounts of the reality that, under strict conditions, they were enabled to apprehend, evaluate in comparison to other experience, and finally, relate as a comprehensive system of thought, which he terms perennial philosophy. Huxley relates that, throughout history, these individuals have generally come to be named saint, prophet, sage, and enlightened one, by those who knew them.[277]

In an holistic consideration of context, in this case, the context of spirit, we discourse the realities of accessing the mysterious and relatively unknown reality of spirit. First, and foremost, we are told that ultimate spiritual reality is essentially unknowable through language. At a literal level, this poses a paradox. It is both true and untrue at the same time. It is true that we cannot know ultimate spiritual reality in a meaningfulness sense on the basis of words alone, and yet it is untrue that we cannot know of or about it; for we can gain a measure of vicarious experience of it through language. Thus, while language as a representational tool is

---

[277] Huxley, p. ix.

not adequate to the task of knowing in the experiential sense; that is, knowing it with one's whole sense of being, since we cannot see, feel, hear, taste, or hold an abstract concept with our five concrete senses; it nonetheless provides us with a measure of symbolic approximation.

Like art, like poetry, like scientific and mathematical symbolism, language is a tool of conveyance, a means of conveying actual experience, which, however inadequate to the task, aids and abets communication. The imperative which Huxley defines is that intellectual honesty requires that we be clear about the difference between actual and vicarious experience. Symbolic representation is not a substitute for actual experience, and while we may come to know of or about an abstract unknown in a roundabout way through language, we are still missing the fullness of experiencing the thing directly. In Huxley's view, words are not the same as things; a knowledge of words about facts is in no sense equivalent to a direct and immediate apprehension of the facts themselves.[278] In short, there is no substitute for experience.

The reason why this difference is so important is that knowledge of ultimate reality derives from a change in one's experience. We are able to know it; as opposed to knowing of it; to the extent that we are able to experience it, and to experience it is synonymous with undergoing an altered state of perception. Altered states of perception of this kind do not occur just because we know they exist and are possible; they occur because of manifest capabilities to have them, and because of channeled capabilities to acquire them.

Knowing, in the modern sense, tends to be characterized by the scientific, which translates into left-brainedness. Such knowing is based on thinking. When knowing is characterized by thinking, what derives is the tendency to believe that this is the only way to know. Given that the left hemisphere of the brain is also the locus of language processing may

---

[278] Ibid., p. 126.

contribute to reported inadequacies of language to convey the experience of ultimate spiritual reality.

Holistically speaking, knowing is not limited to left-brain reasoning. In the case of creative individuals, for instance, brain activity focuses in the right hemisphere of the brain; indicating a difference between left-brain knowing by thinking and right-brain knowing by awareness. In clinical practice, it is not uncommon to hear women complain about male significant others' lack of understanding. This common complaint derives, in part, from the fact that women have a greater tendency than men to rely on the right sides of their brains for knowingness. One might well say that the right side is the sensitive side of the brain; where insight, perception, and the like are processed; in contrast to the logical left side of the brain; where calculation, reasoning, and the like are processed.

The matter of knowing ultimate reality, then, is complicated by this societal preponderance of left-brainedness. The more adept we become at flexibly processing information, exercising both the left and right hemispheres of our brains, the better we are able to perceive in holistic terms. The brain activity of some individuals has been found to be diffuse and nonspecific, fostering a greater degree of flexibility, although this is the infrequent case. Given that we cannot truly know a thing unless we experience it ourselves, cultural left-brainedness can be seen to impede holistic comprehension. In this, it is a reflection of the attentional eccentricity of our age. For this reason, while there are many church-goers and religious followers, few are currently able to experience spiritual reality. This preponderance of left-brainedness may explain why so many persons are depressed in response to current life conditions, as opposed to feeling hopeless. In prior ages, the reverse was true; right-brainedness was favored, resulting in a flourishing of masterful artistry that is historically unparalleled; it was the era of the grand masters. It is not surprising that the era of cultural right-brainedness was also a time when religious experiences were prevalent, more readily accepted, and more readily understood. To compensate for this lack of right-brain development in this cultural era of left-brainedness, requires exercise; in the same way that one must physically stretch, taut, or otherwise utilize one's muscles in order to tone them, one must exercise one's receptive right-brain capacity in order to develop it. For this reason, contemplation, meditation, creative activities, art and music appreciation serve as developmental counterbalances to left-brainedness.

In testament to the human capacity for faith; believing and trusting; human history records the persistent awareness of and belief in the existence of an ultimate, more often than not unperceived, reality, and the knowledge that experience of it is possible. Documented experiencers have conveyed that the experience is not accessible in the usual manner of learning or studying a thing, but is rather achieved through an alteration of inner being such that the divine essence within the soul, which is pure spirit; that is, timeless, bodiless, Godlike; is inspired and liberated. Shankara states that liberation cannot be achieved except by the perception of the identity of the individual spirit with the universal spirit. It cannot be achieved by the physical training of Yoga, by the speculative philosophy of Sankhya, by the practice of religious ceremonies, or by mere learning.[279]

Accordingly, in order to get in touch with universal spirit, one must alter one's inner being, allowing the spirit source to recognize one's individual spirit; freeing it to extend more fully within oneself. In the process of this manifesting, one experiences more fully the connection between the individual and the universal spirit. One becomes more actively connected to the world of universal reality, and one becomes more amenable to being affected by it.

Shankara states that it is because we do not know who we are, because we are unaware that the kingdom of

---

[279] Ibid, p. 6.

heaven is within us, that we behave in the generally silly, the often insane, and the sometimes criminal ways that are so characteristically human. In his estimation, we are saved, liberated, and enlightened by perceiving the hitherto unperceived good that is already within us, by returning to our eternal ground, and by remaining where we have always been without knowing it. It is a curiosity that, much like the lack of human knowingness of the answers to the eternal questions about who we are and where we come from, that we are so relatively unaware of our own capacities of soul.

Shankara refers to Plato; where, in his treatise, the *Republic*, he states that the virtue of wisdom more than anything else contains a divine element which always remains; and where, in his treatise, Theaetetus, he makes the point that it is only by becoming Godlike that we can know God, that to become Godlike is to identify ourselves with the divine element which in fact constitutes our essential nature, but of which in our voluntary ignorance we choose to remain unaware.[280] Plato's assessment that our ignorance is voluntary speaks to an unexplained tendency; man's persistence in ignoring his own true nature. One may well wonder why this is so. The reasons are numerous; from knowledge of God's denial of Job and other such castigations of Man by God in antiquity, which would suggest the avoidance is due to a fear of God's reprisal. We already know of the reason of difficulty with achievement; many desiring persons find it difficult to accomplish. We further know of the reason of cultural distraction; so many are immersed in the ways of the world that the ways of the spirit do not beckon. We now know of the reason of left-brainedness; the prevailing preference for scientific versus spiritual knowledge, and the effects of this preference upon human development. We find that the reasons are many and overlapping; posing the moral dilemma that in order to truly know oneself the individual must choose a different fate.

---

[280] Ibid., pp. 14-5.

In reflecting upon the human condition, we find a considerable tendency of choosing to steer a course that is not consistent with humanity's true nature. This context makes such extent realities as human genetic decoding comprehensible. In the name of science, from the skewed perspective of left-brainedness, modern man, in attempting to eradicate disease is creating the possibility of his own destruction through genetic manipulation. The caveat that derives from historical hindsight is the potential for destructive extremism; such was the case during the era in which the skewed perspective of right-brainedness resulted in censorship and the banning and burning of books; many learned and scholarly works were lost to the cultural milieu of intolerance for what was not notably right-brain oriented. The potential for left-brain oriented extremism similarly exists in the current era. One may well wonder what the world would be like if, in the future, man ever becomes more brain balanced.

It is remarkable that, in light of the fact that knowledge of the human soul's potential for transformational experience has existed for *more than twenty-five centuries,* the potential has not been more extensively actuated. To appreciate the historical significance of this fact regarding human spiritual attainment, consider it in the context of Huxley's discussion of the evolution of human consciousness. Huxley states: *human minds have proved themselves capable of everything from imbecility to Quantum Theory, from Mein Kampf and sadism to the sanctity of Philip Neri, from metaphysics to crossword puzzles, power politics and the Missa Solemnis.* According to Huxley, there is good reason to suppose that there have been no considerable changes in the size and conformation of human brains for a good many thousands of years. Therefore, he concludes, that human minds in the remote past were capable of as many and as various kinds and degrees of activity as are minds at the present time. Following Huxley's reasoning, given that the biological

233

thinking apparatus of man has remained essentially unchanged over the course of millennia, differences in human consciousness and thought across human history must be attributable to something other than evolution.

Analyzing differences in human cognitions, past and present, Huxley proffers the following explanations. In part, he says, they are due to absence in the past of appropriate language and the framework of an appropriate system of classification, which rendered some present-day thoughts inconceivable, and thereby, inexpressible. In additional part, he says they are due to the absence of incentives to develop the instruments or invent the means for certain kinds of thinking to occur. According to Huxley, throughout prehistory and history, there are long periods during which people don't pay attention to problems or matters that their predecessors considered interesting, despite their capability of doing so. Thus, during the time period of the 13th to the 20th centuries, man turned his attention from certain aspects of reality to certain other aspects, and developed the natural sciences. This attentional shift was predominantly away from religion and towards science, as explanatory frameworks for comprehending the world and individual life experience.

It is, according to Huxley's line of reasoning, our will that is the primary impetus for shifts in thinking over time. He states that, our perceptions and our understanding are directed, in large measure, by our will; we are aware of and think about those things which, for whatever reason, we want to see and understand. That, *where there's a will there is always an intellectual way*.[281] The reader may take note of the parallels between Huxley's 1,945 C.E. remark, Marshall McLuhan's statement regarding the capacity for thought to transcend circumstance, and the adage, *Where there's a will, there's a way*. The influence of Huxley's percept upon intellectual thought is undeniable. We find that the factor

---

[281] Ibid., pp. 16-7.

of human will is relevant to an holistic consideration of the context of spirit.

Reality, like a diamond, is multi-faceted. Each facet provides a partial view of the gestalt, or totality, of all reality. Thus, at any given point in time and history, man tends to perceive reality from the perspective of facets that represent certain, but not all, aspects. These facets serve as windows unto the world for man's perception. There exists a tendency for man's attention to be differentially attracted; at any given moment in time, the facets of the diamond of reality, with their capacities to refract and reflect light, attract our attention; upon these lights of thought we then focus. As in the case of diamonds; whereby perception of light reflecting capability requires movement, a shifting of the diamond to enhance visibility of its reflectivity; thereby providing a more complete appreciation of its subtle complexity; so too, might we view the nature of all reality. Without movement to shift our focus across aspects, we remain focused upon one or another, delimiting our perception of the totality.

We find that the matter of spiritualization is affected by a number of factors; including language capable of its expression, perceptual receptivity, translation of experience, prevailing interest, and human willingness. The 20th century witnessed a new era in the history of human consciousness; a willingness to accept as scientific the perspective of extrasensory perception, sparked by Russian interest in researching the phenomena. This willingness created opportunities for focusing awareness on areas previously ignored; inspiring a revisiting of prior knowledge while opening vistas that provided increased comprehension and insight. While the willingness continues to exist, the willing are relatively innumerous, particularly among the academic, where funding sources now tend to be tied to the practical and the applied, as opposed to the exploratory and the esoteric. Despite this trend, with regard to where we are in terms of such knowledge, humanity is in a learning phase; riding on the wave of the statistical S-curve that represents the stages of learning. When one considers the context of what is known, we find that much of what is known began with first, unexpected, and unusual encounters that led to more systematic exploration of the phenomena. In this, they may aptly be regarded as frontiers of human awareness. So derived a number of diverse, yet similarly esoteric knowledges; knowledge such as the existence of extraterrestrial life forms, knowledge that human beings and alien beings have interacted, knowledge that human beings have been abducted by alien beings, knowledge that there are multiple dimensions of existence, among many others.

The fairly recent acquisition of such knowledge spurred renewed interest in matters of religion and spirituality. The adage, *It put the fear of God into me*, addresses the experience of bewilderment that accompanied such realization. More than at any other known time in human history, the reality of alien presence during the 20th century significantly impacted human consciousness; generating new questions and reconsiderations of old answers to the eternal questions of who we are, where we came from, and where we are going. The newly added question of How do aliens fit into the picture? generated a variety of considerations; some thoughtful, some hysterical, some concerned with the implications for defense of the planet, some concerned with the implications for religion; Where is God? What did he think about alien visitations? Was God an alien? For such considerations to have occurred indicated a high degree of startled human awareness.

The unexpected impetus of alien phenomena led to a reconsideration of the polarized roles of science and religion. Science began to explore religion in earnest; if alien beings could exist when none had been anticipated, then, science reasoned, so could angels, demons, and other unusual forms of life previously considered the realm of religious experience. The presence of alien life forms on the planet had the impact of a rude awakening; *We are not alone* was the message that shockingly transmitted. The implications are mind-boggling; a challenge to our limited understanding of where and how we fit into the scheme of life. In addition to our incapacity to answer the first set of eternal questions pertaining to our planet of birth, we now faced a second set of eternal questions pertaining to the cosmos of existence. Suddenly, we faced the realization that we didn't know much about origins; it was a humbling experience for all.

Accompanying this expansion of extraordinary knowledge, was a dawning comprehension of the necessity for further developing the capacity for spiritualization as a prelude to organismic and cosmic growth. As new learning melded with old, we acquired a deeper, more profound understanding of the essential nature of life; perceiving more clearly the vital role of the spirit in facilitating access to other aspects and realms of reality; and to comprehending them. The immaterial facet of soul; that aspect with which contact with spirit occurs, has acquired new relevance.

It is interesting to note that, since the 1990s, when, all around the planet, experiences with aliens occupied the mainstream of conscious thought, in a matter of a decade, people have become otherwise distracted. While some may continue to ponder the pertinent questions, most of us have relegated such thoughts to the back burner of consideration; presuming the danger is past, since we no longer hear about persons being abducted. The same sort of response occurred following the first official announcement of alien encounter in the 1930s. The human response to such intermittent phenomena indicates a homing of attention; an attentional redirectioning that attends and then redirects to the lastest news. We find that, while the reality of alien phenomena has been integrated in human consciousness, it is not at the forefront of conscious thought.

With regard to the relationship between humanity and the future, with greater awareness that the realm of the soul, the dimension of the supernatural, and the reality of the alien pertain to the lifescape of the future, what we face is the need for a greater individuality. That is, the development of self and the actualization of spirit; given the reality that the processes involved in eventuation are person specific. The factor of human will is relevant to such actuation.

With regard to the relationship between science and religion, we find that the historic shift in focus; focus being that orientation held in the popular mind; from religion to natural sciences; natural science being that knowledge concerned with the physical world and its phenomena; fostered a perception of dichotomy; that science and religion are antithetical and incompatible, a perception which predominates. A prime example of this is the unresolved difference in perspective regarding creation; attributed by science to the big bang and evolutionary process, attributed by religion to God and creationism. The fact that such incongruity exists and persists speaks to what Kurtz and Ketcham referred to as the paradoxical human nature; indeed, many persons believe that both attributions are relevant.

We find that humanity generally has a high degree of tolerance for its own paradoxical and contradictory nature. An holistic consideration of the human nature is highly relevant to understanding the confused and confusing picture of human society. When one considers the extensiveness of human contradiction, one might venture to say that people are walking contradictions. This reality of contradictory nature speaks to the human imperfection. Life is replete with examples; from the preacher who believes that brotherly love and taking advantage of his followers are compatible, to the politician who believes that exposing his opponent and accepting questionable support for doing so are compatible, to the media pundit who believes that freedom of speech and violating privacy are compatible, to the nobel prize contestant who believes that winning a prize and taking credit for someone else's accomplishment are compatible. Such paradox of contradictory nature has been the hallmark of humanity; it has served to harrass, to haunt, and to hound mankind from the beginning. Whether human tolerance for its own paradoxical nature derives from human nature itself or from human awareness of human limitations is unclear.

In the wake of the shift from religion to science, beginning with anatomy and natural science, matters of scientific interest took the forefront in the human mind and imagination. The devaluation of the religious solution in recent history; as the means by which to answer the as yet unanswerable; speaks to the human preoccupation with answers. Science captured the forefront of our collective attentions as a possible solution. This shift, like the shift to religion previous to it, led to the paradoxical development of good and bad science. Good science focused on improving life and longevity, bad science focused on exploiting life and disease. Were it not for the existence of bad science, our knowledge of biowarfare would be limited to an understanding of microscopics; the study of those entities that engage in activity at a microscopic level; as is the case with lymphocytes; the cellular mediators of immunity; B-cells and T-cells; in order to prevent disease and fight infection. Such knowledge would never have been applied as a weapon of warfare. At the same time that exploratory anatomy and surgery provided new comprehensions of the body for use in saving lives, it also provided knowledge for use in what has been termed *mad science*; hence, historic attempts to artificially replicate life; through the animation of dead bodies, as portrayed in the story of Frankenstein. Such application followed from the discovery of electricity, and efforts to apply animating principles to the deceased. From its early mad scientist beginnings, the knowledge has led to modern means of resuscitation by electric shock; as is done in cases of cardiac arrest and severe brain-behavior abnormality. The current dilemma of medicine is the push-pull between the good and bad science of genetic decoding and the cloning of species; with outcome unknown.

Like the dawn of a new day, poised at the beginning of a new millennium, we bear witness as scientific and spiritual comprehensions coalesce, expand, and transform our consciousness of who and what we, our world, and the cosmos really are, in the universe of all possible realms and dimensions of existence.

Matthew Fox, a theologian, and Rupert Sheldrake, a biologist, report that after centuries of divergence, the worlds of science and spirituality are recognizing a new creation story.[282] According to Fox and Sheldrake, the passages of St. Thomas Aquinas in *Summa Theologica*; where Aquinas states that *when an angel moves, it leaves one place, and it appears in another,* and that such movement can only be detected through its action; is identical to the actions of quantum particles, as defined by the physics of quantum theory. Quantums, according to Webster's, are very small increments or parcels into which many forms of energy are subdivided.[283] And quantum theory in physics is based on the concept of the subdivision of radiant energy from finite quanta, which is applied to numerous processes involving transference, or transformation of energy in an atomic or molecular scale.[284]

In between movements, say Fox and Sheldrake, the angels and the photon quantum particles, are in a timeless state. Einstein is credited with the discovery of the timelessness of the photon, which is a quantum of radiant energy.[285] Einstein may have been familiar with the works of St. Thomas Aquinas and his belief in angel travel; travels

---

[282] Scheinin, Richard, "Science and spirituality", *Houston Chronicle*, January 6, 1996, 1E and 3E.

[283] Webster's New Collegiate Dictionary, p. 937.

[284] Ibid.

[285] Ibid., p. 857.

in timeless immortality. We find from the science of physics that undetectable movement is a matter of transitioning between states of existence; between the mortal and the immortal, the timeful and the timeless; and that such is the action of angels and quantums.

In July 1,996 C.E., upon completing the first version of this book, I underwent hypnosis, and mind-traveled to the state of timelessness. My exact words of comment during the experience were, "It's utter chaos". In the process of revising, I decided to include my experience, and looked up the dictionary definition of the word chaos. The first definition is *chasm, abyss.* The second is *a state of things in which chance is supreme; especially, the confused unorganized state of primordial matter before the creation of distinct forms.* The third is *a state of utter confusion.*[286] Apparently, while under hypnosis, I accessed the state of timelessness. I find it interesting that my description under hypnosis is consistent with a dictionary definition of primordial matter, the unmanifest matter of creation; the creative potential that exists in the universe. I also find it interesting that my description is redundant; given that chaos is defined as a state of utter confusion, and I referred to it as utter chaos; indicating a strong impression regarding the chaotic nature of the timeless state. It is relevant to note that at the time of the experience, I was comfortably relaxed; I had no physical or emotional reaction to the witnessing, I was simply cognizant of it; indicating the experience was one of pure consciousness. Given my own experience and what is known about the primordial, if Fox and Sheldrake are correct, and angels have indeed traveled in this manner, it is a wonder that they are able to do so; the experience, traveling unscathed through a state of perpetual motion with the constant potential for being bombarded by primordial matter, is unusual to say the least, and would require supernatural capacities of survival.

---

[286] Ibid., p. 184.

What the fundamentalists Lee and Nee have stated, that God has difficulty finding us; this they inferred from the biblically reported question posed to Adam by God after the committing of the first sin; *Where art thou?*[287] which Lee and Nee attributed to Man's distancing himself from God through sin; is relevant to our consideration. Reflecting upon the biblical report to which Lee and Nee have called our attention, we may consider their belief, derived from the biblical record: *Therefore the Lord God sent him forth from the garden of Eden, to till the ground from whence he was taken*, as an explanation for the barrier between mortality and immortality; the garden of Eden representing paradise on earth, relegated exclusively for immortal beingness after the failures of Adam and Eve. The bible also states: *And the Lord God planted a garden eastward in Eden; and there he put the man whom he had formed*[288], implying that man was incapable of entering the garden God created of his own volition. In these passages of Genesis, one finds reported barriers of two types; the barrier of God at a distance, calling to Adam without seeing him, and the barrier of the garden paradise, unaccessible to man after his fall from God's good graces.

When one further considers the biblical passages of Genesis: *And God made the firmament, and divided the waters which were under the firmament from the waters which were above the firmament: and it was so (1:7); And God called the firmament Heaven. And the evening and the morning were the second day* (1:8), one may well wonder wherein exists the firmament of Heaven, since it is not visible or discoverable by humankind. One may well presume that God's calling unto man was done from the separate firmament of Heaven, of which little is known. From the perspective of modern science, one may postulate that such firmament constitutes a separate dimension of existence.

---

[287] Lee and Nee, p. 22; Genesis 3:9.

[288] Genesis 2:8.

The matter of distance; evidenced by God's communications from afar, and God's location in a different place in time and space, supports the notion that angels and other immortal beings must traverse a barrier of some kind in order to appear to mortal beingness. Consideration of this fact lends credence to the notion that immortals have the capacity to traverse time and space in a manner inconsistent with and superior to mortals. One may wonder whether the creative field of primordial matter constitutes a form of invisible barrier between heaven and earth; although this is not its purpose, its purpose being one of providing sustenance for creation.

Fox and Sheldrake contend that scientists are turning into awestruck mystics as they plumb the expanding universe and the subatomic world, stating that a new cosmology is unfolding that recognizes the mystery of creation and God's presence in it. As they see it, the findings of quantum physics represent the vacuum state from which the Godhead underlies creation; such that the traditional notion of soul is now scientifically being established as the field of animating force that gives order to creation.[289] We find from this 1,996 C.E. report an interesting feature; an example of the persistent difficulty with language usage pertaining to spiritual phenomena to adequately convey meaning; in its attributing to *soul* what we have found to be the nature of *spirit*. Such interchanges in usage of terminology may be confusing. The report serves as a powerful example of the way in which two divergent knowledges; the knowledge of religion and the knowledge of science; have coalesced through the medium of a relatively new science, into a newly found comprehension; adding scientific credence to religious belief.

The holistic concept of mind and body has achieved a place of recognized acceptance in prevalent thought after a period of 2,500 or so years since it was expounded by Socrates. We may well appreciate the duration of time

---

[289] Scheinin, p. 1E.

that has passed before it gained a general acceptance. Galileo's notion that the earth was round and not flat, as presumed in his time, was more readily discoverable, and became accepted after a far shorter time period. It is quite remarkable that it has taken humanity 2,500 years to accept as true something that was known so long ago. One may similarly remark about the relatively recent support from science for the religious belief in creationism. One may hope that acceptance of the holistically heartful concept of spirit/mind/body will take less time.

With respect to addiction, it is the soul; that aspect of the individual capable of becoming enspirited which is most in need of attention. Spirit is a constant; eternally available to those who seek it. Soul is an inconstant; with potentials for existence at varying degrees of development. We have found that soul has the capacity of attuning to and attending to spirit, and becoming affected by it. In this respect, spirit and soul may be considered creative elements; they have considerable capacity to alter the course of human lives. Among substance abusers, addicts, and others easily and customarily distracted by the inconsequentials of life, this is the realm; the realm of the spiritual; where intervention is most beneficial.

In this day and age of increasing uniformity, we may consider the relevance of heeding the differences inherent in marginalization; as has historically been the case with substance abusers; in so doing we might catch a glimpse, in the reflection, of aspects of our own humanity; enhancing our holistic perception of the truth of who we are. The ages-old adage, *There but for the grace of God go I*, reflects the graceful recognition of fortuitous intervention in one's life unshared by another. Such attitude comprehends the human vulnerability without discomfiture or indifference. Given that vulnerability is a prerequisite for affectability, and therefore, for genuineness of experience, we may presuppose the potential for those affected by addiction to overcome it, with the aid of spiritful soul.

CHAPTER FOURTEEN

The Holistic Perception of Society

In considering the reality of spirit, having discussed its role in the lives of human beings and the reality of spiritual existence, we turn our attention to the matter of spirit in society. At the level of quantum awareness, we will find that vibrational energies transmit and receive. Further, that at an unconscious level, we automatically process and respond to the transmissions. In this manner, it is known that we transmit telepathic signals of which we are only semi-consciously aware.

This speaks to the reality of affectability; the fact that persons encounter other persons with whom they may or may not get along. One may recall the expression describing the instant affinity of one person for another that, *It was chemistry*; as if biochemistry were the reason for *love at first sight*. In reality, what we find is that it is rather a matter of spirit; of an unrecognized compatibility based upon an unseen and typically unknown telepathic transmission. Without observing it, we automatically transmit, one to another, an unseen communication of who we are and receive an unseen communication about the other.

It is relevant to consider that this is the manner in which much of what is termed natural communication occurs; we have discussed that such is the nature of sound, and we know from entomology that such is the nature of insect communications; life communicates with energy. Life is apparently vested with such capacities of utilizing the physical world for survival-enhancing communication. The reality of man's greater consciousness indicates that such conveyance of communication processes will convey more conscious communications; the processes themselves, at all levels of life, are undeniably sophisticated.

It has further been demonstrated that what I will call energetics; the capacity of communication through energy; is not limited to communications between living beings, but also occurs between the living and the deceased. Examples of this, are the energetic transmissions of ghostly phenomena; which are said to function as energetic remnants of the past; a form of energy signature residing in a realm of time and space not quite our own. Such energies are capable of communicating in the same vibrational manner as when their embodiments were alive. We have found that persons may be more or less affectable by such transmissions; the capacity for such receptivity varying across individuals. From this we find that the individual may persist in residence, even with the departure of the body; constituting an energetic manifestation of the soul that is eternal unless it chooses to depart.

According to Hans Holzer, the majority of ghostly manifestations draw upon energy from the living in order to penetrate our three-dimensional world. Ghosts, reports Holzer, are different from spirits in that ghosts are like psychotic human beings, unable to reason for themselves or take much action; whereas, spirits are capable of continuing a full existence in the next dimension, and can therefore, think, reason, feel, and act.[290] From parapsychology, we learn that ghosts and spirits are energetic beings with differing

---

[290] Holzer, Hans. *Ghosts: True Encounters With The World Beyond.* Black Dog & Levanthal Publishers, Inc.: New York, 1997, p. 25.

capacities for affecting the dimensional reality of everyday existence. Holzer credits Albert Einstein's discovery that energy never dissipates, it only transmutes into other forms as the explanation for *the electromagnetic fields uniquely impressed by the personality and memories of the departed one*, in the manifestations we call ghostly phenomena.[291] The energetic realities of ghosts and spirits have been explained by science; the corroboration supports the notion that spirit is communicative.

A further indication of the communicativeness of spirit is provided by experiences pertaining to telepathy. John Hick, in *Philosophy of Religion*, offers a tentative explanation for the process of mental telepathy. He reports that one theory has tentatively suggested that our minds are separate and mutually insulated only at the conscious and preconscious levels of awareness, but that at the deepest level of the unconscious we are constantly influencing one another, and it is at this level that telepathy takes place.[292]

Consciously, pulses of information register in the form of hunches, intuitions, dreams, and gut feelings. Michael Murphy writes that what happens would be better described by saying that the sender's thought gives rise to a mental echo in the mind of the receiver. That this echo occurs at the unconscious level, and consequently the version of it that rises into the receiver's consciousness may be only fragmentary and may be distorted or symbolized in various ways, as in dreams.[293]

According to Lynn Allison in *How To Talk To Your Cat*, cats are clairvoyant; the only animal species besides man that are capable of psychic communication.[294] Allison states

---

[291] Holzer, Hans, p. 26.

[292] Hick, p. 127.

[293] Murphy, p. 259.

[294] Allison, Lynn. *How To Talk To Your Cat: And get it to do what YOU want.* Globe Communications Corporation: Boca Raton, Florida, USA, 1993.

that we owe a debt of gratitude to the ancient Egyptians for their recognition of cats' special abilities, which, according to Allison, have been scientifically documented. She cites experimental psychologist, David Greene, who states: *Whether it's an alley cat or a prize-winning Persian, any cat can perform absolutely astonishing mental, physical and extrasensory feats.*[295] Greene has chronicled cat case histories that include *predicting natural disasters long before they happen; saving people and other animals from death or injury; tracking owners over incredible distances; and carrying out complex tasks with superhuman intellect.*[296]

Dr. Michael Fox, scientific director of the U.S. Humane Society in Washington, D.C., has collected, according to Allison, *hundreds of examples of the astonishing intuitive ability of cats to read the moods and feelings of their owners. And there are volumes of evidence that cats possess remarkable powers.*[297]

Given what we know about the unconscious nature of the telepathic communication between animals, we are able to regard intuition with a new-found respect. Intuition is defined by Merriam-Webster as *quick and ready insight.*[298] Such insight in the form of intuition may reflect a form of telepathic communication; with others, with soul, and/or with spirit. If one considers, particularly in this day and age of left-brainedness, the tendency to discount or ignore one's intuitions, one becomes aware of a propensity to close an available avenue of awareness. Closing oneself to the possibilities of insight renders one less able to know in the holistic sense. When one considers that just as many of the significant discoveries of science have been due to insight as they have to accident, the relevance of intuition becomes

---

[295] Allison, Lynn. *How To Talk To Your Cat: And get it to do what YOU want*, p. 87.

[296] Ibid., p. 87.

[297] Ibid., p. 87.

[298] Merriam-Webster, Incorporated, p. 614.

clear. In the personal sense, insight may serve as a guide to the individual; steering one away from a decision and/or situation that may not be suitable, even when the outward indicators say that it is.

Failure to ascribe credibility and meaning to intuitive sources of knowledge hampers human awareness by interfering with a vital source of knowledge relevant to human existence. The criticism raised by women that patriarchy has suppressed and at times, oppressed, is, in this regard, justified; patriarchy being defined as, social organization marked by the supremacy of the father in the clan or family, and broadly as, control by men of a disproportionately large share of power. [299] Patriarchal bias against intuition; what has come to be regarded, in the dichotomous thinking that has developed regarding what is male and what is female as women's ways of knowing; has, at various points in time, discounted intuition as a dubious and inferior way of knowing. Women have struggled against this prejudice; defined as adverse opinion without just grounds or before sufficient knowledge; to assert the place of the intuitive in consciousness; while patriarchy has struggled against women's intuition shaping the thinking of the day. Such attitudes, like attitudes towards addiction, have waxed and waned throughout the course of human history. Science, in modern times, by substantiating the validity of intuition, has altered the course of human perception.

Over the course of time; the 2,000+ years since the beginning of recorded history; prejudice has had considerable impact upon thinking. The historic arguments; of which scientific versus religious argumentation over how the world was created, rational versus intuitive argumentation over valid ways of knowing are a part; speak to the reality of man's ignorance and tenacities of belief; the truths that we believe more than we, at any given point in time, are able to know, and beliefs that are often persistent and discordant;

---

[299] Merriam-Webster, Incorporated, p. 850.

such truths being evident in the recorded discourses and arguments of history.

We may see from these truths about variable human ignorance, belief, and prejudice, how processes of selective attention and inattention have played a significant role in the shaping of human thought and consciousness. As Aldous Huxley so insightfully informed us, we are aware of the things which we want to see and understand. From this perspective, we may more fully comprehend the impact of biblical records; their prominence in human consciousness throughout the ages; as a testament of prophecy relevant to the human future. They persist because we are cognizant of our own ignorance; the records of prophecy provide us with a portend of the future; we selectively attend to their potential because of their relevance to our existence; in this, they constitute, above and beyond an historic record, the transmittal through time of a prophetic communication. We find that the human will is strongest when the matter pertains to the futurity of humanity.

Having considered spirit in society; its manifest in consciousness, intuition, and will, we turn our attention to the holistic perception of society with regards to the spirit/ mind/body phenomenon of addiction. Comprehending the light-extinguishing impact of our inattention to what don't want to see or understand enables us to better comprehend addiction in the context of culture. Society, as a general rule, is adept at ignoring what it wishes would go away; historically, these have included corruption, insanity, poverty, and to some extent, addiction. Given our theme of addiction, we will continue to weave through philosophical considerations which foster a more holistic comprehension, and consider those pertinent aspects of society that we wish would go away that are relevant to our understanding.

There is a particular dynamic; an interactional style of relating; that exists pertinent to perpetrators of abuse and their victims; wherein, the perpetrator places the blame upon the victim as the source cause of the problem, without which the instance of abuse would not have occurred; and wherein, the victim of the abuse, regardless of expressed accusations and anger at each instance of abuse, fundamentally blames her- or himself as the accountable party, with a tendency to repeatedly excuse and forgive the perpetrator, in light of this belief. We may see this dynamic unfold in instances of child abuse, sexual abuse, and spousal abuse; wherein, the child, partner, or spouse believe they are largely to blame.

In truth, the dynamic, a psychological form of hostaging, holds both perpetrators and victims in a kind of perpetual boxing match from which there seems to be no escape. The perspective of those hostaged by the dynamic tends to be one of, who, outside of them, would understand? When aid is sought, it is often sought for the purpose of either blame or revenge, unless forced by law or trauma, rather than for an end to the dynamic; which is more frightening to the parties than the dynamic itself. Having originated in early childhood, the dynamic, for those to whom it applies, constitutes the way of the world. That this dynamic exists to the extent it does is testament to the revolving door phenomenon of faulty parenting. With respect to society's perceptions of responsibility; these have varied at different points in time, tending towards a distorted and skewed perspective of the phenomenon; in favor of the victimizer, as was the case when women and children were considered to be the property of their fathers and husbands, or in favor of the victim, as has been the more recent case since women's emancipation. The reality of the folles au deux; that the folly is inherent in the pairing; is born of impressionable childhood. Such is the nature of many relationship dynamics; some benign, some destructive; including that of the addict and the codependent. Since women's emancipation, it has tended to be the victim who bears the burden of social responsibility for the problem; considered to be primarily a woman's and a children's problem, although this is not exclusively the case. The burden of seeking professional and/or legal help, the burden of paying for such help, the burden of proof in prosecution, the burden of scrutiny with regards to the help-seeker's psychological functioning, and, if they have children, parental functioning. Through intuition and reason, we may come to discern a general inequity or unfairness in the situation, as though God has chosen to play a dirty trick upon the pair; locking them into positions of difficult to escape burdensomeness.

From a different perspective of spirit; that of the Tao, defined as the unconditional and unknowable source and guiding principle of all reality;[300] which practice derives from the mystical philosophy of 6th century China, wherein harmony is believed achievable through unassertive action and simplicity; with respect to the spirit/mind/body phenomenon of addiction, we become aware that substance abusers and addicts, and generally-speaking, the consumers of addictive culture, tend to be similarly burdened. We perceive that the reality of addiction is skewed towards the complicated, and that actions taken to alleviate it tend towards the unsuccessful. On an intuitive level, we may appreciate the impact of this skewed relationship, and sense its import for our culture, given that the reality of culture is yet more complicated than that of addiction.

From a practical perspective, one may consider that alternative approaches may provide benefit; as is the case with the problem of mind-blocking. That is, when the mind is blocked from finding a solution, an alternative approach may be indicated. A familiar example of this is the well-described case of writer's block, wherein a writer experiences a form of mental freezing; an arresting of creative thinking and reasoning processes; that interferes with a particular piece of work. The advised solution involves a change of perspective; taking a break in order to take one's mind off the problem, engaging in alternative activities, et cetera.

---

[300] Merriam-Webster, Incorporated, p. 1201.

Given the entrenched nature of the problem of addiction, in consideration of the advice given in cases of mind-blocking, and awareness of the spirit as experienced through taoism, we encounter the possibility that benefit may derive from the adoption of a less assertive, less complicated approach to the matter.

We know that the experience of addiction is complicated. We know that responses to addiction are complicated. And we know that the environment of culture is a complication. In the midst of all the complicatedness, the action of uncomplicating one's life experience may serve to alter the reality.

There are many possible ways of responding to this awareness. We may, for example, stop blaming the victims of addiction; as a partial remedy to lessen the role of culture in perpetuating the cycle of abuse. We have learned that to do the opposite is not effective. While society holds substance abusers responsible for using substances, it tends to ignore the reality that we share responsibility for the fact that culture promotes consumption and consumptive addiction. Blame serves the purpose of pointing to the so-called guilty party; as in, *It's your fault.* Given the lengthy legal history of humankind, one may rightly conclude there is a human propensity to point the finger in accusation. While codes of law originated out of a perceived necessity for the maintenance of orderliness in society, the fact of their existence rendered them instruments for committing injustice. There is irony in this human paradox; that to deter and punish wrong-doing, we established a means by which wrong-doing could be legally committed.

Guilty verdicts constitute a form of judgment, and thereby, of blame. In the legal sense, such judgment is deemed appropriate for the maintenance of social order. In the social sense, there is disagreement regarding the appropriateness of rendering judgment. The rendering of judgments about others, on a social basis, has become common practice;

perhaps, in imitation of legal practice. Gossip about members of society is a mainstay of media communications; who did what to whom and when and why and how, et cetera. While celebrity status renders such gossip public, it reflects the nonpublic societal norm; gossip about friends, neighbors, spouses, et cetera. When gossip becomes judgmental, which it frequently does, it conveys a sense of blame. The historic societal tendency towards blaming, and at times, shaming, is not helpful with respect to addiction; indeed, it is a common problem of relationships in general; therefore, while we are cognizant of its relevance, we find that such approach is not a fruitful one. Uncomplicating life may, in this regard, involve disengaging from processes of blaming and shaming.

Beyond this, simplification may involve taking stock of ourselves and our lives. Like the personal inventory required of alcoholics and other addicts who participate in the Alcoholics and/or Narcotics Anonymous treatment programs, we may elect to assess, in a personally relevant way, the manners in which we are unthinkingly affected and unthinkingly affect; this pertains to personal life experiences as it interacts with family and significant others and as it interacts with society. Conducting a personal self-inventory of this kind, like reading a book, is an unassertive behavior, which has the potential to yield new insights; as such it is in keeping with the adopting of a new approach, in this case, one consistent with spirit; an exploration that invites spirit into one's life.

From such exploration, one may find that spirit attracts one's attention in a new direction, perhaps even a direction that is inconsistent with one's current manner of living. The caveat in exploring spirit is that one is well-advised to be aware that inviting spirit into one's life has the potential to result in life-changing impacts, for which one may or may not be prepared. Once spirit has touched us in this manner, there is no going back; we become affected in the process. While spirit in and of itself is not harmful, and allowing oneself to be affected by it is not directly dangerous, it may prove unsettling with regard to the outside world; others, particularly others to whom we are close, may not understand the change that has taken place, and may or may not respond favorably to it. In this regard, relationships may become affected.

To become enspirited is to unassertively allow the all-knowingness of life to affect one's relation to life, and in this manner, to guide without giving directions. This is the true meaning of the Christian notion of *Ask and you shall receive*; the materialistic view of asking God to bestow one with favors is not the correct view of the nature of spirit; rather, it represents the inviting or asking of spirit to enter one's life, and thereby, receiving its affect. One never knows in advance of such affect, how one will be affected, and it is for this reason that caution is stated.

A prime example of spirit in action, is what sometimes occurs in mid-life and is referred to as mid-life crisis; wherein a person arrives at a point in time and place when life ceases to satisfy, and they begin to explore the reasons for the dissatisfaction. From a societal perspective, the circumstances of the individual experiencing a mid-life crisis are neutral rather than negative; many have accomplished goals they intended, yet arrive at a point where they find that something is missing. At this point of reckoning, spirit is nudging for attention. If attended, it will enable the individual to address the need for something else in life. Spirit has the capacity to provide us with the nudge and the guidance; we may choose to ignore its efforts to affect us, or we may elect to allow the affecting process to begin; the decision is ours.

If we find, in experiencing spirit, that the consumptive nature of society is detrimental to us personally, we may make changes in the way that we live our lives. When life ceases to feel as if one is living for oneself, and begins to feel as if one has no control over one's life, this is an indication

निम

of the absence of guiding spirit. Recognizing the relevance of this experience, we may seek help from the source of life itself, and thereby, reorient in a manner consistent with who we really are.

The reader will recall John Carmody having raised the matter of peacefulness of soul; the need for the individual experiencing trouble to seek peace of mind. If one reflects upon the reality of society, one finds that life is generally not peaceful. The hustle and bustle of life; the noises, activities, and interruptions; given that life is generally crowded with people, is not conducive to finding peace of soul. It follows from this, therefore, that persons are challenged to seek personal means of remedy in times of need. This too, constitutes a form of uncomplicating one's life, mayhap temporarily, on an as needed basis. People who have experienced a troubling of the soul within the context of such conditions of interference understand the reason why so many persons go on retreats, take vacations, or spend time alone; for respite.

In keeping with this perspective of the tao, we may consider another aspect of society that we wish would go away; the phenomenon of missing persons. Exactly how long the matter of missing persons has existed is unknown; over the past decades, there has been a growing awareness of the phenomenon. When its occurrence reached a point of significance, it gained attention as a phenomenon in its own right, rather than as a corollary statistic of crime. It became understood, with an increase and regularity of prevalence, that something else was going on.

Initially, it was discovered that there were persons who went missing in order to escape the law; this was found to be true in some instances of contentious child custody, wherein, one or the other of the parents of a child or children would "disappear" in order to avoid the mandate of law that granted sole custody to the other parent. There were several such well-publicized cases in the 1970s and 1980s;

the phenomenon documented by media. At the time, in consideration of context, we find that custody laws were being changed, and that government was becoming more actively involved in the role of *in loco parentis*; defined as acting in the place of a parent[301]. Such practice in America began in the 20th century with the formalization of the national public school system. It followed on the heels of child labor laws, which prohibit the employment of children under fourteen years of age, due to the earlier-in-time labor abuses previously mentioned. From this protectionist policy on the part of government, a protectionist attitude developed at the level of education. What began with government, was enacted into law, affected public schools, continued wielding influence; affecting the public sector's involvement in the lives of families.

The treatment of the child in society has become a major body of law. As such, it has repeatedly run into conflict; from the perspective of publicized knowledge, primarily with religious bodies who have contended that government has overstepped its bounds in its efforts to protect children; resulting in an overcontrolling of matters best left privately decided by families. Matters of custody being particularly contentious, many justice systems have adopted the intervention practice of mediation, in an attempt to mitigate the contentiousness. The past several decades has also borne witness to the struggle for control over education, and the re-granting of the right to parents to home school or self-educate their children, provided they meet the government-mandated standards of achievement by test. We find a context of increased government involvement in decisions that affect families, and to some extent, contentiousness regarding such ordinance.

The matter of missing persons has become a national concern; by the turn of the century, the National Center for Missing and Exploited Children reported that 100,000

---

[301] Merriam-Webster, Incorporated, p. 601.

persons, including children and adults believed responsible for their abductions in the United States, go missing every year.[302] While this number reflects only approximately three ten thousandths of the total population, it is sizeable enough to attract attention. In cases where persons are affected by family members kidnapping family members, and the lives of the departed become that of fugitives from justice, it is difficult to perceive an uncomplicated response. The primary response of government, family members on the run, and family members left behind is assertive. From the perspective of tao, such assertion has generated considerable stress for all involved. One may wonder what impact spirit might have upon such lives, and whether the unassertive action of simplification may positively affect the current stressful reality. There are no ready answers; we know that spirit affects those who contact it; we also know the effect is individual.

From an holistic perspective, these realities that society wishes would go away reflect a present-day dissonance between the rights of the government and the rights of the individual; a kind of jurisdictional tug-of-war over who has the right to make certain kinds of decisions. The matter is an ongoing one; upon reflection we find that such is the nature of the contest of wills. Reflection upon recent history shows us that this is true. The cases of contesting the Vietnam war draft in the sixties and seventies, of contesting Internal Revenue Service seizures of assets in the eighties, of Texas attorneys contesting the tax-filing deadline in the nineties, et cetera, share the common denominator of the battle of wills between government and individuals. Given what we have discovered about individuals reflecting manners of government; as we found to be the case of accusations within relationships; it is not surprising to find individuals and groups of individuals contesting government in the manner of government. What

---

[302] National Center for Missing and Exploited Children, 1-800-THE LOST.

is self-evident in such instances is the exercise of human will in the service of differing perspectives.

Three well-publicized cases from the eighties and nineties serve as prime examples of the modern-day struggle in the case of the government versus the individual; each case involving sizeable fortunes and Texas heirs. The first case occurred in the 1980s, when the heiress of the Brown and Root Company fortune was deemed unfit to manage her own affairs on the basis of a diagnosis of manic-depressive disorder; a legal guardian was appointed to manage her considerable estate.[303] The second case occurred in the 1990s, when the divorced heiress, Barbara Bauer, was appointed a state guardian by court decree to oversee the management of her fortune; the decision rendered on the basis of a diagnosis of alcoholism and contention that Mrs. Bauer was unfit to manage her own affairs.

The third case reads like the Hollywood script for a frightening movie. It occurred in the 1990s, with the disappearance of the fortune of Tyler, Texas wildcatter, William Joseph "Bill" Amis, Sr. Considered to be one of the last of the Texas oil tycoons, Amis, a World War II army veteran made millions of dollars drilling oil wells; first for Shell Oil in Oklahoma and North Texas, later as an independent driller. At the age of 67, he suffered a stroke. When he failed to fully recover, he was assigned guardianship under judge David Hunter Brown; who obtained Mr. Amis' signature on a spendthrift trust putting Judge Brown in charge of Mr. Amis and his estate. The decision was rendered on the basis of his prior spendthrift history and debilitated mental condition. Subsequently, Mr. Amis was sequestered by the judge and his associates; controlling contact with others, including prior friends and family. Amis' son battled the judge for jurisdiction, and obtained legal guardianship; the judge

---

[303] Both the Brown & Root heiress and Bauer heiress incidents were reported in the *Houston Chronicle* newspaper, published by the Hearst Corporation in Houston, Texas.

however refused to relinquish custody of the father. In a western movie style scenario of holdup and shootout, the junior Amis orchestrated a rescue that resulted in his firing a shot at the judge, who died from complications of pneumonia following the shootout.

Amis Sr. died of a heart attack eight days after the shooting, Amis Jr. went to jail for murder in 1,992 C.E., $553,000 in estate monies went missing, the multimillion dollar trust was declared bankrupt in 1,992 C.E., Amis Jr. died in prison following a heart attack and a bout of pneumonia in 1,999 C.E., and his seventeen year-old daughter inherited his social security pension.[304]

The reality of persons falling victim to the struggle between government and individuals, or to the struggle between individuals over matters of jurisdiction; in these three cases, jurisdiction over assets; is relevant to our consideration as one of those matters we wish would go away. The matters we wish would go away are those which portray the paradox of human nature; the benevolence/malevolence; the knowing/unknowing, et cetera; in so doing, they frighten us with their exposure of who we imperfectly are; the reality they reflect is not the whitewashed version we would like to believe; the indication being a general intolerance of the way we are, of our own human nature. The awful truth, to use a modern phrase, is that we are uncomfortable with the reality of ourselves; that we do not like ourselves in the sense of the reality of who and what we, as human beings, are. In the holistic sense, we find meaningfulness in the intolerance; the human discomfort with its own paradoxical humanity, reflected in those matters we wish would go away. We are comfortable to the extent that we can pretend the problem is someone or something else, rather than humanity itself; with its complicated paradoxical nature. In this respect, our condemnations of others reflect condemnations of ourselves;

---

[304] Moore, Evan. "The Judge And The Wildcatter", In *Texas*, Houston Chronicle Magazine, January 14, 2001, pp. 8-18.

those aspects we disdain and would prefer did not exist. We find in an holistic consideration of society that the fundamental problem of society lies with the paradoxical nature of human beingness; and the intolerance engendered by the ages-old realization of this reality. From a philosophical perspective, societal intolerance derives from the awareness of man's true nature; a less conscious man would not engage in such consideration. One may therefore say that man's elevation in the realm of the animal kingdom, in the form of the modern species of homo sapiens, with its greater capacities of consciousness, has enabled such reality.

In addressing the matter of societal responsibility, we come to understand the underlying reason for the prevalence of contentiousness in human society; beyond the struggle of the human will for the benefit of the individual soul attempting to realize its true self, there lies an even greater struggle; the struggle of the human paradox, which society most notably observes in relation to the dichotomy of good and evil. Given this reality, one may well consider the question: To whom does the matter of responsibility appropriately fall; to whom do we most wisely entrust the care of society itself? We have mentioned the conflict between the individual, the religious, and the governmental over jurisdiction; we may now comprehend the conflict in light of the question regarding belief about appropriate responsibility; the views undoubtedly differ.

In an holistic consideration of the matter of appropriate responsibility, we consider the unorthodox psychiatric perspective of M. Scott Peck, who expounded the view that a new category of mental disorder, classified evil personality disorder, is warranted in order to identify and diagnose persons who perpetuate deliberately evil intentions in a pathological manner. Peck's perspective addresses the limitations of psychiatry/psychology. Whereas, diagnoses of conduct disorder indicate troubled development in children, providing a forewarning of the potential for a troubled adulthood; and diagnoses of sociopathy indicate troubled development in adulthood; these diagnostic categories, based upon explicated behavior, are limited in their scope. Peck's novel suggestion speaks to the limitation; the absence of adequate identification of a qualitatively different dangerousness of personality; a recognition of a reality based upon professional experience; which he terms evil.

In light of Peck's perspective, one may consider the fact that, within psychology, the 20th century witnessed the development of a new treatment direction; that of the psychology of exploitation. We find, in America, evidence that much of the attention of the treatment community underwent a refocusing upon areas of human abuse, exploitation, and torture; abuse of the mentally and physically challenged, children, the elderly, spouses, sexual abuse, et cetera. The reality of such refocusing by the treatment community speaks to the recognition of the existence of a problem in society that would not go away. In this regard, what began within the field of psychology as an effort to address and treat the emotional aftermath of world wars; post-traumatic stress disorder; evolved into an effort to address and treat the emotional aftermath of cruelty in society.

In 2,008 C.E., I was invited to attend a guest lecture luncheon on Women and Philanthropy featuring Tracy Gary, a national charismatic speaker, at the University of St. Thomas in Houston, Texas.[305] In the course of her speech, Ms. Gary presented the research findings of Strauss and Howe regarding millenial turnings.[306] The current time period,

---

[305] Gary, Tracy, Charismatic Lecturer. "Inspired Living, Inspired Giving: How we can transform our families, communities and the world," Women and Philanthropy Lecture Series. University of St. Thomas, Houston, Texas: April 22, 2008.

[306] Strauss, William and Howe, Neil. *The fourth turning: an American prophecy: what the cycles of history tell us about America's next rendezvous with destiny.* 1st Ed. Broadway Books: New York, New York, 1997. Neil Howe, *The Fourth Turning.* .Broadway Books: New York, New York, 1996. Based upon the *The Millenial Saeculum.*

beginning with the year 2,007 C.E., has been predicted to be an age of crisis per Strauss and Howe, who revisit *The Millenial Saeculum's* posited millenial transitions as applied to current history. They relate the cycle of four transitions termed *turnings* that affect the world approximately every eighty years; from a first turning, termed High, towards confident expansion; to a second turning, termed Awakening, towards spiritual exploration; to a third turning, termed Unraveling, towards individualism; to a fourth turning, termed Crisis, towards passage through a great and perilous gate in history. From this philosophical perspective of millenial turnings, we may perceive indications of occurrences in society that are coincident with this analysis. Holistically speaking, such context is relevant to comprehending the impact upon human struggling; while the struggles persist, they persist within the context of a kaleidoscopically shifting backdrop. Usual manners of responding may lose effectiveness under such conditions of change, rendering consideration of spirit, including tao, all the more noteworthy, in that spirit provides a kind of lifeline not otherwise available during such societal transitionings.

CHAPTER FIFTEEN

The Illusion Perspective

Disillusion is the condition of being disenchanted or left without illusion.[307] The experience of disillusionment is that of being stunned; of being overcome or overwhelmed by what is revealed when illusion falls away. In the ages-old search for truth; about ourselves and our world; we may, in the process of discovery, encounter the experience of disillusion. The euphemism, life is not always what it seems, is an apt characterization of the experience of disillusionment; of discovering the truth underlying a believed illusion.

Awareness of the reality and experience of illusion has existed since antiquity. It is the underlying reason for the appeal of magic; a psychological means of coming to terms with a frightening reality over which we have no overt control. Magic tricks, performed by magicians, and illusions of magic presented in media, enable us to visit these phenomena in the comfort of knowing that we are safely unaffected. In this way, they satisfy a natural human curiosity about a phenomenon we know exists which, were we to encounter it directly, would prove frightening. In this regard, the vicarious experience of enchantment serves the

---

[307] *Webster's New Collegiate Dictionary*, p. 325.

purpose of desensitization, enabling us to better tolerate actual experiences of disillusionment.

Not all experiences pertaining to disenchantment involve magic. We know, for instance, from repeated incidents in history, that the greatest financial swindles of all time have involved illusion; the falsification of appearances in the service of conning persons out of their money. When the reality of the worthlessness of the allegedly lucrative investment becomes known, the impact of the disillusion is shocking. Persons not generally known for gullibility wonder how they could have been so well-deceived. Such is the nature of illusion; it deceives with a sudden shock upon realization of the discordant truth.

Not all experiences of disillusion involve swindle. The experience of disillusion may be as simple as the sudden realization that the person one married is not the person one thought one had married; an experience which occurs frequently, particularly in this age of mobility when families no longer marry among families they have known for generations. The experience, after the initial shock wears off, is a disheartening one, with the similar reaction of wonderment; how could one have allowed themselves to be so fooled? To some extent, this reflects the nature of the process of disillusionment following infatuation which occurs in nearly all relationships. In the benign case, it is the point of reckoning when the partners are faced with the reality that their perceptions were enchanted by infatuation, and they must now accept the truth that the partner is not as perfect as they had initially perceived or believed. Were it not for this enchantment effect of falling in love, persons may not so readily and willingly engage in committed relationship. In this, it seems, that human nature has thrown us a curve ball intended to encourage the propagation of the species. The fact that this is generally the case in matters of love speaks to the human sensitivity to the experience of disillusionment.

The experience is not always as benign as seeing a normal partner without the effect of love's enchantment. I recall the therapy case of a woman who unknowingly married a scoundrel. After successfully wooing her into marriage, he proceeded to amass significant marital debts; which, when he absconded, became her legal responsibility. She was saddled with debts for purchases she did not possess; she went home one day to the rude awakening of an empty house. Her shocked reaction after a year of marriage was typical of the experience of disillusionment; she could not comprehend how she could have allowed him to deceive her in this manner. There was nothing in the way of a warning sign to alert her; he was in every way an attentive and well-behaved spouse, he was not overtly charming or manipulative, and other persons they knew similarly failed to perceive any untoward behavior or remarks that might have cued her. One day, he just simply upped and went away, taking with him most of their worldly possessions. Whether or not this man had a history of such conduct remained a mystery. From a purely behavioral perspective, it was as if he had flitted in and out of her life like a wild bird staying long enough to roost for a houseful of furniture and a new car, and then went on his merry incognito way. She learned that she would have to legally divorce him in absentia to rid herself of the affiliation, which she promptly did, after which she sought therapy to work through the emotional upset and regain a sense of normalcy.

In 1,993 C.E., while living in San Antonio, Texas, I experienced a different version of disillusionment. During a conversation with a retired military psychologist, the subject turned to recent, rather sensationalistic, reports in the media pertaining to reported alien encounters. He inquired if I thought they were true. I was somewhat skeptical regarding their veracity. I believed in the reports of alien craft sightings, which were well-documented, but was skeptical that human beings were being abducted and tortured by alien beings.

Viewing the time, place, and circumstance from the perspective of a play, the setting was one of hysterical hypermode. From what seemed like one day to the next, the country's attention had turned from the usual and customary to the unusual and alien. Books, conversations, film, and media reports refocused upon the new center of attention; reports by human beings that they had been abducted into alien spacecrafts, experienced the conducting of forced medical procedures, and were subsequently released. What does one think in the face of such sudden and unusual report?

As a civilian psychologist working in what was at the time, a predominantly military community with five local air force bases, I had been exposed to considerations of current conspiracy theories. Affected by this context, I wondered if someone was conducting a secret experiment to assess the human reaction factor, and said so. I was familiar with the reported outcome of Orson Welles' CBS radio broadcast at 8 p.m. Eastern Standard Time on Halloween eve in 1,938 C.E., based on the novel, *The War of the Worlds*, by H. G. Wells.[308] The broadcast occurred 9 years prior to the well-publicized incident of the Magdalena, New Mexico, alien craft crash in the Plains of San Agustin on July 5, 1,947 C.E.,[309] commonly referred to as the Roswell incident; and 23 years prior to the Betty and Barney Hill abduction experience en route from Montreal to New Hampshire on September 19, 1,961 C.E..[310] Given that the radio station did not state that it was broadcasting a fiction at the outset, the

---

[308] Sklar, Robert. *A World History of Film*. Harry N. Abrams, Inc.: New York, 2002, p. 201.

[309] Good, Timothy. *Alien Contact: Top Secret UFO Files Revealed*. William Morrow and Company: New York, 1993, pp. 96-110.

[310] Callimanopulos, Dominique and Mack, M.D. John E. "A Historical and Cross-Cultural Perspective on Reported Encounters", In Mack, M.D., John E. *Abduction: Human Encounters With Aliens*. Rev. Ed. Ballantine Books: New York, 1994, Appendix B, pp. 446-7.

broadcast had the powerful effect of convincing many radio listeners that Martians had invaded New Jersey. Accounts of the phenomenon indicated it induced widespread fear and panic, due to the fact that listeners believed the events were genuinely occurring at that moment in time. I wondered whether a similar phenomenon were occurring.

Much to my surprise, I was informed that the matter was no hoax; the United States Air Force knew alien abductions of human beings were real; the psychologist with whom I was having the conversation told me he himself had conducted therapy with persons who had had such experiences. I was stunned; my perception of the reports I was hearing, reading, and seeing changed; the knowledge that life was not as I perceived it to be was shocking.

Shortly thereafter, I received a booklet addressed to mental health professionals. It was sent to my private residence, as opposed to my place of business, and advised persons in positions such as mine to be open to the possibility of reports of alien encounters from patients; to seriously consider them if and when they occurred. The booklet constituted a second form of confirmation. Meanwhile, in the public eye, commentary vacillated between hysterical reports by individuals, discrediting of abduction tales, modulated reports by newscasters, and government denials of coverup. Persons were understandably alarmed, concerned, and uncertain about the truth; in the words of the judiciary, was what they were hearing the truth, the whole truth, and nothing but the truth, so help them God?

In the same way that, from one day to the next, a sudden change in experience may be noted, there arose in San Antonio a state of hyper alert and excited agitation. Following on the heels of the change in ambiance, it was rumored that an alien presence has been sighted in a lake in South Texas and local military personnel had been mobilized. This brought the matter closer to home; the impact was a noticeable increase in the numbers of hushed conversations.

I recall experiencing a mixture of awe, curiosity, and stunned awareness. The experience constituted a third form of confirmation.

The reality of an alien presence nearby gives one pause for reflection; in what seemed like an instant, the world had changed. The illusion of normalcy vanished, and I experienced the disillusionment of knowing the truth; there were more than the usual and customary beings on the planet. I was surprised by the truth that I was called to face; a truth which unnerved my previously unshaken perception of reality as essentially human in nature and origin. This, despite having grown up with knowledge of the existence of UFOs; unidentified flying objects; and talk about alien visitors from outer space. Exposure to television shows like the 1,963 C.E. CBS television series, *My Favorite Martian,* in which the actor Ray Walston, portrays Uncle Martin, a Martian who lands on Earth, looks human, speaks English, invisibilizes, moves objects at a glance, and evidences an advanced knowledge of technology;[311] constituted an abstract intrigue, not a close-to-the-cuff report or direct experience of what government terms EBEs; extraterrestrial biological entities. This was no minor reckoning; it serves as an example of the nature of the experience of disillusion.

The documentary, *The Phoenix Lights: We Are Not Alone*, documents the reality of an alien visitation that occurred in the state of Arizona in the United States of America.[312] The testimonials provide a glimpse of the experience; documenting the reality, providing a source for

---

[311] *The Encyclopedia of American Television: Broadcast Programming Post-World War II to 2000.* Lackmann, Ron (Ed.). Facts on File, Inc.: New York, 2003, p. 248.

[312] Kitei, Lynne D. *The Phoenix Lights: We Are Not Alone*, a Vanguard Cinema release. Steve Lantz Productions, LLC: Buena Park, California, 2008. Based on the book: Kitei, Lynne D. *The Phoenix Lights*. Hampton Roads Publishing Company: Charlottesville, Virginia, 2004.

understanding. The film stands as one human story in the saga of human-alien encounter experiences.

The truth is that, whether disillusion involves facing realities of alien existence, paranormal experience, or normal phenomena, it is, in fact, a normal aspect of growth; specifically, of a growth in consciousness. As an aspect of growth; it is not a particularly pleasant experience. It is, however, essential to the growth process. One may well wonder why the *Spirit in the sky*, as it has been referred to in song[313], presents us with such growth experiences, but, like it or not, they happen, and when they do, we are faced with a reckoning; whereby, in the dissipation of illusion followed by the experience of disillusionment, consciousness expands.

Belief in spirits and the spirit extends to prehistory; it is part of the ancient lores of tribal peoples, including those of Africa, such as the Dinka of Sudan who believed in Sky as God and Spirits that took possession of individuals, and the creation mythology of the Bambara of west Africa, who believed that Faro or God formed the sky and Pemba or Spirit formed the earth; those of Central and North America, such as the Aztecs who believed that the primal creator was a god/goddess that created the Lord and Lady of Duality who reined highest, and the Incas who believed in sacred spaces (places) that were continually surrounded by malevolent spirits lying in wait, and the Mayans, who believed in a patron deity of royal lineages; all of whom believed in the capacity of their shaman priests to travel between the earthly and spirit worlds. The Amazon and Chacoan peoples also believed in multiple spirits; both earthly and celestial; that influenced people's lives. The belief in spirit also has prehistoric roots in the Shinto or *way of the gods* religion of Japan, who believe in the existence of kami; the Japanese word for spirits, who exist in all forms of nature. We find that from the beginning; including in prehistoric times; human

---

[313] Greenbaum, Norman. *Spirit in the sky.* Studio City, California: Varese Sarabande Records, 1967.

beings have believed not only in the existence of a creator, but also in the influences of spirits. Human consciousness of spiritual reality derives from our prehistoric origins. We believe that spirit exists, communicates, and affects us, and have so believed from the beginning of human time. We find that ancient beliefs do not die with the collapse of old civilizations; they merge into the new and become modern beliefs; reflections of the persistence of spiritual reality and the extension into the future of human consciousness.

Without the spirit-driven experiences of disillusionment that result from looking truth in the eye, we remain psychologically blocked and spiritually ignorant. Of necessity, we face the truth of our own origins of consciousness and accept the mixed-up-ed-ness of our beliefs, deriving as they do from ancient sources not entirely our own; we, the peoples of planet earth have a rich and varied spiritual history of contribution to human consciousness. The antithesis of disillusion is delusion; the state of self-deception. It is sometimes tempting, in the face of uncomfortable truth, to resort to the self-deception of denial, rather than face what is uncomfortable truth. Substance abusers and addicts know this experience well. The escapist solution may take the form of another drink, pill, syringe, et cetera; a decision to postpone the reckoning. Like the character, Scarlett O'Hara, in the movie, *Gone With The Wind*, based on the novel by Margaret Mitchell, after the North has pummeled the South during the American Civil War; her home and life in ruins; when she decides to postpone dealing with the terrible truth of the war-torn circumstances, declaring she will think about it tomorrow. One may well say that under such circumstances, a temporary postponement of the reckoning is a healthy response to a tragic circumstance, in that it provides breathing room; a time to recoup from the initial shock, a means of gradually sensitizing to the reality one must face. This kind of temporary escapism does not constitute denial, it constitutes coping. It is relevant to consider that when escapism includes psychological denial, the truth is that it, too, constitutes a form of coping. The reality of weather-torn lives around the world over the course of the past several decades speaks to a higher-than-normal incidence of such reckonings; wherein the illusion that dissipates is one of a false sense of security. This comprehension enables us to better understand the escapist solution of the substance abuser, as a form of coping with the realities of life.

In the usual and customary sense, persons often choose a form of psychological escape. As previously stated, persons generally prefer comfort to discomfort; and this preference for comfort fosters a tendency to avoid certain truths that may be unconsciously known and consciously suspected. People, generally, are not so far apart in this regard as is perhaps the tendency or the preference of belief. The fact of the matter remains that truth is faced in the perceptual shift from self-deception to disillusion; in the shedding and letting go of our psychological and physical defenses; whence we may confront it directly, without a protective barrier or shield. Then, and only then, may we see truth as it is; in its unadulterated, undisguised true form.

Within the experience of facing truth through disillusionment lies the seed of a greater potentiality. There is assurance in the knowledge that the perceptual disruption that is the experience of disillusion is the way to a more holistic comprehension, a greater degree of spiritualization through enhanced consciousness, and a striving towards ultimate wellness in the wholeness of being sense.

Nonetheless, the experience of disillusion can be of sufficient stun to render us temporarily unable to perceive the inherent potential in the midst of what may manifest as an existential crisis; what does it mean that this has happened?. Following the dropping of the perceptual veil of illusion, the temporary state of lost perspective which may follow has the potential to obscure understanding; rendering the experience confusing. As we experience the reckonings that come with the territory of being alive; whether these follow from deliberated exploration in search of truth or from the force of happenstance; we journey most wisely when accompanied by awareness that a veil of disillusion exists; for us and for most people; prepared in this manner to recognize the experience for what it is, if and when it occurs.

Our journey of holistic reflection upon the matter of spirit and illusion, leads us to a consideration of the notion of human suffering; we know it exists, but why? The matter has puzzled scholars and philosophers since antiquity. One may consider the fact of human suffering as the ultimate disillusionment; why does God, spirit, et cetera, permit us to suffer? John H. Hick in *Philosophy of Religion*[314] examines the point of suffering as it relates to the idea of hell. He states that, the idea of heaven in Christian tradition is balanced by the idea of hell. He considers that in the same way that reconciling God's goodness and power with the fact of evil requires that out of the travail of history there shall come in the end an eternal good for humanity, it would likewise seem to preclude eternal human misery. Hick reasons that the only kind of evil that is incompatible with God's unlimited power and love would be utterly pointless and wasted suffering, pain which is never redeemed and worked into the fulfilling of God's good purpose. Unending torment would constitute precisely such suffering; eternal by definition, it could never lead to a good end beyond itself. In Hick's consideration of the Judaic-Christian perspective, unending torment is not compatible with the belief in God's unlimited power and love; it does not reconcile with the notion that human suffering has to come to a good end.

How do we comprehend the notion of unending torment? If we accept the conceptualization in which the notion of unending torment is equated with the notion of hell, we confront this dilemma head-on. We are hard-pressed to

---

[314] Hick, pp. 124-5.

reconcile the image of the raging inferno with the belief, expressed by Hick, that endless, pointless torture is unacceptable. How do we resolve this dilemma?

First, we consider that the conceptualization of hell as the endless torment of fire is valuable as a symbolic, representational truth; based upon the bible. We find that, according to The Holy Bible, in *The Revelation of Saint John The Divine*, heaven and hell exist as different dimensions of reality. The notions of fire and brimstone that we typically associate with hell arise from a dream-like vision of the future to which John is exposed; wherein the Lord upon the throne in heaven, representing divine goodness acts against the fallen badness that is attempting to lay claim to the world. John witnesses a prophesied enactment of a good versus evil war of the worlds; the visioning is panoramic.

Documented reports from some of the alien abductees of the 1990s express that they experienced a phenomenon we may note is similar to the one described in Revelation; they report having been shown by alien beings a vision of future happenings of world proportions that involve considerable conflict on the planet; their visions are similarly panoramic. The validation of such visions is not a matter of public record, however, publications of the experience provide us with the knowledge that persons in modernity have shared a similar experience as that of the saint, John the Divine. From these reports one may gather that mortal beingness is being informed of events to come; whether such portends constitute inevitability remains to be determined, in large measure by events which have yet to unfold.

As prophecies about the future, their occurrence will depend upon the actualization of the possibilities that have been foreseen; whether or not, for instance, an anti-Christ arises intent upon seizing power in his own name; the depiction is one of the deliberate slaughtering of existing saints and prophets, and the drinking of their blood in an act of conquest. According to the revelation to Saint John, the Lord avenges his saints and prophets by smiting the world, condemning *the dragon, that old serpent, which is the Devil, and Satan,* to be bound for one thousand years in the dimension of *the bottomless pit* (Revelation 20:1, 2, 3). During the thousand years that the devil is bound, Christ reigns upon the earth. When the thousand years expire, the entity called the devil is supernaturally released back into the realm of mortality; God casts him and death into the lake of fire (Revelation 21:10,14), destroying the first heaven and the first earth, whereupon a new heaven and a new earth come into being (Revelation 21:1).

Notions of fire and brimstone derive from references to the bible, although such portrayals in modernity may not accurately reflect the biblical record; wherein it is the hell created by God, and the minions he sends as avenging angels that spew smoke, fire, and brimstone; in the latter case, upon the earth against the minions of the usurping devil. We find, in everyday thought, the existence of a generalized confusion; a belief in an eternal unending torment in a place called hell. Considering the concern which Hicks has expressed about the existence of unending torment; that it must ultimately end in good to be compatible with our notions of God; according to biblical prophecy, the torment of hell does in fact, end. The matter becomes one of prophetic fulfillment; whether in fact, the prophecy of a second triumph of the *good* of the gods over the *evil* of the devils comes to pass. According to prophecy, the dilemma is ultimately resolved with the elimination of hell and the curse that was placed upon humanity in antiquity, rendering possible the immortalization of persons upon the earth.

There is, however, as Hicks alludes, the possibility of the existence of an unending torment not of God's creation. Indeed, one may consider the possibility as the hypothetical outcome of a triumph of devils over gods; the human record clearly states that the gods have triumphed in the past and will do so in the future; were/should this not be the case, unending torment would be a conceivable reality. Dominion of the planet by devils; what the bible terms beings that engage in abominations; would certainly be conducive to the creation of a condition of hell upon earth. When we consider the notions of abominators; theologic; and of hell on earth; literary; we find that the tormenting of human souls by evil doers; black witches, feral demons, satanic cultists, and the like, is a much considered perspective reflecting the human angst, concern, horror, and terror that such beings exist and have existed, and may, as prophesied, wreak havoc on earth as was done in the past. In this regard, such entities are regarded as joiners with the devil. In another regard, in typically paradoxical human fashion, there exists a kind of play on words; wherein persons seeking to differentiate themselves from the norm, in the spirit of rebellion, are known to adopt such paraphernalia and symbology; common among adolescents; as a means of defiant self-expression. Other forms of expression, such as the saying, *The devil made me do it* in response to an acknowledged mistake speaks to a spirit of independence from self-judgment; an expression of esteem within the context of religious understanding. We find there exists on earth the true nature of the beast, as it is referred to in the bible; attributed to human possession; as well as varieties of caricature and reference.

Viewed in this way, the application of the biblical concept of torment defined as hell, to the concept of hell on earth, may be considered to be a representation of the experience of enslavement by evil; a force in the universe with the power to consume and dissipate the human spirit, through the sheer force of its will to dominate. In astrological terms, fire consumes air, and the spirit is airy in nature. A force which consumes the human spirit; driving out the eternal life aspect; could metaphorically be conceived of as being fiery in nature. Hell, as experienced in life, may be construed as a state or condition of experience. Such view is compatible with the Judeo-Christian perspective of God's alternate reality;

although in mortal experience, we have no direct means of knowing; such accounts as are contained in the biblical record constitute reports from supernatural beings to mortal beings. In testament to human belief and the human will which has ensured the transmission of the biblical record throughout history, and in reflection of the application of such shared immortal knowledge, the understanding of hell and torment is one which humanity has historically comprehended. We comprehend that immortal beings may pass judgment upon us at death, and that we may be relegated to the alternate reality of hell; a form of castigation for mortal sin; reflecting a mortal comprehension of inferiority in relation to immortal superiority.

We further comprehend what may be characterized as the experience of hell on earth. In the metaphorical sense, hell on earth may be likened to the experience that is forced upon others by Darth Vader, the character in the 1,983 C.E. movie, *Return of the Jedi,* from the George Lucas Star Wars Trilogy. Darth Vader, portrayed by James Earl Jones, personifies the devil in his enslavement of the human will to the dark side of evil, with its insatiable need for all-consuming control; the movie a battle of moral positions between good and evil. The character of Luke Skywalker, played by Mark Hamill, the defender of the light, personifies the light side of good. In this, the Star Wars Trilogy may be viewed as a futuristic personification of the biblically-prophesied battle of the gods of good and evil; providing a glimpse of hypothetical experience; conveying the message that before the final battle is won, the struggle that translates into experiences of hell on earth, has the potential to extend to outer space.

We know, from human experience, of the existence of evil characters in the world who employ the force of their will to dominate and control; subsuming the will of others towards their malevolent aims. In the biblical report, the persona is the devil or Satan, the immortal being to whom the evil that exists on earth is attributed. According to *Encarta Encyclopedia*, the term, *the satan,* is a translation of the Hebrew term *ha-satan*, which was originally used as the title of a member of the divine court who functioned as God's roving spy, gathering intelligence about human beings from his travels on earth.[315] A functionary angel feared by humans because of his capacity to black list them, Satan becomes, in later Jewish tradition and early Christianity, an adversary not only of human beings but also of God, with whom he has a falling out. As the original fallen angel, Satan comes to be viewed as the supreme spirit of evil, who rules over a kingdom of evil, with followers of his own. We may conclude from the perspective of theology that the torment of domination by an evil that enslaves is the essence of the experience of hell on earth; for which the devil and his minions are held to be responsible. One may well wonder, from the perspective of theology, how it is that Satan, an immortal angel, could corrupt; the expectation being that immortal goodness is incorruptible, while mortality is corruptible. I plead ignorance of theological considerations of the matter; I have not encountered them. Did Satan's role as a human tabs-keeper; keeping tabs on the sins of man; roaming the earth, monitoring sinners, play a role in his demise? Such wandering did not corrupt Jesus the Christ; why, then, would Satan have corrupted? The ancient lores may provide clues for human understanding, as in the pre-Christian lore of the battle between the gods of good and evil. The historic legend contains the seed of the later developments; the continuation of a spiritual struggle between good and bad, originating with the gods themselves. In this, one may well state that the human condition is a reflection of the godly condition; divided as it were, and as yet unresolved. This matter of reflection is manifestly evident; from the mimicries of hierarchy, intelligence gatherings, judiciary judgments, parental punishments, practices of worship, and et cetera,

---

[315] *Encarta Encyclopedia*, Standard Edition, 2004.

to the good and evil divide. We find that consciously and unconsciously, humanity has sought to imitate the divine. We find that the holy bible is relevant to our consideration of spirit; in the portend of the coming of the second and final war on earth between the immortal spirits of good and evil; the prophesied end of the old earth and the creation of a new; it speaks to the historic matter of the human spiritual struggle, providing us with the means to put the struggle into context.

We have considered the matter of unending torment raised by Hicks from the biblical perspective of an ultimate resolution, as well as from an experiential perspective of hell on earth and in outer space. We now consider the matter of hell itself with respect to differences in theological perspective. *Encarta Encyclopedia* defines hell, in theology, as *any place or state of punishment and privation for human souls after death. More strictly, the term is applied to the place or state of eternal punishment of the damned, whether angels or human beings.*[316] We learn from the encyclopedia that belief in a hell was widespread in antiquity and is found in most religions of the world today.

For the early Teutons, hell signified a place under the earth to which the souls of mortals, good or bad, were consigned after death. The early Jews had a similar conception, termed Sheol, where all the problems of earthly life came to an end, in the depths of the Pit. Among early Christians, the term hell was variously applied; as a designation of a state of limbo for unbaptized infants, as a state of limbo for the souls of the just who died before the advent of Christ, as a place of purgation from minor offenses, as a place of punishment of Satan and the other fallen angels and of all mortals who die unrepentant of serious sin.[317] The concept of hell is also found in the pre-Christian lore of the ancient Icelandics, among whom Hel, in the Nordic pantheon of gods, was the

---

[316] *Encarta Encyclopedia*, Standard Edition, 2004.
[317] Ibid.

name of the goddess of death.[318] While not exhaustive, this purview provides us with the comprehension that notions of hell are ancient, various, and pertinent to beliefs about death and souls among both early non-Christian peoples and later Christian peoples. The belief in a place or state that is hell, associated with what happens after death, is an ancient aspect of the human consciousness.

In the context of the body of knowledge we may regard as the lore of hell, the concern of unending torment raised by Hicks may be seen to be variably relevant with respect to the notion of hell. According to Encarta Encyclopedia, *the duration of the punishments of hell has been a subject of controversy since early Christian times.*[319] The 3rd century Christian writer and theologian, Origen, taught that the punishments of hell were purgatorial, proportionate to the guilt of the individual, that in time, the purifying effect of hell would be accomplished in all, even devils, punishment would cease, and everyone in hell would eventually be restored to happiness.[320] The doctrine of Origen was condemned by the Second Council of Constantinople in 553 C.E.; it was replaced by a belief in the eternity of punishments among Orthodox and Roman Catholic churches.[321] Such beliefs persist amidst controversy regarding the nature of the punishments of hell. Encarta informs us that *Opinions range from holding the pains of hell to be no more than the remorse of conscience to the traditional belief that the "pain of loss" (the consciousness of having forfeited the vision of God and the happiness of heaven) is combined with the "pain of sense" (actual physical torment).* From an holistic perspective, the context of variances in human belief about hell and punishment post-death renders the philosophical

---

[318] Thorsson, Ornolfur, *The Sagas of Icelanders: A Selection.* Viking Penguin: New York, 2000, p. 70.

[319] Ibid.

[320] Ibid.

[321] Ibid.

concern about unending torment an unresolved debate in the human mind and consciousness.

Having considered the dilemma of equating unending torment with the notion of eternal hell, we consider the notion of spiritual enslavement; a form of assumption of dominion over the life of a human being. This concept, reflected in the belief of the possibility of human possession is also an ancient one; it exists in early rabbinic thought as a belief in *evil impulse* linked to Satan.[322] The concept of possession involves satanic access; a utilization of the individual in a manner consistent with satanic wishes, independent of the individual. Possession is considered to be an assumption of control over the will of an individual; it constitutes an involuntary affectedness, as opposed to the notion of voluntary surrender to evil forces. The belief that human beings can be possessed by the devil or his subordinates, the demons, is found in both Judaism and Christianity.[323]

The concept of possession differs from the notion of regression; that individuals deviate from an original state of grace at birth, rendering possible future decisions to engage in serious sin. The notion of possession carried to the extreme of death, is characterized in the Harry Potter book series by J. K. Rowling, wherein entities termed dementors invade the minds of their intended victims, with the deliberate intention to kill the human will, and thereby the self of the individuals they attack.[324] These towering, hooded figures glide and hover, sucking the happiness from their victims, filling them with icy, debilitating dread that renders them incapable of self-sustainment.

In this portrayal of the human experience of possession, the minion of evil drives the eternal spirit out of the body in

---

[322] Ibid.

[323] Ibid.

[324] Rowling, J. K.. *Harry Potter And The Prisoner Of Azkaban*. Harry Potter Book Series. Scholastic Press: New York, 2001, pp. 17-8.

order to capture the soul, resulting in a dulling of the mind and the closing of the portal to unitive knowledge and creative transcendence. While most persons have not experienced possession, accounts of such occurrence within a variety of cultural contexts exist, indicating the reality of the potential. It is relevant to address the difference between possession by an evil force and possession, as in the mediumistic sense, by a benign spirit. Documentation of experiences by mediums; persons receptive to psychic possession by spirits; has demonstrated that such occurrences involve a desire to communicate on the part of the spirit; the individual who serves as the medium for the communication comes to no harm, although they may experience such physical effects as fatigue subsequent to the episode. We know, from experience and the recordation of experience, that spiritual possession of human beings is possible; and that the possessing may occur as the result of either malevolent or benevolent spirits.

In the everyday regard, most people don't think about the possibility of either type of possession, or about the possibility of inviting the divine spirit into oneself. In a functional sense, we tend to live our everyday lives operating behind the veil of illusion that life is as we directly perceive it; we do not generally walk about witnessing the presence of demons, ghosts, and spirits. Those who do are in the minority; their life experience is without a doubt, different from that of the norm. I remember my surprise, as a child, while visiting with my maternal grandparents, that I was affected by a ghostliness I did not understand. My psychic grandmother, sensing this to be the case, informed me the ghosts were harmless, regular visitors. She was one of those persons whose perception included the spiritual; most of us know such possibility vicariously from reading books or watching movies.

The greater our distance from spirit, the easier it is for us to believe that we are immune to such happenings;

living without conscious awareness of such reality is, in a sense, self-protective, but it provides us with a false sense of security. It also has a tendency to shield us from the realization that we are not the ultimate authority or creation or power in the universe; the humbling knowledge that we are less in charge of our world than we may choose to face or care to accept. In relation to the power of creation, we are as incapable of such power as plants are incapable of our power of perception. Shielded by the veil, we develop a greater tendency for hubris, perhaps even failing to accept the truth of our lesser form of existence, believing in our own quite capable powers as if these were the equivalent of those of the gods. In this way, we render ourselves more easily fooled; a form of self-deception; that we are more powerful in our human state than we actually are. The attraction of evil becomes comprehensible from the perspective of its proffer of unnatural power. The failure to accept the human state of existence such as it genuinely is, while believing in a greater state of existential possibility, renders human exploitation possible.

This is the heart of the human dilemma which pertains to human relations. Viewed non-holistically, human experience is perceived as an end-all, be-all, and one means of achieving personal power under such perceived conditions, is through the exercise of the will in the service of dominating others, thereby to gain access to a better present for oneself. Viewed holistically, human experience is perceived as a journey towards a condition of greater existence, and one means of achieving personal power under such perceived conditions, is through the exercise of the will in the service of dominating ourselves; our own selfish tendencies, our own unhealthy psychological defenses, our own weaknesses; and thereby to gain access to a better future. Human experience, viewed in holistic terms, enables us to grasp the existential meaning of the observation that there are true paths in life; one has but to discover one's true way in the world, to derive soulful benefit.

Whichever path we choose has potential ramifications; for good and for evil. Linda Goodman, in *Love Signs: A New Approach to the Human Heart*, states that every astrological sun sign contains a strength that can be reversed into a weakness, and every sun sign contains a weakness that can be reversed into a strength, through the law of positive-negative polarity.[325] In the same way that astrological inherencies of personality can veer positively or negatively, towards strength or weakness, so too, can the actions we take as we journey along the path of life to which we are intended. It is relevant to consider that the practice of astrology has ancient origins; whether or not one overtly believes in such cosmic influences of birth, astrology has had a far-reaching influence upon human thought, and is a generally accepted aspect of human consciousness.

One of the original forms of astrology was developed by the Chaldeans, who lived in Babylonia; the current Iraq; circa 3,000 B.C.E. The present-day signs of the zodiac are believed to have originated in Mesopotamia circa 2,000 B.C.E. The Chinese independently developed what is referred to as the Chinese calendar; an astrological chart with animal designations; circa 2,000 B.C.E. The Aztecs independently developed a system of astrology similar to that of the Chinese. Other forms developed in India and among the Maya of Central America. Circa 500 B.C.E. astrology spread to Greece, and from there to Europe. In the 1500s, the science of astronomy successfully refuted some of the original foundations of astrology, and this led to a general scepticism among scientists, which persists to this day. We find, from an holistic perspective, that astrology has played a significant role in the shaping of human thought for at least 5,000 years. Given its independently

---

[325] Goodman, Linda. Love Signs: *A New Approach To The Human Heart*. Ballantine Books: New York, 1978.

repeated development across cultures; a condition requisite for scientific validation; we may conclude that spirit has played a role in its manifestation, and for purposes of holistic comprehension, include it in our considerations.

We may recall Huxley's observation that we are aware of what we want to see and understand. We have discussed the human tendency, at differing points in history, to differentially focus upon aspects of experience. We have historically tended towards positions of hubris in our certainties. Cognizance of this limitation is essential to an holistic consideration of human consciousness, its development over time, and the impact of spirit upon consciousness. One may well comprehend how it is that we do not want to see and understand the truth of our inferior human beingness in the universe of existence, particularly in light of what we have learned about the existence of alien beings. Recognition of the truth is humbling. Yet, in the humility of experiencing this truth, lies a certain strength, and the possibility of aligning our individual, cultural, and species purposes with the purpose of the universe of all life; which is survival; including with that which is superior to us; mayhap, even with alien life forms.

Beyond the disillusionment that arises from suffering betrayal, loss, torture, and heartbreak, lies a profoundly disturbing truth; the trespass of what is not divine; the trespass of evil. Evil is devoid of love. It has no love or care for the vitality that generates from the spirit of other living things. It is egotistically predatory. We have no illusion about what constitutes evil; in that we have a clear understanding of what evil is; we do, however, have the capacity to be fooled by it; to fail to recognize evil when it manifests; and to be used by it; to fail to protect ourselves from its possession.

Murphy cites Socrates' contention in the *Charmides* that all good and evil originates in the soul and overflows from there; for the head and body to be well, cure must begin with the soul. Accordingly, Socrates attributed ignorance of the cures for many of the diseases of his time to physicians attempting to cure the body without the soul.[326] From the Socratic perspective, the soul is the means of comprehending what ails mankind. We find in Socrates an example of holistic thinking applied to the practice of human healing. Logically reasoned, we find in this Socratic thinking the belief that the problem of evil in individuals may be cured by curing the soul. The application of this belief was common practice in the days of New World exploration, when European peoples, horrified by some of the murderous practices encountered among native peoples, attempted to convert them to Christianity as a means of saving them from a perceived evil.

Given what has been historically learned about Satanic evil, we have come to an understanding that such evil cannot effectively function without minions; immortal and/ or mortal. We know that, in modern mortal experience, evil can and does often function independently. We may comprehend that such creeds for rightful living such as the Hebraic Ten Commandments[327] or Decalogue, which were the precepts given by Yahweh, the ancient Hebrew name for God, to Moses, the Hebrew prophet, on Mount Sinai located in modern-day Egypt, which were later adopted by the Christians, were an attempt to establish a foundational bedrock for goodness to prevail over evilness through the establishment of codes of conduct for rightful living. The prevalence of violent crime in society speaks to a greater number of evildoers than in times passed; and the reality that with an increase in population generally, there will be a concomitant increase in evildoers specifically. Society is well aware of the problem that exists with respect to violent crimes, and the limitations of law which require the committing of an offense in order for prosecution to occur. In this respect, law is retroactive not proactive. There exists a tendency of thought which expects the law to *solve* the

---

[326] Murphy, p. 259.

[327] *The Holy Bible*, The Old Testament, Exodus 31:18).

problem of violent crime, which it is in fact, unable to do. We find from this consideration that resolution of the problem of evil does not lie within the scope of the legal system. One may well ask, If this is so, wherein lies the resolution?

According to Socrates, the resolution lies with a healing of the souls of evildoers, which poses a moral dilemma; how does one go about healing the soul of one who does not want to be healed? As clear-cut as we may consider such matters of society to be, they are in fact, less simple than a matter of right and wrong, and more complex than a proffered solution might indicate. In the shedding of the illusion that evildoing may easily be resolved, we confront the truth of our inadequacy. Beyond the realization, we look with hopefulness at the possibility of affecting individual lives, through the power of spirit to affect human will.

The concept and matter of evil is generally not addressed in the treatment of substance abuse and addiction; to do so may be regarded as a form of moral positioning. The reality of extent evildoing in the lives of many an addict, renders the topic both touchy and relevant. For those substance abusers touched by evil in their lives, discussion of evil strikes a resonant chord of experience. As a former patient of mine once explained, her drug addiction was a necessary evil; the only means she had of coping with the greater evils in her life; those of surviving economically through nude dancing and occasional prostitution, which she otherwise would have found psychologically intolerable. The dilemma she thought she faced was the threat of being fired because of her drug addiction; in reality, it was one of facing the truth that without drugs, she would not be able to continue in her line of work, and would have to seek alternative employment. Parentless, with no one to whom she could turn, she feared destitution. From a spiritual perspective, one might say that spirit sprang her from a form of human bondage; facilitating her towards her true path in life, something she had been unable to do for herself.

It is relevant, in our consideration of illusion in the context of spirit, to consider the unique perspective of the Buddhist; as an aspect of the totality of human consciousness. Buddhism teaches that the individual soul is an illusion produced by various psychological and physiological influences; in Buddhism, there is no conception of a soul or self that can survive death.[328] From the perspective of Buddhism, what many other religions term the soul is a reflection of the psychology of the individual; a perspective compatible with the Christian belief that the soul represents individuation. Theologically, the belief that life is cyclic, leading to rebirth speaks to the perennial question of human beingness; *Is there life after death?*; differentially answered. The relevance of Buddhist thought to our holistic reflection is its contention that the matter of soul is an illusion; that persons are subject to continual change and therefore there is no permanence of an independent self or soul.[329] From the perspective of Buddhism, based upon the original teachings of Buddha, human beings perpetually stream through renewed existences; reborn anew without transmigration. Since the time of Buddha's personal spiritual reckoning circa 528 B.C.E., 18 different sects of Buddhism have emerged and evolved; each with their own variations of belief. The method by which Buddha arrived at his comprehension of life consisted of meditations by which he achieved successively greater levels of altered consciousness until he arrived at an understanding. According to *Encarta Encyclopedia*, *Buddhism does not recognize a conflict between itself and modern science. On the contrary, it holds that the Buddha applied the experimental approach to the questions of ultimate truth.*[330] We find the concepts of illusion and delusion to be anciently comprehended; with differences in the applied comprehensions.

---

[328] *Encarta Encyclopedia*, Standard Edition, 2004.

[329] Ibid.

[330] Ibid.

If we believe in the existence of ultimate truth, as resides within all-comprehending spirit, whether we differentially believe in the avenue of the soul (Judeo-Christian, Islamic, Orthodox), in the path of right living (Buddhist), in the advice of the ancients (Nativist), et cetera; differential means; we fundamentally believe in the capacity of the truth provided by spirit to heal us. Regardless of the means that are employed, there is a consensual human belief in the significant other that is spirit. It follows from this that our individual and collective health and well-being necessitates that we invite spirit into our lives. Through spirit, we accept our differentness; the differentness that is humanity; that we may eventually emerge from the experience of life as a phoenix risen from the ashes, in the evolution or transmigration, however one chooses to believe, that is human maturation in the service of human survival. Revitalized by the experience of spirit, we are imbued with a sense of awe at the majesty of creation; as profound as the awe one experiences in the witnessing of childbirth; we fundamentally comprehend the wisdom of spiritual awareness, become empowered to enact ourselves in the service of a continuing survival. It is in this manner that the enspiriting of the individual takes precedence over race, creed, government, religion, and science, as Shankara contended. Beyond the veil of illusion and the experience of disillusionment, in the comprehension of recognized truths pertinent to our human existence, emerges hope in the nature of an evolving human consciousness.

CHAPTER SIXTEEN

The Persistence of Spirit

Spirit has a way of persisting through the fog of our closed and clouded consciousness, despite our many and varied efforts to deny its entry into our lives. Whether we choose to actively welcome its presence or avoid it like the plague, we may find ourselves caught by its insistence to make itself known. Suddenly, without warning, spirit calls and shakes our sense of reality. Welcome or not, when spirit calls, we generally respond. I attribute this tendency of response to the nature of spirit; its inherent truthfulness, to which we naturally respond with an instantaneous recognition.

Such callings of spirit are readily recognizable. Interestingly, they do not only pertain to persons. I share the following anecdotes from personal experience. As a child, I had a tiger cat named Tippy for the characteristically Siamese bend at the tip of his tail. He was an avid hunter; regularly bringing home various and sundry *catches* as presents. One evening, he appeared at the front door, meowing oddly, as if injured. Upon being let inside, he promptly deposited a tiny field mouse upon the terrazzo floor. I watched in stunned amazement as the mouse, apparently upset by the intervention of my cat, stood upon its hind legs and squeaked a vociferous complaint at my cat. Affected by spirit, the mouse did not respond as expected; it did not immediately scurry and hide; rather, it turned and faced the cat in contentious confrontation, unafraid. The incident made a lasting impression upon my young psyche; here was a tiny field mouse acting with a volition of self-assurance not typically encountered.

Another anecdote involves a recounting of the experience of a physician I met while volunteering in South Florida in the aftermath of Hurricane Andrew. I had paid him a compliment based upon an interaction I had witnessed with a hurricane survivor. Well-adjusted, he remarked that he had come a long way in his own personal development; that I would have considered him to be a basket case had I met him years prior when he was going through his own personal experience of hell following the unexpected death of his wife. As he spoke about his bereavement and thoughts of suicide, he was filled with reminscent feelings of gloom and sadness. He related that he owed his life to a dear friend of his, who, concerned about his despair, suggested he go back to school to take his mind off his grief. As he shared this, and his subsequent decision to attend medical school, his body and countenance filled with smiling and a serenity of spirit that was contagious. He stated simply and knowingly, that the decision had saved his life; to experience his telling of it was to know that spirit had played a vital role.

A third anecdote is that of a Jewish woman I met. She was well-adjusted and content in her life as a divorced mother. She recounted that at one point in the course of her marriage life had, for no apparent reason, become suddenly unbearable; she could no longer continue functioning as she had. She was overcome by a disturbing awareness that were she to continue as she was she was going to die. She had no way of explaining what was happening to her; life was fine, her marriage was stable, her husband caring; in short, she felt that she had achieved a good life for herself. She saw no point in consulting anyone, because there was nothing to say. She was overcome by something she could not control or ignore. It was sufficiently powerful that she took to her bed and stayed there for a month, refusing to engage in the activities of normal living, leaving her husband and children to fend for themselves. She was not depressed, anxious, disturbed, or distraught; she was confused, and needed time to think. Unable to shake her powerful feeling, she decided to seek a divorce, shocking everyone who knew her. Once she had made the decision to go her own way, the feeling of unbearableness lifted, and she resumed living normally under different circumstances. She reflected that she had never experienced anything like it before in her life; it was as if something had grabbed hold of her in such a way that she could not escape facing the message it was trying to convey. Overpowered by spirit, she acknowledged a truth for which she had no other basis, and changed her life. In light of what is known about premonitions, she felt convinced that in heeding the forewarning she had prevented leaving her children without a mother to raise them.

The experience of the persistence of spirit is immortalized by Doris Lessing in the character of Martha Quest, an English expatriate living in pre-World War II Africa.[331] Martha's rebellious adolescent spirit seeks and finds comfort in nature and books amidst the isolation and poverty of her family's life. Her experience of immersing herself outside of her frayed-around-the-edges family and the dilapidated thatched roof dwelling they call home renders her open to communion; occaisionally attracting the power of the spirit without, by which she becomes periodically possessed, as described in the following passages:

Suddenly the feeling in Martha deepened, and as it did so she knew she had forgotten, as always that what she had been waiting for like a revelation was a pain, not a happiness; what she remembered, always, was the exultation and the achievement,

---

[331] Lessing, Doris. *Martha Quest: One.* Simon & Schuster, Inc.: New York, New York, 1952.

what she forgot was this difficult birth into a state of mind which words like ecstasy, illumination, and so on could not describe, because they suggest joy. Her mind having been formed by poetic literature (and little else), she of course knew that such experiences were common among the religious. But the fact was, so different was 'the moment' from what descriptions of other people's 'moments' led her to believe was common, that it was not until she had come to accept the experience as ordinary and 'incidental to the condition of adolescence' as she put it, sourly, and with positive resentment, that it occurred to her, Why, perhaps it is the same thing, after all? But if so, they were liars, liars one and all; and that she could understand for was it not impossible for her to remember, in between, how terrible an illumination it was?

There was certainly a definite point at which the thing began; It was not; then it was suddenly inescapable, and nothing could have frightened it away. There was a slow integration, during which she, and the little animals, and the moving grasses, and the sun warmed trees, and the slopes of shivering silvery mealies, and the great dome of blue light overhead, and the stones of earth under her feet, became one, shuddering together in a dissolution ofdancing atoms. She felt the rivers under the ground forcing themselves painfully along her veins, swelling them out in an unbearable pressure; her flesh was the earth, and suffered growth like a ferment; and her eyes stared, fixed like the eye of the sun. Not for one second longer (if the terms for time apply) could she have borne it; but then, with a sudden movement forwards and out, the whole process stopped; and that was 'the moment' which it was impossible to remember afterwards. For during that space of time (which was timeless) she understood quite finally her smallness, the unimportance of humanity. In her ears was an inchoate grinding, the great wheels of movement, and it was inhuman, like the blundering rocking movement of a bullock cart; and no part of that sound was Martha's voice. Yet she was part of it, reluctantly allowed to participate, though on terms—but what terms? For that moment, while space and time (but these are words, and if she understood anything it was that words, here, were like the sound of a baby crying in a whirlwind) kneaded her flesh, she knew futility; that is, what was futile was her own idea of herself and her place in the chaos of matter. What was demanded of her was that she should accept something quite different; it was as if there were a necessity, which she must bring herself to accept, that she should allow herself to dissolve and be formed by that necessity. But it did not last; the force desisted, and left her standing on the road, already trying to reach out after 'the moment' so that she might retain its message from the wasting and creating chaos of darkness. Already the thing was sliding backwards, becoming a whole in her mind, instead of a process; the memory was changing, so that it was with nostalgia that she longed 'to try again.'

There had been a challenge that she had refused. But the wave of nostalgia made her angry. She knew it to be a falsity; for it was a longing for something that had never existed, an 'ecstasy,' in short. There had been no ecstasty, only difficult knowledge. It was as if a beetle had sung. There should be a new word for illumination.

She saw that she was standing off the road, in the grass, staring at the two little buck, who indifferently flicked their tails and grazed their way off into the bush. Martha thought she had often shot these little creatures, and that she would never do so again, since they had shared the experience with her. And even as she made the decision, she was as helplessly irritable as if she had caught herself out in a lie which was pointless. She felt, above all, irritable; not sad, merely flat and stale; the more because not five minutes after 'the moment' it had arranged itself in her mind as a blissful joy; it was necessary, apparently, to remember the thing as an extremity of happiness.[332]

As we live our lives in everyday fashion, perhaps only semi-conscious of holistic reality, we may consider the following perspectives on the matter of spiritualization as pertains to everyday living.

Ernest Kurtz and Katherine Ketcham tell us that learning how to live with other human beings is one of the grand, classic problems of human be-ing.[333] They state that most of us tolerate each other by identifying with and seeking out those with whom we share strengths, ignoring or avoiding

---

[332] Ibid., pp. 52-3.

[333] Kurtz and Ketcham, p. 198.

those whose strengths are not our own. For instance, those who enjoy the competition of sports seek out other sports enthusiasts, professors other academics, coin and stamp collectors other collectors, automotive buffs others who like automotives, art appreciators other art appreciators, et cetera; in each case looking for and socializing with those whose interests and skills make shared enthusiasms possible.[334]

Instead, Kurtz and Ketcham contend, it would be wiser to connect with each other most healingly and most healthily on the basis of shared weaknesses rather than shared strengths.[335] The reason, they state, is that the crux of human connection is at the most fundamental level of our human-ness; it is our weakness which makes us alike, our strengths which make us different. Thus, by acknowledging our shared weakness Kurtz and Ketcham contend that we create a rooted connectedness, a sense of common beginnings. Accordingly, we will grow in different directions with our different strengths, but our roots will remain in the same soil; the soil of our own imperfection.[336] Kurtz and Ketcham contend that this vision of our shared imperfection is the beginning of spiritualization. If we can see our own mixed-up-ed-ness and see the mixed-up-ed-ness of people we love and respect, and accept this reality, we can then move toward an acceptance of the mixed-up-ed-ness of those whom we find difficult to love.[337] We find, from the perspective of Kurtz and Ketcham, that human beings are most similar with regard to the common denominator of human imperfection; a fact of mortal beingness; all else is a difference. From this understanding, spiritualization in the service of humanity, as different from spiritualization in

---

[334] Ibid.

[335] Ibid.

[336] Ibid.

[337] Ibid.

the service of individuality, derives from awareness of the common human denominator of imperfect beingness.

Tolerance is defined as *the sympathy or indulgence for beliefs or practices differing from or conflicting with one's own.*[338] Tolerance, according to Kurtz and Ketcham, is important for human connection to occur. One may regard the matter of tolerance as a which came first conundrum. Kurtz and Ketcham advise that tolerance is necessary for human connection. Yet, a sense of human connection is essential in order for tolerance to occur. In other words, if one does not feel connected to human beingness, one will not be inclined to tolerance; and if one is not inclined to tolerance, one will not feel connected to human beingness; which comes first? For the purpose of comprehension, we may understand that both are relevant; whether we are affected by a sense of being connected to our human beingness, or whether we are affected by a sense of tolerance of human beingness in general, the affect will influence our manner of being in the world.

This speaks to the psychological notion that in order to love another, one must first be able to love oneself; if one truly loves another, the presumption is that one also loves oneself. From this perspective, the matter of tolerance is a reflection of the manner and degree to which we are, at any given point in time, enspirited. It is relevant to acknowledge the fact that human spiritedness, like human energy levels and biorhythms, waxes and wanes; to become enspirited does not automatically translate into a perpetual state of spiritual affectedness. In the same way that we rely upon memories of good and happy times to tide us over in bad and unhappy times, experiences of spiritual affectedness serve to tide us over and guide us in times when it seems that spirit has all but abandoned us. In this regard, references to *living in the spirit* do not necessarily mean that one lives

---

[338] Webster's New Collegiate Dictionary, p. 1218.

in a state of constant rapture; such condition is not typical; it means that one lives in the wake of knowingness, guided by the truth that spirit has embued one with. One is also not limited in the experience of spiritualization, and may experience many such occurrences, at different points in one's life, which facilitate one's life journey.

The matter of tolerance, then, speaks to the matter of accepting human imperfection; our own faultiness, frailty, weakness, et cetera. We are able to accept weaknesses in others to the extent that we are able to accept weaknesses in ourselves; regardless of liking, for tolerance is not a matter of liking. We can be tolerant without liking; this is an important point; conflict arises from the unrealistic expectation that one must like in order to tolerate. Tolerance, like love, cannot be forced. We sometimes confuse tolerance and respect; expecting tolerance where respect is called for, as in legal rulings of fairness which require respecting the rights of others. For example, we may respect another's right to express their view without feeling particularly sympathetic or indulgent; that is, without tolerance for their view. This speaks to the difference between spirit and law.

Human intolerance is an ages-old circumstance. While civilization encourages tolerance of a kind, it also acknowledges the existence of intolerance. The matter of tolerance is particularly relevant during periods of parenting. Parents come to learn what they will and won't tolerate in their children; with considerable differences between them. What one set of parents will tolerate, another will not. So, too, the matter of punishment; what constitutes acceptable forms of punishment. Like God, who tolerates and indulges us, but also gets angry and castigates us, parents individually determine where to draw the line on indulgence. According to biblical record, God indulged Adam and Eve with the Garden of Eden, but did not tolerate their disobedience; expulsion was the consequent punishment. Humanity has long followed such example.

The matter of obedience is at the heart of the conflict between spirit and law. Jesus the Christ was executed for his disobedience of the law in Judea; his enspiritedness conflicted with the law that prohibited his practice of Christianity. From the perspective of law, one could reasonably argue that he could have left Judea, practiced independently, and avoided the conflict that resulted from secretly held meetings in violation of the prohibition. Instead, his decision to bring Christianity to the people of Judea placed him in a position of confrontation.

During the Middle Ages in Europe, when legal censorship was instituted; banning books whose perspectives were deemed dangerous; enspirited priests turned against the church and the law, secreting copies for posterity, and became regarded as heretics. From the perspective of law, their offenses were punishable by death.

In both instances, spirit and law conflicted over the matter of obedience. Given that there is no magic formula; or scientific formula for that matter; for the purpose of determining the ideal equation, that is, the ideal relationship between spirit and law, humanity vascillates, as it has done from the beginning. The contradiction exists that while most Christians believe in upholding the law, they also revere Christ, who broke a law punishable by death. How does one reconcile the contradiction? The matter of reconciling the calling of spirit is a personal one. We find that tolerance waxes and wanes, and differs between persons.

The examples cited address historic situations wherein tolerance of disobedience was viewed as disruptive to society, which disobedience, in hindsight, is viewed as beneficient. The conflict that may arise between spirit and leadership; as between child and parent; is addressed by the following example from literature.

Without established leadership, as William Golding portrayed in the novel, *Lord of the Flies*, civilized society crumbles into the recklessness and brutality of anarchy.[339] It is a fictional account of a group of children who are shipwrecked upon an island, with no surviving adults, and the conflicts that emerge. The group divides into civilization rule followers and civilization rule breakers; each going their own way with an emergent leader. The struggle to survive results in warring between members of the subdivided group, with disastrous consequences, before the surviving children are rescued. Enspirited by the absence of an overriding adult authority, Golding's 1,955 C.E. portrayal presents a prophetic vision of ensuing childhood chaos; paralleled by modern-day youth gangs.

While creativity, like insight, is sparked by impulse; by, one may say, a surge of spirit, it's actualization in society requires tolerance. Without tolerance for difference; for creative perspectives, insights and discoveries; we do not grow to new levels of being, understanding, and achievement. Imagine what the effect would be, for example, if on the basis of intolerance, we reacted against an evolutionary quirk of nature that birthed a man decidedly different from other men, even when that man could be the link to our evolutionary future. A strange thought perhaps, but a relevant one, as Michael Murphy, co-founder of the Esalen Institute in California informs.

Murphy states that there is potential creativity in certain human activities which at first sight seem strange or unattractive, that certain life-giving attributes emerge first as sickness or eccentricity, that if we take a strictly reductionist or materialist view of human nature, we are not likely to see that certain upsetting or perverse-looking episodes have a tendency toward the release of capacities than can support activity for the sake of others, that to know such episodes might be first signs of creative capacities can help

---

[339] Golding, William. *Lord Of The Flies*. Capricorn Books: New York, 1955.

us integrate them into our everyday life.[340] Seen in this light, intolerance of the creative human potential poses a possible threat to humanity.

We find support for this point in Peter L. Bernstein's analysis of *the controversy between quantification based on observations of the past and subjective degrees of belief.*[341] According to Bernstein, *the mathematically driven apparatus of modern risk management contains the seeds of a dehumanizing and self-destructive technology.* Bernstein cites Nobel laureate Kenneth Arrow's warning that knowledge foments a dangerous belief in certainty; a form of self-delusion of invincibility. While Bernstein's focus is the world of finance and risk management, his comprehension based upon Arrow's contribution to thought is relevant to our consideration of the conflict between spiritual and known reality; which, at this stage of time, is predominantly scientific.

The reader will recall the earlier discussion of the paradigm shift towards science and mathematics which began during the Renaissance; the effect of the emergences of new ways of thinking had a profound impact not only upon science and mathematics, but also upon economics. According to Bernstein's description of modern finance, since the discovery of probability theory in 1,654 C.E. by Chevalier de Mere, a French nobleman with a penchant for gambling and mathematics, finance has evolved into forecasting the outcome of the roll of the dice; a quantified form of predicting future financial events called risk management. We learn that probability theory is a form of risk management intended to predict the likelihood of a financial outcome. What de Mere devised as an intellectual exercise; a form of intellectual puzzle; evolved into a standard of practice, based upon the belief that attending to the odds of probability could serve

---

[340] Murphy, p. 199.

[341] Bernstein, Peter L. *Against The Gods: The Remarkable Story Of Risk.* John Wiley & Sons, Inc.: New York, 1996, p.7.

to reduce the risk of financial loss. Since then, forecasting instruments; financial and otherwise; have proliferated.

The problem with the modern application of probability theory, according to Bernstein, is its tendency to support a perspective of scientific certainty; what we may term a false positive. While risk management is a useful and valuable tool, danger arises from the perception that such tools will enable us to determine, and thereby control, the future. It is relevant to note that financial investments include the caveat that past performance does not guarantee future results; indicating the financial industry's understanding that financial analysis is an indicator of the past, not the future. As long as we accept the truth of the uncertainty, we can not be fooled into a false sense of certainty.

Bernstein describes the dilemma as an historical controversy between two competing perspectives; *those who assert that the best decisions are based on quantification and numbers, determined by the pattern of the past, and those who base their decisions on more subjective degrees of belief about the uncertain future.*[342] We are supported in our search for holistic comprehension by Bernstein's recognition of an unresolved controversy pertaining to decision-making; whether it is best to rely upon science or belief as the better prognosticator of the future. What has prevailed is a duality of beliefs; it is up to the will and the spirit of the individual to determine how best to base decisions. While the controversy persists, many of us tend to base our trust in science, and our faith in belief; in effect, increasing the odds in our favor of being right. When we straddle the two diametrics, we stand a better chance of a positive outcome; a diversification of thinking that is analogous to a diversification in one's financial portfolio.

We find that while humanity continues to diverge upon the matter; the two diametric perspectives certain of the

---

[342] Bernstein, Peter L. *Against The Gods: The Remarkable Story Of Risk*, p. 6.

rightness of their own positions; an holistic perception of the reality shows us a different picture; one of a prevailing uncertainty, given the unresolved status of the controversy. Perhaps, this is as it needs to be; to be otherwise puts us in the position Adam and Eve confronted; attempting to be as a God by accessing forbidden knowledge, with negative consequence. While we may bemoan the reality that we are, as the saying goes, mere mortals, and while in our mortal beingness we may emulate and imitate the divine, until we earn or gain the right of supernatural passage at immortalization, we remain mortal and uncertain, lacking in omniscience.

As Bernstein warns, *Our lives teem with numbers, but we sometimes forget that numbers are only tools. They have no soul; they may indeed become fetishes. Many of our most critical decisions are made by computers, contraptions that devour numbers like voracious monsters and insist on being nourished with ever-greater quantities of digits to crunch, digest, and spew back.*[343]

The quest for spiritualization predates the beginning of recorded history. This spiritual questing is as persistent as human nature; having firmly progressed into a decidedly scientific present. The tenacity of the human spirit speaks to an irrefutable fundamentality that spans time, peoples, and cultures of all kinds.

It is a quest for the answers to what Robert Coles of Harvard called the eternal questions. Coles stated that the questions are three; Where do we come from? What are we? and Where are we going? He further stated that these are the very questions which children repeatedly and subtly ask.[344]

It has been said that, as children, prior to the completion of the process of socialization, we are closer to the truth. A

---

[343] Bernstein, Peter L., p. 7.

[344] Coles, Robert. *The Spiritual Life of Children.* Houghton Mifflin Company: Boston, MA, 1990, p. 37.

rational explication is that as we mature, and grow further away from the source of our birth, we forget what we originally know, as our thinking and perceptions of reality are altered to fit the conventions of the day and times. This was the message of the child's book, *The Emperor's New Clothes*, [345]in which it took a child to comment that the emperor was not wearing clothes, to break through the denial of the royal empire, which accepted what it wanted to believe, that the emperor would only be dressed in the finest of clothing, when in fact he was wearing nothing at all on his royal personage.

Could it be that the reason children are closer to truth, and the asking of the eternal questions, is that their state of being is closer in time to the original birth state; and in so being, closer to the primeval state? In which case, we have mistakenly attributed the etiology of this phenomenon to the state of innocence which is a reflection rather than the source of the capacity of the child. If God, by any name, is the epitome of conscious knowledge and goodness; a penultimate positive; and immortality is a right of passage into eternal beingness that accrues from stages of living, then, it stands to reason that the soul's challenge in a given lifetime is how to retain the innocence with which one is born while acquiring consciousness relevant to the stage of the soul's journey. Accomplishing the unity of innocence and consciousness is the penultimate challenge of human-beingness.

A related aspect of spiritualization is the effect that *accessing God* has upon mortal beingness. We have discussed the effect on consciousness or mind; we now proceed to discuss the effect on physiology or body. Given that accessing God constitutes an act of accessing timelessness, and the reality of such accessing is known to effect consciousness, it stands to reason that timelessness

---

[345] Andersen, Hans Christian. *The Emperor's New Clothes*. Houghton Mifflin Company: Boston, MA, 1949.

similarly effects physical beingness. In one respect, we already know that this is true; the timelessness of creation is the source of all birthing; it is the source of our becoming, without which natural bodies would not exist. We know, too, from aeronautical experience, that human beings age more rapidly when exposed to outer space; for this reason, astronautical exposures to space are time-limited, to minimize the effects of aging. What this tells us is that timelessness and space are polar opposites; timelessness gives birth to life, space disposes of life. The cosmos harmoniously generates and degenerates life; in effect, constantly cleaning and restoring itself. If angels, like photons of light, are able to traverse space, it is because they are impervious to disintegration.

From this, we may reason that accessing creationism is holistically restorative; having a vitality enhancing impact upon mentality and physicality. Comprehending this, we understand the ages-old legends and beliefs in the fountain of youth; the search for a supernatural source of extending life akin to the tree of life of immortality described in the bible.[346] It lends the credence of scientific rationalism to the biblical record of Genesis, wherein we are told that generations of Adam lived to be hundreds of years old. As a case in point, Abraham, whose communications with God are documented, lived to be *an hundred, threescore and fifteen years*; 175 years of age.[347] The bible documents the long-livedness of the generations of Adam; reported to have lived to be 930 years of age. While we may reasonably conclude that contact with the Godhead has the impact of slowing down or reversing the body's aging process, the role of genetics in the longevity of the generations of Adam is indeterminate.

The case of Dorothy Eady provides additional support for this theory; the source is contact with a non-Christian deity.

---

[346] *The Holy Bible*, Genesis 2:9.
[347] The Holy Bible, Genesis 25:7.

Dorothy Eady reportedly spent the night burning incense for and praying to the ancient Egyptian god and goddess, Osiris and Isis, in whom she believed, having proclaimed herself to be the reincarnation of a priestess of the ancient temple of Kom el Sultan.[348] This occurred in 1,952 C.E., at the Temple of Sety the First, Egyptian pharaoh or God-king of the 19th dynasty, who lived from 1,306 to 1,290 B.C.E. According to historical records, when Dorothy emerged from the temple the next morning, the watchman swore that she looked twenty years younger.[349]

From the perspective of a theorized polarity of creationism and destructionism deriving from the known religion of creation, that is, the creative nature of inexplicable life; the known science of cosmology, that is, the consumptive nature of space matter, including black holes; and the known methodology of single case research studies; we may conclude that immortal omniscience has the capacity to restore life. The apparent natural/supernatural answer to the quest for restored youthfulness is spiritual; it lies with contact with the Godhead. The alternative is scientific; the anti-aging remedies of modern medicine, which proliferate for obvious reasons.

In our quest to comprehend the persistence of spirit, we look to Kurtz and Ketcham's contention that at least from the time of the Greek Delphic oracle's first admonition to know thyself, the arch-foe of spirituality has been recognized to be denial; the self-deception that rejects self by attempting to repudiate the essential paradox that is our human be-ing.[350] We are, in Kurtz and Ketcham's words, perfectly human,[351] which is to say humanly imperfect. The search for spirituality they contend is first and foremost the search for reality, for

---

[348] Cott, Jonathan, pp. 42-45.

[349] Ibid., p. 68.

[350] Kurtz and Ketcham, p. 19.

[351] Ibid.

honesty, for true speaking and true thinking.[352] Not knowing or being certain of the truth, we seek it. In questing through this book for an holistic comprehension of reality, the reader is, from the perspective of Kurtz and Ketcham, unknowingly engaged in a spirituality search.

The process of awakening to a higher consciousness; a more spiritual self; is akin to the metamorphosis of a caterpillar into a butterfly; through a transformational cocoon state. Metaphorically speaking, in the cocoon state of spiritualization, we become pupas of possibility; our human potentiality activated with the essentials for transforming into resplendent human butterflies; on our way towards becoming angels of innocent knowingness. The meaning of *kokkos*, the Greek word from which the term cocoon derives, is grain or seed.[353] Like a cocoon, human beingness is essentially a seed-like condition of possibility, with the potential for ultimate transformation into the angel-winged human butterfly of immortality. If we believe in immortality, as most persons do, we can appreciate that the process of transformation towards the possibility of immortalization is influenced by deciding actions in the spiritualized mortal pupa state.

We hold the keys that decide our individual futures; for the doors that will open to us in the next stage of the journey that is life; in this and in future lifetimes. When Queen Isabella of Spain consigned Christopher Columbus to journey to the outer limits of existence, at a time when the majority of humanity believed the earth was flat and sailing to the edge would mean falling off the precipice to certain death; her decision turned the key to the door of a new future; a more conscious awareness of genuine reality. The realization that the world was not as we thought it was stunned humanity with its comprehension; Isabella, in effect, opened the door

---

[352] Ibid.

[353] *Webster's New Collegiate Dictionary*, p. 214.

of comprehension to a truth unknown to Europeans at the time.

In consideration of Peck's psychiatric perspective regarding evil personalities, it is mindfully wise to consider, with respect to human transformation, the reality that throughout history there have existed persons whose malevolent intentions are such that they serve to interfere with the holistic process of transformative spiritual growth; advertently or inadvertently arresting human potential. This arresting effect; most notable in cases of childhood abuse and notorious criminal conduct; is analogous to the arresting of the transformative developmental process of the silkworm for the purpose of harvesting its silk. Whether or not one cares about the fate of moths, into which the silkworm would naturally transform, the point of the analogy is that human malevolence has the potential to arrest human maturation. Human history is replete with examples of the effects of such malevolence. As we consider the tenacity of spirit and the vitalizing impact of spiritualization, we take wise heed of the opposite; the potential for possession by malevolence.

From an holistic perspective, we may consider the truth that on a cosmic scale, human beingness is not the only intelligent life form in existence. We know from military documentation of the existence of alien life forms. The possibility of human subjugation to superior life forms exists; for good or for evil. As human beings, we pray for the supremacy of benign supernaturality among deities, and we closely follow news reports of alien activities for evidence of benign or malignant intention. The movie, *E.T.*, about a benign extraterrestrial who kept saying, *E.T. phone home* because he was homesick affected the human populace with its sensitivity, and the possibility that alien presence could be benign. The popular movie had a significant impact upon perspectives, opening our minds to positive as well as negative possibilities, at the same time that it served to prepare our children for a different future reality.

307

Confronting the reality of the superiority of the supernatural and the alien over the human contains the potential for an experience of fear, and the danger of overreaction. While knowledge of such fear and its consequences may mitigate overreacting; desensitizing us to the experiential reality; it cannot eliminate our experiencing the emotion of fear altogether; we are instinctively hard-wired to react to perceived danger for survival. The response does not constitute a response of spiritual nature, it constitutes a response of animal nature. Given that the experience of encounter with superior beings for most human beings is vicarious, rather than actual, most of us do not know how we would react; with animalistic fear, with spiritual recognition, or in some other manner. We are wise to face the truth that we do not know how we would react in such circumstances, rather than to assume or presume the outcome. This realistically applies to potential encounters with immortals; angelic, demonic, and godly; as well as with alien beings. In terms of human survivability, facing the truth of our natural human reactivity is an important consideration. From an holistic perspective, we confront, recognize, and accept this truth about human beingness.

We cannot be spiritually affected by what we do not perceive; the reality of this is expressed in the adage, *Ignorance is bliss.* Spiritual ignorance is a two-edged sword; the first edge cuts us off from growth-enhancing awareness that may prove painful, allowing us to remain deluded about our true selves without the burden of responsibility that comes with knowingness; with knowingness, we face the inescapable fate of what it is that we must soulfully do. The second edge cuts us off from achieving the true purpose of our individual lives; our soul's lifetime mission; inhibiting our progression towards immortalization. According to the ancient Greeks, we are bound to repeat the mission of the soul of a given lifetime until we learn the intended lesson; conceivably recycling through similar life experiences, like the retaking of various versions of the same test, until we finally achieve mastery. We do not progress to the next spiritual level of beingness without mastery of the prior levels; there are no shortcuts in the journey of the soul.

The reality of this speaks to the spirit/mind/body phenomenon of addiction and the unique position of the addict. One may consider that the addict is mired in a kind of current lifetime holding pattern; unable, unready, and/or afraid to face and complete the mission of her/his soul. Perhaps, the reality of experience has proven too daunting; sending them scurrying to hide behind substances like frightened mice. When one considers how daunting are the missions of the soul, one wonders not that so many cower and hide in the face of it all; facing the gods is a daunting prospect. It is as unrealistic to expect all men to face the prospect of soul missioning as it is to expect all men to be leaders or heros or saints or sages. As we look to the prospect of our respective journeys through life, we may consider the relevance of readiness, willingness, and ableness; in order to proceed we must be ready, willing, and able. The reality of this prerequisite speaks to the importance of the individual; the pursuit is neither game or triviality, it is dependent upon individualistic conditions at once determinate and indeterminate.

The crux of our species leanings and yearnings for spiritualization lies with the reality of the soul's true purpose. Our desire is an inspired intuition of the need to spiritualize and comprehend the truth of our evolutionary situation. The human situation has three potentials; the potential for failure; the failure to evolve, which includes evolution towards evil rather than towards good; the potential for stasis or repetition; the static repeating of one's past until the soul matures; and the potential for success; the achievement of the aims of the spirit through the soul towards evolutionary metamorphosis. Our quest for truth through spiritualization is the quest for survival; for understanding that will enable us to better actuate ourselves in the present towards an uncertain end. We know within the deepest levels of our being that we are capable of transforming into beings of superior spirit. Our ancient memory enables us to intuit that this is so. We yearn for the lightness of being of a superior spirit, and freedom from the material burden of aging. We attain superior spirit through the desire; the seeking of it; and through self-honesty; by breaking through the self-delusion that prevents us from perceiving genuine reality.

Kurtz and Ketcham state that individuals we regard as sages and saints concerned themselves greatly with the matter of hypocrisy and self-deception because they knew the simple but essential truth that human beings find it extremely difficult to know the truth about themselves; that just as we cannot see our own face without some kind of mirror, the mind, the soul, cannot directly know its own nature; access to spirit enables us to know ourselves truly. The authors contend the Russian proverb; *You cannot kiss your own ear*; is analogous of the fact that we cannot directly know our own being.[354]

Accordingly, Kurtz and Ketcham state that the answer to the quandary of what to do in order to be is to listen to stories, because stories are mirrors of human be-ing which reflect our essence back to us, that in the mirror of another's story, we can discover our tragedy and our comedy, and therefore our very human-ness; the ambiguity and incongruity that lie at the core of the human condition.[355] These, they state are wisdom stories that will satisfy our hunger by sustaining a spirituality of imperfection.[356] From this perspective, we better comprehend why it is that we relish reading books and watching movies; for they portray, in its various aspects, the human condition. Through the mirror of spiritualization, through the aid of the eternal spirit, we can experience and know the truth of our own being. In this way we may extend our reach for self-actualization to realization of the spirit.

---

[354] Kurtz and Ketcham, p. 63.

[355] Ibid., pp. 63-4.

[356] Ibid., p. 64.

Life is a journey. Whether or not we delude ourselves regarding our own true natures and purposes as individuals and inhibit our own self-actualization, whether or not we allow ourselves to become mired in the muck of psychological game-playing that substitutes for a more mature and responsive-to-spirit life, whether or not we engage in the pursuit of self-discovery and self-actualization in quest of spiritualization and the eventual maturation of our souls, from the moment of conception, we have embarked upon a solitary journey. We are individually responsible for our own evolution, in the mysterious journey of our soul's progress through life, and collectively responsible for the evolution of our species, in the grand journey of Homo sapien's progress through time. From an holistic perspective, the journey through life is facilitated by spiritualization, the journey through time is facilitated by reproduction, and survival is a paradox; a matter of evolutionary creationism wherein the maturation of our souls and the survivability of our bodies depends in great part upon the capacity of our minds for consciousness. The concept of spirit/mind/body speaks to the reality of human existence.

Whether or not the foretellings prove true, there exists a remarkable parallel between the biblical prophecy of the end of days,[357] and the scientific assertion that our Milky Way galaxy will end in collision with the Andromeda galaxy in 2 billion years.[358] It is mind-boggling to consider that: 1) such capacities for foretelling, both religious and scientific, exist, and 2) that they coincide. They stand as testaments to the human spirit's desire to know its own fate, a reality that animates all questing.

---

[357] "And I saw a new heaven and a new earth: for the first heaven and the first earth were passed away; and there was no more sea." REVELATION 21:1. *The Holy Bible.*

[358] NOVA, Thomas Lucas Productions, Inc. MONSTER of the MILKY WAY: A Supermassive Black Hole. WBGH Educational Foundation, 2006, 2007.

EPILOGUE

When I first began writing *Addiction In Context*, it was 1,996 C.E. I was dis-employed as a corporate mental health care director, ousted by the industrial changes taking place across the country and around the world. Unable to find comparable professional employment in the midst of the closures, I turned my hand to writing; in an effort to make sense of it all. Mental health was in a tumult; the high costs of health care resulted in demolition of the service sectors; across America, psychology and psychiatry professionals found themselves tossed overboard to sink or swim without life boats as primary care medicine assumed the role of official care provider; the takeover occurred at warp speed; by way of example, according to the Houston Chronicle, 200 psychiatric hospitals closed in the city of Houston in the year 2,000 C.E. In the course of a few short years, the Zeitgeist changed; the meaning of therapy for one's woes was redefined.

The sudden, drastic, and forced nature of the change in the professions was shocking. A new set of circumstances, with a new set of rules, replaced the post-WWII stability, wreaking havoc as it upended 55 years worth of tradition. With globalization in process; big fish eating little fish; corporate medicine shut down the perceived waste factor (aka extravagance) of psychiatry/psychology in favor of primary care physicians offering medicaton as a practical cost-effective solution.

I suffered the unexpected, along with a large cohort of other Americans, who all seemed to be losing positions at the same time, from union workers to medical professionals. Given my natural intellectuality, in due course, I analyzed the emergent reality. As I acquired insight into what had happened to me, what was happening to the country, and why, I came to the conclusion that life is not what it seems; those at the top may understand, but most others do not. Most of us amble through life without thinking beyond the perimeters of our circumscribed life circumstances. As long as all is well within this personal life boundary, the tendency is to ignore the seeming irrelevancy of other circumstances. As people, we tend to live perceptually isolated lives, ensconced within the microcosms of our individual life circumstances.

This realization led me to reconsider the matter of writing a book to answer the question of recidivism in addiction treatment from a somewhat different perspective. My life had changed, my perspective had broadened, and intuition suggested that my hypothesis that the source of the addiction problem was cultural pertained to the source of my career problem; that it was in the nature of present-day societal reality to create such calamities. There are so many factors that enter into the equation of why things are the way they are, that to assess a problem, one must either pragmatically limit the focus of study by concentrating on a known or hypothesized portion of these; or redefine the boundaries in order to remove the restrictions placed upon the identification and analysis of possible sources of influence. For the sake of holistic comprehension, I chose to do both.

To approach the subject matter holistically required considering addiction from a variety of views, or angles of perception. While at first consideration, such a proposition may appear easy, it is not. The more one considers the possibilities, the more one comes to appreciate the complexity of the phenomenon. In this regard, the endeavor is just that, an endeavor. It is by no means exhaustively all-inclusive. It is, however, sufficiently expansive as to render the philosophical perspective possible and comprehensible. It constitutes a contribution to the world's body of knowledge, such as it is, and to thinking about thinking, which it is. To the reader, I caution that it is far better to follow whatever course comes naturally than to follow in another's shoes, be it a much-traveled or a less-traveled road.

Since beginning *Addiction In Context* in 1,996 C.E., many unexpected and unstudied changes in this and other cultures have occurred which have impinged upon the way things are; they serve as a reminder that the impacts of conditions which motivated me to write this book persist, that life goes on, and that a paradox exists with regards to the inevitability of change. In this respect, I have gained a sense of validation that the intellectual urging I had at the outset was an inkling of something out there that I hadn't yet fully perceived, but sensed was relevant and important to comprehend.

My contention that things are not always what they seem holds just as true now as it did when I first set out to write *Addiction In Context*. Denial of reality as a psychological construct is just as prevalent and prominent in our thinking today as it was yesterday and yesteryear; perhaps it always will be. The relevance of this perspective derives from the human tendency; from the mind and culture of Man.

The relevance of the philosophical perspective derives from its attendance to this matter of human nature; its development and evolution over time; including recognition of the contextual inseparability of spirit/mind/body. These are relevancies which will persist throughout time. In truth, one can say that humanity's response to addiction has been as eccentric and habitual as the phenomenon itself. In keeping with the Delphic oracle's admonition to *know thyself*; *Addiction In Context* holds an holistic mirror to the phenomenon that we may come to better comprehend the human reality.

I conclude this epilogue with a final comprehension, acquired by serendipity upon completion of this work. It is stated in *The Holy Bible*[359]:

Beloved, think it not strange concerning the fiery trial which is to try you, as though some strange thing happened unto you.

But rejoice, inasmuch as ye are partakers of Christ's sufferings; that, when his glory shall be revealed, ye may be glad also with exceeding joy.

In this light I comprehend the strangeness of what I have experienced; perhaps the divine intended it that I might better comprehend what was difficult to perceive.

#

---

[359] *The Holy Bible*, 1Peter 4:12,13.